Making Crime:
A Study of Detective Work

RICHARD V. ERICSON

UNIVERSITY OF TORONTO PRESS
Toronto Buffalo London

© University of Toronto Press Incorporated 1993
Toronto Buffalo London
Printed in Canada

ISBN 0-8020-6981-9 (paper)

First published in 1981 by Butterworth & Co. [Canada] Ltd.

Printed on acid-free paper

Canadian Cataloguing in Publication Data

Ericson, Richard V., 1948–
  Making crime : a study of detective work

  ISBN 0-8020-6981-9

  1. Detectives – Canada.   2. Detectives – Canada –
  Case studies.   3. Criminal investigation – Canada.
  I. Title.

  HV8021.E74 1993   363.2'5'0971   C93-094856-4

To Dianna. She too has sacrificed for this.
And then there is Edward Greenspan,
head of the Centre of Criminology's Special Services Division,
along with Professors Doob, Edwards, Leyerle,
McCulloch, Mewett, Saywell, and Waddams.
In generously providing their time and advice they have
furthered my education on the meaning of duty and discretion.

Contents

Preface

In this book we explore general investigation detective work and its place within policing, crime control and wider processes of social control. We accomplish this through an observational study of detectives operating within two general investigation detective offices in a Canadian municipal police force, and by relating our findings to the socio-legal literature. While general investigation detectives represent only a small fraction of a police force membership (less than 10 percent of the Force we studied), they have an important role within any force. They are assigned the task of routinely processing cases brought to their attention by others (usually uniform patrol officers), and of arriving at a conclusion for the cases by giving them specific designations (e.g., whether a "crime"; type of offence; clearance category; type of charge). This work of "making crime" is particularly important to the extent that the policing mandate, and the legitimacy that flows from it, is defined primarily in terms of the control of "crime" and "criminals."

While there have been a multitude of studies on the patrol police and some other aspects of contemporary policing, there are few studies on detective work. Moreover, the existing published socio-legal studies have been conducted only in American jurisdictions and have been based largely upon interviews, document analysis, and/or unsystematic observation (Skolnick, 1966; Greenwood et al., 1975; Sanders, 1977; Wilson, 1978 and Manning, 1980). The present study is a contribution to the understanding of an area of policing that is only beginning to be explored and documented. It contributes to a comparative examination of detective work in that it is the first study in the context of Canadian legal and social organizations. It also contributes through the use of systematic observation methods along with document analysis.

There are several themes in the book which are interconnected to develop a portrait of detectives at work. In their routine, everyday work detectives deal primarily with cases in a reactive manner, that is, after they have been brought into the police organization and been made into police property by patrol officers. The detectives' task is to make what they can of these cases within the organizational criteria of the police force and the wider organization of crime control. Detectives work cases that they see as promising and disregard or finesse others which have little apparent prospect for investigative payoff. They are motivated to do this to gain organizational reward, control the level of their work, and achieve satisfaction from what is often a routine and boring job.

Detectives are skilled at doing this, largely because they work within an enabling environment. At least compared with their patrol officer colleagues, detectives have autonomy from their supervisors. They also have autonomy within the law, as they learn to use the ostensibly controlling procedural law to their organizational advantage. Furthermore, they have a "positional advantage" (Cook, 1977) vis-à-vis other segments of the police force and the other organizations of crime control. This comes about because they operate in conditions of low visibility, which in turn places them in a powerful position via the control of information.

In these circumstances, detectives are able to transform citizen conflicts into the property of the police organization (Christie, 1977), to be used according to various criteria of their own detective units, the police force, and the wider organization of crime control. When they decide not to work a case, or to unfound it, or to re-interpret it, there is little or no review that might challenge what detectives have made of the case. When they decide to proceed against a "criminal" who can be identified with a "crime" in a case, detectives are typically able to accomplish outcomes that are consistent with their objectives. Justices routinely grant warrants, releases, and bail conditions in accordance with detective requests. Defence lawyers and Crown attorneys cooperate with detectives in working out plea settlements and sentence recommendations so that most accused plead guilty and receive a disposition within a predictable range. Along with judges, the other agents of the court typically accept the detectives construction of cases, and the organizational actions of the courts rest in important ways on the facts of cases as presented by detectives.

As discussed in Chapter 1, from the inception of the new police in 1829 most of these elements have continually been a part of detective work. While detective work only gradually became institutionalized as an integral part of public police forces, it has always been characterized by the relative autonomy of its practitioners through enabling rules, low visibility, and information control. In contemporary settings these elements are the foundation of the detectives' working environment and shape their working ideology and practices.

While there is a certain durability of these elements, we differ somewhat from the emphasis given to them and their implications for detectives' discretion (power) as depicted in some contemporary accounts of detective work. Contrary to the portrayal of many (e.g., Skolnick, 1966; Reiss, 1971; Wilson, 1978), but in accordance with Greenwood *et al.* (1975) and Manning's (1980) findings, we document that detective work is largely reactive rather than proactive. Detectives working in general investigation detective units respond mainly on the basis of occurrence reports submitted by patrol officers who in turn have received complaints from citizens. Obviously the existence of the complaint, the nature of the account given by the complainant, and the filtering of this account by the patrol officer, are things which are usually created externally to detective units. Moreover, detectives are rarely able to proceed with an investigation which starts out "cold" and ends up with a chargeable suspect. Rather they are dependent on others to identify and produce suspects, and their main work is routine processing and preparing documents on suspects who have been produced by others. *Initially* detectives are reactive, although they may later do some proactive work to validate, deflect, or alter the complaint; at least initially, the control of cases is in the hands of persons other than detectives.

Once a case is taken on by detectives, what is made of it is very much in their control (for a supporting study, see Sanders, 1977). The only real threat to their control is the possibility of a citizen complaint that they did not perform their duty properly. Thus, an important part of detective work is expending energy on cooling out citizens and otherwise finessing cases to minimize this threat.

Detective discretion lies in information control: the investigations they do or do not undertake; the questions they do and do not ask; the interpretations they do and do not give to the answers; the written accounts they give and what they leave out; the formulations they give to other actors and their ability to predict that these will be routinely accepted by others as legitimate for purposes of action. Detective discretion also resides in enabling legal rules and other organizational rules, which provide them with a framework to formulate legitimately their actions and their accounts.

Our study provides rich and unique data on how detectives accomplish case control once they have received it. While they do their work routinely, they are not automatons in the way that some accounts suggest (e.g., Greenwood *et al.*, 1975). Our portrayal is of workers who are subject to controlling influences; who work in response to these controls and sometimes find ways around them to accomplish their organizational tasks as they see them; and, who in turn exert considerable control over the process. This is a dialectical process between organizational structures and the persons who respond to them and constitute them.

Obviously, our study is not an evaluation of a particular detective operation nor of detective work in general. Our interest is in understanding the organization of general investigation detective work and its implications for understanding crime, criminality, and processes of social control.

We conclude that there are senses in which detectives have both more and less power than other researchers have documented or other commentators have imagined. We stress that the various policy alternatives that are usually debated (e.g., changing the law, changing the structure of the police organization, professional socialization of officers) are not as simple and straightforward as they sometimes appear to be. For example, there is a very different legal context in Canada, with procedural law which has generally developed in more of a "crime control" direction than in the United States. Yet, our data suggest that general investigation detectives in Canada operate in similar ways to their American counterparts, and achieve similar outcomes. Apparently the procedural law makes little difference, functioning in both jurisdictions *for* crime control (McBarnet, 1979).

Perhaps most of the proposals for reform have little impact because reformers know too little about what it is they are trying to reform. Even the most concrete proposals for reform do not take up the concrete facts about the nature of detective work. These facts and control of them are embedded in many constraints other than those usually talked about. First and foremost detective work is conducted within organizational contexts (as defined by Silverman, 1970), including the community policed, the law and court apparatus, and the police force. If one understands these organizational contexts, one can readily appreciate the inevitability of such things as detective control over the process, the point that "crime" is not an entity constituted independently of the organizations established to deal with it, and the realization of the limited capabilities of detectives and other members of crime control organizations to deal with the "crime problem" through deterrence and detection.

It will be appreciated that this study is about one very small segment in the total machinery of State control. This book must be seen as only one step in a continuing project which examines all aspects of "policing," defined in terms of all governmental efforts for controlling, developing, shaping, and refining the population.

Based on one reviewer's reading of an earlier draft of this manuscript, I am disposed to make one more point about the nature of this project. In the description and analysis of the data there are, of course, some things which some audiences might view as questionable activity on the part of detectives or other actors. For example, comments with racial overtones, "colourful" language, flexible use of time on duty, and questionable exercises of authority are occasionally included as they form a natural part of the description and analysis that inform the central issues of the book. This research did not take a survey orientation to these phenomena by counting them up, analyzing them, and providing a commentary on them. These things occasionally appear as part of detective work, as they do in all other occupational settings.

Toronto, Ontario
August 1980

Richard V. Ericson

Acknowledgements

This research would not have been possible without the cooperation of many organizations and people. I am very grateful for the access granted in the jurisdiction we studied. The Police Commission cooperated in formulating an agreement and permitting the research to take place. The Chief of Police deserves special mention for encouraging the project at all levels in the force, and for "paving the way" in this pioneering venture. I also acknowledge the cooperation of the senior officers who helped us as we embarked upon the fieldwork. Of course, I am extremely grateful to the detectives who allowed us to observe their activities; more than anyone else, they provide the substance of this book.

I am indebted to many colleagues at the Centre of Criminology, University of Toronto, for their encouragement, support, and intellectual contributions. We all owe a lot to John Edwards for having created the Centre as an active research environment. Gordon Watson, Director of the Centre at the time this research was initiated, helped in many ways to support the project. Anthony Doob, the current Director, has been extremely supportive at several key stages in the project. I benefited from a year in the scholarly environments at Churchill College, Cambridge, and the Institute of Criminology, University of Cambridge, during which time I began a major revision of this book.

I am indebted to Hans Helder, who engaged in seven months of fieldwork for this project and who subsequently assisted in data analysis. His skill as a fieldworker, and his many insights, have influenced this book in numerous ways. Lynn Bailey has been of enormous help in organizing the data, and in typing successive drafts of the manuscript.

I am extremely grateful to James Wilkins for access to his materials on the work of Crown attorneys, and to Dianne Macfarlane for access to her interview material with lawyers who became involved in cases described in this book.

Many persons have influenced the shaping and refining of the manuscript through various drafts. At one or more stages, I have benefited from the comments of David Bayley, Maureen Cain, Anthony Doob, David Downes, James Giffen, Hans Helder, Peter Manning, the late Pauline Morris, Albert Reiss, Paul Rock, Peter Solomon, James Wilkins, and a representative of the police force studied. I think each of these persons will find instances in which I have followed their advice and instances in which I have not. My interaction with these persons has resulted in a product that is more than the sum of their parts; in light of this, they cannot be responsible for what has been produced.

The research for this book was supported by substantial grants from the Donner Foundation, the University of Toronto, and the Social Sciences and Humanities Research Council. I wish to express my gratitude to these organizations.

Finally, I am fortunate to have become associated with Butterworths, a supportive and efficient publisher. I am particularly thankful for the encouragement given by Mr. David Hogg, Managing Editor (Academic Division) at Butterworths in Toronto and for the editorial skills of Valerie Bulanda.

I trust readers will find that the substance of this book matches the substantial support it has received from so many sources.

List of Tables

Chapter 1

Detectives and the Making of Crime

Detective Work in Perspective

In the evolution of the "new police" after Peel's reforms of 1829, detective work had a very secondary role. While the new police were explicitly established to penetrate civil society and keep surveillance over the population (Silver, 1967: 12-15)[1], this surveillance was to be done by *visible* uniformed beat officers. Indeed, in the beginning there were no detectives who were part of the new police. For the first ten years the task of criminal investigation remained with the magistrates and Bow Street runners, who continued the previous practice of doing work on a fee paying basis, and who explicitly combined the police and judicial functions (Moylan, 1929: 13-14; Cobb, 1957: 72; Miller, 1979: 15).

The early years of the new police were chaotic. There was an enormous turnover rate as the new commissioners responded to discipline problems by the multiplication of disciplinary rules backed up by the punishment of dismissal.[2] One problem stemmed from the fact that while Commissioner Mayne explicitly defined effectiveness in terms of crime reduction, he had no officers trained in criminal investigation. His officers either established lucrative liaisons with the Bow Street runners, or simply had their cases "scooped" by the runners. Moreover, many of the more serious and notorious cases they worked on failed to produce convicted offenders. These problems, combined with perceived threats from Irish political groups, provided the basis for the argument that the new police required their own investigative branch.

The first traces of a detective branch appeared in the work of an Inspector and Sergeant who were assigned to a series of murder cases in the late 1830s. This *de facto* detective team was incorporated into the first detective branch, which was established in 1842 with six sergeants and two inspectors. However, this branch remained within the general administration of the Force, and even by 1868 only 15 out of the 8000 members of the Metropolitan London Police were designated for detective work. In 1877, an inquiry revealed that three senior detectives were involved in illegal gambling operations; this led to the establishment of a House of Commons Committee, which in 1878 recommended and had accepted a proposal to establish a distinct

1

detective operation (Criminal Investigation Division or "Scotland Yard").

In short, it was almost 50 years following the inception of the new police that a distinct detective operation was established. Moreover, while detectives were assigned rather more specialized tasks relating to criminal investigation and enforcement, their goals were defined in terms of the overall function of the new police as reproducers of order. While there were occasional experiments of appointing "gentlemen of good education and social standing" directly to the detective branch (e.g., from 1878-1884), these experiments were judged a failure. As a result, all detectives were socialized into the police occupation by extensive work on the beat as uniformed officers, thus ensuring similarities in organizational outlook between uniform officers and detectives. This outlook was related to the stated goals of reproducing order, which included the containment and control of crime through *surveillance* and *criminal law* enforcement.

Even in the earliest days, this work of patrolling and controlling the population was no more exciting for detectives than it was for uniformed officers. The essence of work was routine surveillance and mundane information processing.

> [My analysis] suggests that, as compared with the tasks of Sherlock Holmes, or Dr. Thorndyke, [CID work] is not exciting. The detective side of police work, in an English force at all events, is, it must be admitted, a somewhat matter-of-fact occupation, in which hard work and knowledge of the criminal classes are essential. Crime in real life is largely the work of professional criminals of poor intellectual capacity, no social accomplishments or charms, and little imagination, though they may have a great deal of low cunning. To cope with them successfully, powers of abstract reasoning and scientific knowledge or apparatus serve less than the more commonplace resources which may be summed up in the word 'information,' including under the term not merely the assistance derived from informants but close and constant personal observation of criminals, their ways, haunts, and associates, backed by an efficient system to ensure the identification of old offenders. It may need a 'master brain' to defeat the machinations of 'master criminals,' but, as someone has said, it requires an ordinary policeman to deal with ordinary crooks, and it is from them that society has most need to be protected.
>
> (Moylan, 1929: 178)

A major reason why the detective branch took so long to become established, and why it was kept with a low level of manpower and other resources, was the British cultural resistance to State control that was not visible. The schoolmaster standing in front of his pupils, the prison warden standing in the control tower of the panopticon, and the uniformed police constable standing on the street observing and being observed in "public," posed no threat to those who put these agents in their positions. However, the idea that these agents would not be visible was abhorrent. The very idea of a plainclothes police was strongly attacked, and even after the detective branch was established much of the continued criticism of their work could be interpreted as reflecting an underlying resistance to a "secret police."

The old police had been in plainclothes, but once the new police were established in uniforms, any plainclothes operations were viewed as the ominous beginnings of a secret police. One indication of this fear is the fact that in the first 40 years of operation, police officers in the Metropolitan London Force were not allowed to appear in plainclothes, even when off duty, without special permission (Moylan 1929: 152). Initial attempts by the Force to use plainclothes officers in anti-crime patrols were attacked by magistrates, who refused to prosecute people accused of assaulting plainclothes officers (Reith, 1943: 82, 102). In 1833, a Select Committee of the House of Commons inquiry into the case of a police officer who infiltrated a working class union, expressed its strong disapproval of the officer's actions and emphasized that deployment of plainclothes officers should be limited to specific cases of crime detection and prevention where no other means are available. Moylan (1929: 152-153) argues that this case had a major effect in forestalling the development of the detective side of police work.

By the 1860s and 1870s, growing public debate and concern over the problem of serious crimes and the inability of the police to deal with them created an enabling environment for the expansion of the detective operation. As Miller (1979: 20) expresses it, this was the first period in which "fear of criminals outweighed fear of detectives." However, even during this period the relative size of the detective operation remained miniscule and the place of detective work remained under suspicious scrutiny. Thus, in his report of 1869, Commissioner Henderson stated, "There are many great difficulties in the way of a detective system; it is viewed with the greatest suspicion and jealousy by the majority of Englishmen and is, in fact, entirely foreign to the habits and feelings of the nation."

In the 1880s the CID continued to be criticized, although the immediate target for the attack was their inability to catch notorious suspects such as Jack the Ripper. Miller (1979: 21) notes that this led *Punch* to refer to the CID as "the defective police." The criticism continued well into the twentieth century. For example, the MacMillan Committee (1928) on the duties of the police in regard to street offences and the Lee Commission (1929) on police powers and procedure both said that the CID should not be used for detecting "street offences." The Lee Commission also condemned the detectives' "method of bluff," and their use of minor offences for detention of suspects regarding major investigations (Moylan, 1929: 165).

The concerns of the press, and of governmental committees and commissions, indicate that from the very beginning detectives searched for innovative strategies to achieve their surveillance and law enforcement goals. Compared with their colleagues in uniform, detectives had greater autonomy to set their own schedule and priorities, to work away from the watchful eyes of superordinates, and to develop techniques which would produce the information essential for investigation and the production of evidence. As Cobb (1957: 152) states in discussing a case worked on by the first detectives,

> [T]hat crime was one of the many failures of those years. But in the process of failing, Inspector Pearce and Sergeant Otway did something which had not been done in the force before, but which was absolutely essential in detective work: they acted without authority or orders, and even disappeared for several days—exactly as the Police Officers [before the new police] had done.

Along with their colleagues in the uniform branch, the early detectives were faced with the problem of winning public acceptance in order to ease their surveillance and enforcement tasks. This could not be achieved by force; indeed, the ineffectiveness of military intervention strategies for handling civil disputes was one of the factors that led to the founding of the new police (Silver, 1967). Detectives and other police officers had to devise means of establishing cooperation with the citizenry on a face-to-face, day-to-day basis. As Bittner (1970: 98) observes, in the contemporary context, "[T]he most important 'trick' in police work is not to make people obey but to make it possible for them to obey." A version of this "trick" was performed on the first day of operation of the new police. From that day onward, thousands of permutations and combinations of strategies were employed to accomplish and perfect this trick. The legitimacy of the police was no more secure than a house delicately constructed out of playing cards; however, by playing the right cards in their exchanges with the citizenry, and by refusing to withdraw after the occasional collapse, the police managed to build up legitimacy credits and to reproduce the glass menagerie of social order.

> The success of the police, both ideologically and practically, depended on convincing people to accept the official code of illegal behaviour, and to turn to 'official' channels for redress.
> To win this cooperation, the police manipulated their powers of discretion. They often chose not to take their authority to the letter of the law, preferring not to "press their luck" in return for tacit compliance from the community. In each neighbourhood, and sometimes street by street, the police negotiated a complex, shifting, largely unspoken 'contract.' They defined the activities they would turn a blind eye to, and those they would suppress, harness or control. This 'tacit contract' between normal neighbourhood activities and police objectives, was sometimes oiled by corruption, but more often sealed by favours and friendships. This was the microscopic basis of police legitimacy, and it was a fragile basis at best.
> (Ignatieff, 1979: 445)

In the present century, and especially since World War II, this fragile basis of police legitimacy has been reinforced by other forces.

Police surveillance has gradually become institutionalized as a taken-for-granted fact of everyday life (Foucault, 1977). People who have almost given up their lives as soldiers or industrial workers, who have dedicated their lives to unrespectable work in order to appear respectable, have come to view a questioning of the police as more of a threat than anything the police might do to violate their rights (Friedenberg, 1975: 38, 65). In times of economic surplus, the police have multiplied without much public regard to questions of efficiency (cost effectiveness) nor to the wider social implications of their constructive tendencies (Ericson, 1980).[3] The police have replaced cowboys as cultural heroes. The value conflicts, angst, and need to *feel* secure (rather than to *be* secure) among the citizenry is played out and relieved in television "cop shows" that are at the same time episodic and endless (cf. Hurd, 1979). The police hire full time press officers, and organize massive public relations campaigns, using the peoples' resources to convince them that they (the people) would have even less resources through increased crime if they did not accept extravagant police presence in their midst. In short, on the micro-level of police-citizen transactions, the mecro-level of police organizational constructions, and the macro-level of policing as an integral part of the political economy, the police now stand erect on reinforced concrete. Police infiltration into everyday life means people literally accept the saying that "the police are the people, and the people are the police."[4]

In Canada, we have inherited the tradition of public policing that began with London's new police, and we have allowed the public police to become accepted as a major force in our midst. However, apart from a very few research efforts (e.g., Brown and Brown, 1973; Grosman, 1975; Mann and Lee, 1979; Ericson, 1980; Shearing, Farnell and Stenning, 1980), the development and operation of policing has not been examined systematically. Moreover, to date there has been no socio-legal inquiry into detective operations in Canada. Indeed, inquiry into detective work is a neglected area of police studies in all Anglo-American jurisdictions (the five major empirical works to date are Skolnick, 1966; Greenwood et al., 1975; Sanders, 1977; Wilson, 1978; and Manning, 1980). As a result there is inadequate understanding of the detective function as it relates to the uniform patrol function and to other aspects of policing.

A review of the contemporary socio-legal literature provides some general knowledge about the place of general investigation detective work vis-à-vis other aspects of State financed policing. Most large-scale, bureaucratized police forces have evolved a sharp division of labour between their patrol and detective operations. In general, criminal investigation (including the processing of suspects and accused persons) is turned over to detectives at the earliest possible juncture (Cain, 1971: esp. 68; Chaiken, 1975: vii; Ericson, 1980).[5] As a consequence, patrol officers are sometimes viewed as "nursemaids" of detective specialists, and this creates patterns of tension and conflict (Angell, 1971: esp. 192; see also Banton, 1964).

While detectives are still a small minority numerically within a police force,[6] they share a large part of the limelight. Unlike patrol officers (Ericson, 1980), detectives are explicitly in the business of crime work. Although crime work is only one component of police work, and in fact takes up only a small fraction of police time, it is crucial to the police image and to the legitimacy that flows from that image. Therefore, detective work at making incidents into crime is a crucial function for the police force as a whole.

In doing this work, detectives are dependent upon the prior work of uniform patrol officers. The majority of occurrences which detectives receive into their case files have been written up by patrol officers in response to citzen complaints. Patrol officers make an initial decision concerning whether an incident is officially reportable in the first place, and then decide how to influence the career of the report in the police organization by the content of what they write and the label they attach at the head of the report (Ericson, 1980: Ch. 5). Furthermore, patrol officers sometimes have an apprehended suspect who is turned over to detectives in connection with the occurrence (Greenwood *et al.*, 1975: esp. 82-83). Thus, patrol officers frequently make a significant contribution to the detective's work, namely producing suspects who correspond to an occurrence or set of occurrences. Indeed, detectives clear relatively few occurrences by charging suspects through extensive investigation; rather, they depend on patrol officer apprehension of a suspect or an identification from the complainant (Greenwood *et al.*, 1975; Block and Weidman, 1975; Sanders, 1977).

Research has shown that the uniformed police account for a much greater proportion of arrests than detectives (Reiss, 1971: 104). This is partly accounted for by the fact that the uniformed division is much larger; and, by deployment strategies which mean that uniformed officers are usually first on the scene and thus the first to take into custody any available suspects. Moreover, many arrests made by uniformed officers are in relation to their "peacekeeping" duties, and involve the use of minor charges as a device to handle immediate problems of public order (Bittner, 1967b; Bittner, 1970). In these situations uniformed officers are not functioning as law officers but rather as order maintenance officers who use the law as a back-up resource when their authority is threatened. Compared with uniformed officers detectives have fewer authority (legitimacy) problems, partly because they rarely become involved in public order troubles. As law officers, detectives use their authority to produce their goal of criminal law enforcement; as peace officers, the uniformed police frequently use the law to achieve their goal of police authority, and the orderliness that comes with it.

The different organization of their work obviously means that there are differences in outlook and operation between uniformed officers and detectives.[7] However, they have considerable overlap in orientation to their work. As police officers, they routinely work to maximize organizational and personal rewards by proceeding in those cases that cause least resistance (Chambliss, 1969: 86; Ramsay, 1972: 58). While their goals are not the same in all areas, they believe that the ends justify the means, and their practices reflect this belief (Skolnick, 1966: 228). They share the fact that the essence of their task, and their discretion is located in information work (Pepinsky, 1975; Sanders, 1977; Manning, 1977; Manning, 1980). Therefore, much of their work is directed at creating and using rules to guide the flow of information into, within, and out of the organization: when to report something, how to report it, who to report it to, how to avoid the organizational control that comes from committing something to paper, etc. (e.g., Rubinstein, 1973 on patrol work; Sanders, 1977 on detectives). All police officers work in relation to the premises of their particular operational unit as it relates to the wider Force, and to produce the appropriate accounts of their work for official purposes (Manning, 1979: 25). Both uniformed officers and detectives operate in the knowledge that much of their information work as it relates to broader goals is based upon cooperation with the citizenry. Therefore, they collectively do "PR" work in their everyday contacts with citizens, knowing that "service" today increases the potential for citizen cooperation in providing information and allowing surveillance tomorrow.[8]

In summary, detective work has gradually evolved as an established specialized function within the large, bureaucratized police force. The primary work is routine processing of occurrences initiated by uniform branch officers, including the processing of suspects produced by uniformed officers or apprehended on information received from a citizen. Based on the information work he has done, the detective decides whether the case can be made into a "crime"; and, if he has a suspect, whether the suspect can be made into a "criminal." The detective experiences this work as routine. Our subject of inquiry is how he makes it routine.

Detectives as Makers of Crime

It is now accepted socio-legal wisdom, if not conventional social wisdom, that "Crime is a sociopolitical artifact, not a natural phenomenon" (Packer, 1968: 364). The definitions "crime" and "criminality" are powerful tools used by the authorities against "groups and individuals who in any way, inadvertently or deliberately, are resistant to the will of the authorities (as articulated in the behavior of the police and courts) . . ." (Turk, 1977: 11).

The police are at the forefront of this definitional production. They are given organizational capability to produce particular levels of crime, and to produce particular types of crime to the relative exclusion of others. Of course, the authorities place some limits on production by legislating what criminal labels can be applied and by controlling the material resources supplied (cf. McDonald, 1976: 290). Production also depends upon the collective ability of police force members to generate and use the information necessary to make crime (Reiss and

Bordua, 1967: 47; Manning, 1972: 234). In this regard, the discretionary decisions of the police are crucial determinants of "crime" production,

> [C]riminalization is caused by the implementation of decisions made by norm enforcers—especially first-level enforcers—on when and how to use their power to assign criminal status. A criminality rate is—obviously—caused by the criminalization of some proportion of a population. It follows that whatever affects enforcers' decisions and their implementation has 'causal significance' in reference to criminality rates even though the exact nature of the effects has not been, and may never be, fully understood and precisely described.
> (Turk, 1969: 78).

In their everyday decisions, line police officers "commit" crimes to police organizational records and make them available for detective investigators to follow-up or ignore, to "unfound" or verify. Obviously, there are many events which could be made into crimes but are not because a citizen chooses not to call the police (Ennis, 1967; Sparks *et al.*, 1977). Other events could be made into crimes but are not because the police officer decides not to proactively stop and investigate suspects (Ericson, 1980: Ch. 4, 6). Even when police officers are mobilized, their decisions to make complaints or observed conduct of suspects into "crimes" are far from automatic, varying by citizen characteristics and dispute type (*ibid*.: Ch. 5; Skogan, 1976; Sparks *et al.*, 1977). Furthermore, sometimes occurrence reports submitted by patrol officers can be ignored by detectives, leaving open the question of whether the event could be judged a crime; and, after investigation, detectives can decide that the matter was "unfounded" (Sanders, 1977; Bottomley and Coleman, 1979). For all practical purposes, crime only consists of those acts that are so designated by the police for their crime control purposes on behalf of the authorities. *The* necessary condition for crime is the police designation: "the reaction is *constitutive* of the criminal (or deviant) act. In fact, the reaction *is* the 'commission' of the act" (Ditton, 1979: 20).

In this formulation, it is meaningless to use the concept of a "dark figure" of crime. We can study the process by which the police discover things which they make into crimes, and how they do organizational bookkeeping to keep account of crimes, but we shall never know the total volume of things "out there" that could be made into crimes. As Ditton (*ibid*.: 21) argues, "To ask 'how big is the 'dark figure?' is to pose a question of the same logical order as 'how long is a piece of string?' or 'how many grains of wheat are there in a heap?' " While the issue is gradually transformed into black and white once the police have decided to make something into a "crime," the decision on whether or not to constitute it as a crime in the first place has as many shades as a chameleon in a box of crayons. For example, in the victimization survey by Ennis (1967: 87-93), detectives and lawyers agreed only slightly more than half the time on whether victims' descriptions of incidents stated criminal offences let alone what the appropriate label for those offences might be.

In our formulation, the term "underenforcement" is equally absurd. This term implies that all laws will be enforced against all violators at all times (Manning, 1977: 249). The fact is, even with very substantial police resources, certain types of incidents will be systematically excluded from being made into crime (e.g., "domestic" assaults—see Kokis, 1977; Ericson, 1980: Ch. 5), and certain situated features of individual cases will lead to selective decisions not to make them a matter of "crime." This is so because the organizational interests of the police, and/or the organizational interests of the wider network of criminal control and community control, influence the way in which "crime" and "criminal" labels are used by the police.

In carrying out their work of making events into crime, and persons into criminals, detectives operate within four intersecting organizational forums: the community (political territory) being policed; the network of criminal control (the institution of law and its constituent elements, e.g., courts); the police Force; and, the occupational culture of fellow detectives.[9] Each of these organizational forums provides a structural framework from which emanate particular "demand conditions" for detective actions (Bittner, 1967b: 701; see also Silverman, 1979: 134-135). In turn, detective actions, and their interactions with other members of these organizational forums, help to constitute the structural framework within which they operate.[10]

In short, detectives as human actors are not conceived as determined varlets who simply respond to the dictates of organizational structures. This conception is contrary to that of some researchers of the police (e.g., Black, 1968; Pepinsky, 1975, 1976; Sykes and Clark, 1975; Wilson and Boland, 1979), who accept the American ideal that "enforcement responses are supposed to be as automatic as possible" (Bayley, 1977: 224) and who thus portray police officers as automatons emitting responses according to the stimulus of structural forces. We conceive detectives as *enacting* their environment, as well as reacting to it (cf. Manning, 1979: 29, quoting Weick, 1969: 63-64). Therefore, detectives' individual and collective theories about action, interaction, and structure become central to inquiry (cf. Strauss, 1978: 102). How do detectives develop a sense of the rules within each of the organizational forums in order to stabilize their own practices? How do these rules relate to detective action? How do detectives put these rules to use? What do these practices tell us about detectives' sense of order?

As human actors detectives work at producing the organizational realities, which in turn guide their production. This work is carried out in the routine tasks they deal with on a day-to-day basis, and results in a product that is both commodity (e.g., "crime" and other means of case clearance) *and* an established set of social relations (social structure). Detectives consciously and actively create and use structural resources that will allow them to accomplish their organizational tasks with minimal strain. Of course, the constructions of detectives are frequently met with the obstructions of others; this is part of the ongoing process of "negotiating order":

> [I]ndividuals in organizations play an active, self-conscious role in the shaping of the social order. . . . [O]rder is something at which the members of the organization must constantly work. Consequently, conflict and change are just as much a part of organizational life as consensus and stability. Organizations are thus viewed as complex and highly fragile social constructions of reality which are subject to the numerous temporal, spatial, and situational events occurring both internally and externally. . . . [T]here is an implied dialectical relationship in which the informal structure of the organization acts upon the formal structure, producing social change. Concomitantly, events which take place outside of the organization may also have a profound impact on both these informal and formal structures.
> (Day and Day, 1977: 132; see also Benson, 1977; Strauss, 1978)

The detectives' task of making structural conditions which are conducive to their task of making crime involves a perpetual search for *power* resources to be used vis-à-vis those with whom they routinely interact. The question of power—of who has the enabling resources to control the process—has been a focal concern of socio-legal scholars studying the police.[11] The central concept employed in this connection is "discretion," which can be equated with the concept of power. Thus, Black (1968: 25) defines discretion "as the autonomy of decision-making that an officer has," and Davis (1969: 4) states that, "A public officer has discretion whenever the effective limits on his power leave him free to make a choice among possible courses of action or inaction."

In socio-legal studies, discretion (power) is considered to be an element of social organization rather than pertaining to personal characteristics of police officers (Wilson, 1968: 11; Sykes and Clark, 1975: 585-586).[12] The realization that discretion is an inevitable component of every socially structured organization has led socio-legal scholars away from a questioning of its propriety and in the direction of researching its dimensions. The policy question becomes one of judging whether discretion is properly in the hands of particular officials, whether it should be shifted to other officials, and how this can be accomplished (e.g., Alschuler, 1968, 1978).

As stated, discretion (power) is essentially a matter of control over enabling resources that will serve particular interests (Turk, 1973: 4-5). In the process of making crime, detectives have two fundamental resources to work with: (1) *rules,* including enabling legal rules of the criminal law (legislated and judge made), administrative rules of the police Force, and recipe (practical) rules of the occupational culture; and (2) *information control,* including a "low visibility" position within the organizational nexus which allows them to control essential knowledge and the flow of information.

All decisions have discretionary elements and are rule based (Thomas, 1974: 140). The empirical question is to determine which rules are used by detectives, and where these rules emanate from (i.e., from which organizational forum?). The rules may be formal (e.g., legal or administrative) or informal (e.g., emanating from the occupational culture), and using them may be designated as acting legally, extra-legally or illegally (cf. Kadish and Kadish, 1973: 66ff). In any case, there are always rules for action, and it is the researchers' task to fer-ret out these rules as they are conceived and used in the everyday ac-tions of detectives.

Furthermore, all decisions involve the processing of information. A major resource of the detective is the fact that many of his actions are not "legally *or practically* open to re-examination" (Reiss, 1974: 679, emphasis added; see also Goldstein, 1960; LaFave, 1965: 154). The detective operates under a "visibility cover," so that his decision to ig-nore a matter can remain unknown to other organizational members, and his decision to construct a matter in a particular way has to be ac-cepted at face value by other members because there are rarely the means or inclinations to do otherwise. Unlike patrol officers (cf. Ericson, 1980: Ch. 4), detectives are not controlled by having a designated patrol area, by patrol supervisors, and by visible cars and uniforms; detectives are also less controlled by the two-way radio system. Consequently, detective work can be conducted away from the watchful eyes of police superordinates and of citizens who might com-plain. This low visibility-information control nexus means that, con-trary to the situation in most other bureaucracies, discretion increases as one moves down the hierarchy (Wilson, 1968: 7; Wilson, 1978), and specialization tends to extend autonomy rather than curtail it (James, 1979: 80-81).

As background to our analysis in subsequent chapters concerning how these elements are used by detectives, we shall outline the ways in which they have been conceived in the socio-legal literature.

Rules

According to legal ideals, the enforcement of the criminal law is sup-posed to be governed by the rule of law and the principle of legality. Briefly put, the prescription and application of specific legal rules are supposed to operate to reduce arbitrary action by agents of the law. The ideal is to have the law rule, not men.

In practice, the system operates according to men who use laws to accomplish their enforcement tasks. The law is very enabling in this respect, because it is effectively formulated for the pragmatic use and benefit of law enforcement agents, allowing them to accomplish crime control in accordance with their organizational interests (McBarnet, 1979). It is also enabling to the extent that it is silent in some areas, pro-viding no empirical referent vis-à-vis the ideals of the system (Black, 1972).

The system also operates according to the administrative rules and informally developed rules within specific sub-organizations. Therefore, it is a mistake to attempt an understanding of detective crime work solely in terms of the legal rules. To do so is to commit a "category mistake" (cf. Giddens, 1976: 47), "trying to understand the rules of one game by means of assumptions grounded in the rules of another." Detectives, and the police Force on whose behalf they operate, have their own sets of organizational interests, and attendant rules to achieve them. As Skolnick (1966) has argued, detective use of these rules can conflict with the legal rules; moreover, it can substantially discolour the ideals of the system.

A further consideration is that knowledge of the rules—whether legal or police organizational—is of no use *in itself* if one wishes to understand detective work. One has to learn how rules are *conceived* and *used* by detectives as they go about their daily tasks. The primary function of rules, regardless of their source, is to aid detectives in the rationalization of their activities.

In this connection, legal or administrative rules designed to control detective actions cannot be viewed as having a direct impact independent of their translation by detectives. Similar to workers in any bureaucracy, detectives will not respond to a new rule aimed at making their task more difficult by a willing commitment to implement it in letter and spirit.[13] Instead, they will assess the rule in the context of the rule frameworks they have already established. They will then develop strategies to avoid the new rule, to implement it with the minimum level of compliance possible, and/or to turn it to their advantage in easing their task.

We are not arguing that detectives break the rules or even bend them as a matter of routine. Usually such extreme measures are unnecessary because the rules are vaguely written and otherwise enabling enough to get the job done.

It should not be surprising that legal rules aimed at controlling specific aspects of detective work are either deflected or absorbed into the context of other rules. One well researched example of this concerns the right to silence cautions, which have a different legal status in England, Scotland, Canada and the United States, and yet the type of rules seem to make little difference in police practice. After the *Miranda* decision, the law in the United States dictates that the cautions must be given or an accused's statement will be ruled inadmissible, but research shows that the cautions are often not given, are only given in part, or are given in ways ensuring that the suspect will be unable to comprehend them (e.g., Medalie *et al.*, 1968; Ayres, 1970). In England, it was the police who asked for the Judges' Rules regarding the taking statements in order that they could standardize their own practices; these rules have no legal status and, according to several commentators, they do not hinder police interrogation and confession practices (Morris, 1978; Zander, 1978; McBarnet, 1979). In Canada, the English Judges' Rules are sometimes referred to , but they have no legal force and little practical force, and again the police frequently do not inform suspects of their rights (Ericson, 1980: Ch. 6).

Research has also shown how police Force administrative rules developed in support of new policing strategies have been ignored, or reformulated and put to use by line officers so that they can continue their former practices. For example, Chatterton (1979) describes how officers developed rules to circumvent the increased potential for supervision brought about by a new beat patrol system, and James (1979) shows how a special unit set up to meet the demands of "administrative professionalism" was transformed by line officers to conform to their existing practices ("practical professionalism").

For detectives and other police officers, "working to rule" takes on a very special meaning. Detectives work to produce and use rules which allow them to rule, i.e., to control their working environment. Their skill at doing this has been well documented, leading one researcher to observe that rules of constraint imposed by legal or police authorities over line officers can end up strengthening the activity they were supposed to restrain (Skolnick, 1966: 12).

Detectives are pragmatists. They constantly search for and employ strategies that will make complex situations simple, and potentially unusual situations routine, in order to meet organizational expectations with minimal strain. In consequence, they are "highly rule oriented and rule conscious" (Manning, 1977a: 47).

In terms of criminal law rules, detectives are strategists in their use of both substantive law and procedural law as these pertain to particular tasks before them. If we consider the task of dealing with suspects, we can develop this point.

When dealing with suspects, detectives have a choice concerning whether or not they will arrest and/or charge the person. They may decide to arrest and/or charge for a wide variety of reasons, and then use a particular law that will best suit their reasons. The law makes the apprehension possible, explaining why the detective may arrest and/or charge but not why he may want to arrest and/or charge (Bittner, 1967a; Chatterton, 1976; McBarnet, 1979).

This use of the law is especially apparent in minor offence situations, and in particular public order troubles as handled by the patrol police. The law is used as a handy device for dealing with troublesome situations. It is a "residual resource" which is used to assert police authority and/or to patch up interpersonal troubles (Bittner, 1967a; 1970: 109; Ericson, 1980: Ch. 6). A suspect being investigated for criminal assault is eventually charged under a liquor statute for being intoxicated in a public place after the victim refuses to assist investigation; a suspect who throws a chair at a dancer in a bar and strikes her is eventually charged with causing a disturbance so that the police officers do not have to complicate the case with a multitude of witnesses; a husband is provoked into a scuffle and then arrested for assaulting police as a means of removing him from a hostile domestic situation; and so on. Indeed, there is an arrestable offence (breach of the peace) and there are several chargeable offences (e.g., causing a disturbance; obstructing police) which are well suited for use by the police in virtually every circumstance where they feel they need to assert their legal authority.[14] There are many more "substitute charges" that can be invoked if they prove to be expedient in handling a situation (for further examples see Vera Institute, 1977; McCabe and Sutcliffe, 1978).

Police officers can also use the substantive law even when they decide not to arrest and charge (cf. Bittner, 1967b: 702-703). For example, they can make a suspect believe he could be charged but that he is being given a break. This is facilitated by the suspect's general lack of knowledge about police powers, and also by the fact that in many situations the law is ambiguous enough so that alternative interpretations, including the arrest and charge option, are plausible. Giving the impression of a "break" can be a useful means of setting up an exchange relationship with the suspect whereby he agrees to give information to the police as an act of reciprocity (cf. Skolnick, 1966; Rubinstein, 1973: 182). Of course, making the suspect believe he could be charged is also a source of intimidation, serving to make him respect his place vis-à-vis police authority.

These tactical uses of substantive legal rules to generate information, assert authority, and convert suspects into accused persons, are central to the public order tasks of the patrol police (Ericson, 1980). As we document later (see especially Chapter Six), they are also tactical skills useful to the detective task of making crime and criminals.

Another source of legal rules that are of particular benefit in detective work pertain to the procedures for processing suspects and accused persons. It is in this area that the written law does directly relate to practice. "The legal system *is* the procedures not the rhetoric, and procedures do not so much provide safeguards for the accused as powers for the prosecution" (McBarnet, 1976: 178). While we wish to avoid a technical legal discussion at this juncture, it is worthwhile to enumerate some of the procedures indicating that this is the case.

In some areas the law is silent. For example, police officers routinely detain citizens for extended periods on "street stops" while awaiting the results of criminal information (CPIC) checks (Ericson, 1980: Ch. 6). While it is unlikely that persons in these circumstances would officially be judged to be under arrest, it is also unlikely that they feel free to leave the presence of the police officer without running the risk of being charged (e.g., with obstruct police).

Where written procedural law does exist, it is enabling in its vagueness. For example, the justifications for arrests and searches usually contain the element of "reasonable and probable grounds." This amounts to no more than a *post hoc* check on the reasonableness of the police officer's belief that an arrest or search was justified (McBarnet, 1979: 32). Moreover, where criteria are spelled out, they often pertain to offender characteristics, e.g., previous record and domestic and occupational status. Thus, the discrimination which the sociological literature has been so persistent in pointing out is not "extra-legal" after all; it is built right into the procedural law, and this is what police officers orient themselves to in making their decisions (McBarnet, 1979).[15]

When the procedural law becomes more explicit, it aids in generating information and producing outcomes detectives define as successful. In the Ontario context, enabling provisions of the federal *Narcotic Control Act,* federal *Criminal Code* (section 103 regarding weapons), provincial *Liquor License Act* and provincial *Highway Traffic Act* allow police to question suspects and conduct attendent physical searches (Helder, 1978; Ericson, 1980). Moreover, these and *Criminal Code* provisions regarding search warrants can be circumvented by the simple expedient of obtaining the consent of suspects (cf. Freedman and Stenning, 1977). Given the pervasiveness of police authority, suspects are particularly likely to consent (Ericson, 1980; Ericson and Baranek, 1981). Regardless, even in the rare instances where the police introduce evidence in court which is judged to have been obtained as a result of an illegal search, the evidence is still admissible because of the lack of an exclusionary rule (*The Queen v. Wray* (1970), 4 C.C.C. 1; Law Reform Commission, 1973:6-8; Kaufman, 1974: 180-181).

As we have previously mentioned, the law on admissibility of suspect confessions is more enabling than controlling from the police viewpoint (see generally Kaufman, 1974). Failure to inform a suspect of his right to silence, or refusal to allow access to a lawyer while in police custody, are only factors to be taken into consideration by the judge in determining the voluntariness of the statement and therefore its admissibility. A wide range of promises and threats are allowed without rendering the statement inadmissible. Moreover, even if a statement is ruled to have been involuntarily obtained, that part of it which is supported by subsequently discovered fact is still admissible. Not incidentally, statements serve purposes other than as evidence in court; for example, they may help to convince the prosecutor that the police do have a case (Skolnick, 1966), and they are a means of generating information about the suspect and/or other activity that might be made into crime (Zander, 1978).

This enumeration is by no means exhaustive. Further documentation of how procedural law is used by detectives in these areas, and in others, is one subject of the empirically based chapters which follow. However, the point is clear: "due process is *for* crime control" (McBarnet, 1979: 39), not in opposition to it in the way that Packer (1968) and all those who follow his model have formulated it. As McBarnet (1979: 39) concludes in her review of English and Scottish criminal procedures, the principle of legality remains as mere rhetoric because the written procedural law directs the police elsewhere.

> Legality requires equality; the law discriminates against the homeless and jobless. Legality requires that officials be governed by law; the law is based on post hoc decisions. Legality requires each case be judged

on its own facts; the law makes previous convictions grounds for defining behavior as an offence. Legality requires incriminating evidence as the basis for arrest and search; the law allows arrest and search in order to establish it. Legality embodies individual civil rights against public or state interests; the law makes state and the public interest a justification for ignoring civil rights. . . . Deviation from legality is institutionalized in the law itself. The law does not need to change in order to remove hamstrings on the police: they exist only in the unrealized rhetoric.

Low Visibility, Knowledge and Information Control

The use of legal rules and police organizational rules to orient action has both prospective and retrospective aspects (see generally Bittner, 1970). Prospectively, detectives decide upon what actions to take according to how they can cover themselves in case their actions are called into question. They develop "prefigured justifications" (Dalton, 1959) which are formulated with reference to the rules, even if the intent is to deviate from them. Retrospectively, detectives make official accounts of their actions which conform with what they think the rules say should have been done in the circumstances (cf. LaFave, 1965: 428-429; Skolnick, 1966: 215; Buckner, 1970).

This use of rules is interlinked with the low visibility-knowledge-information control resource of detectives. Detectives are able to produce accounts which give the appearance of conformity to the rules because those persons to whom they are giving the accounts (e.g., superordinate police officers, Justices of the Peace, Crown attorneys, judges) rarely have the inclination or the capability to undertake an independent investigation which might produce a different version of events. While they rarely undertake other types of patrol work, detectives constantly work at patrolling the "facts" of their cases. Their "undercover" work is rarely the incognito type of surveillance depicted in popular drama; rather, it consists of prospective and retrospective "covering their asses" by ensuring that their reports make what they do appear to be what the rules say they should do. *The skill of detectives lies in this merging of the 'is' and the 'ought' so that they appear as one.*

In other words, the use of rules by detectives is inextricably bound in with the organizational accounts they give (cf. Carlen, 1976; Manning, 1977, 1977a; Sanders, 1977). Detectives explain, justify, and legitimate their actions with respect to what they think are the appropriate rules, and these rules are used in conjunction with their accounts to orient their actions. This helps us to appreciate why rules are not applied literally. Rules only become applicable in the process of developing an account (cf. Feeley, 1973: 420-421). For example, Sanders discusses a case initially reported as a "burglary" that was re-classified by detectives as a "divorcee-property dispute." Sanders (1977: 95) observes:

Were it the case that crimes are established by literal application of the law or that criminal circumstances exist independent of the work done in an account, it would not be possible to reclassify a case in this manner. In fact, any law is taken to include more than what is written in the penal code, and the sense of what law should be 'used' is embedded in and underlies any reported crime.

As experts in the use of law, and as "accountants," detectives develop their skills through experience on the job. Their skills are embedded in their "recipe knowledge" (Berger and Luckmann, 1966: 56, 83) about the legal and police organizational rules and accounts needed to get the job done, not in the more abstract "specialist knowledge" obtained through formal education and training sessions. Detectives refer to this recipe knowledge as the "common sense" that can only be acquired through extensive experience on the job. It is this "common sense" which the researcher must grasp if he is to provide an adequate account of detective discretionary power and the consequences of it.

The most pervasive and persuasive form of power is the power to define and produce reality. This power is in turn dependent upon other power resources, including access to relevant knowledge, knowledge about how that relevant knowledge is socially distributed, the differential availability of *legitimate* accounts for actions, and the visibility of the process by which accounts are generated (see generally Berger and Luckmann, 1966; Silverman, 1970; Benson, 1977). This power is exercised *over* what might be accepted as a legitimate account of reality, and *through* the particular account of reality that is given as it influences a particular course of action (cf. Hosticka, 1979).

The police organization as a whole has a key "positional advantage" (Cook, 1977) over the other organizations of criminal control because these organizations are dependent upon the police for accounts of what happened in "criminal" events. Indeed, because the processes by which the police produce their accounts are not visible to the other agencies of criminal control (i.e., other agents are not present when victims are interviewed and suspects are interrogated, etc.), these agencies are also dependent upon the police for an account of the procedures by which the police produced their account of what happened. Furthermore, the cases which the police decide not to work on or not to make into "criminal" cases in the first place are not even known to the other agencies.

These conditions of secrecy extend even further when we consider members of the community being policed. Their only possible sources of knowledge are personal experience in an individual case, newspaper accounts concerning "public" aspects of specific cases, and official statistics on what members of the police organization have collectively chosen to make into crime. Operations of the police organization remain well insulated from members of the community, leaving them in a position where they cannot judge what is being done on their behalf, or against them. In other words, secrecy allows the police to mystify and it stands as a potent source of police organizational power (Manning, 1977: 135).

Moreover, within the police organization there are low visibility conditions which allow individuals and sub-units to operate with certain rules that are unknown to other members. They can forge a course of action that meets their own interests as long as they formulate what they did in ways that will be accepted routinely by their super-ordinates. In short, on the level of the police organization as a whole, and on sub-unit and individual levels, "the exercise of discretion is usually not known to any person who might be motivated to challenge it" (LaFave, 1965: 154).

As stated at the beginning of the chapter, the essence of detective work has always been information work. Detectives exercise considerable power over the acquisition of information (Reiss,1971: 124-125). For example, they decide whether or not to interview particular victims, witnesses, informants, and/or suspects, and what to ask these persons in interview. Detectives also exercise power over what happens to the information they do collect, including what to omit from their reports, and how to construct the reports in a way that is likely to produce the outcome they want.

In constructing their reports, detectives are confronted with the task of turning the complexities of a case into a simple account. In this construction, they include what they understand to be organizationally relevant and exclude things which might complicate the case they have decided to make. Herein lies one of the paradoxes of detective work. The detective must be suspicious of the appearances that citizens present to him: "you suspect your grandmother and that's about the strength of it" (Banton, 1964, quoting a police officer). On the other hand, the detective cannot distrust all appearances because he needs to ground his decisions in a reality that will allow him to carry out his investigations (Sanders, 1977: 20). He therefore selects out particular things and transforms a complex and colourful event into black and white. Of course, in the process the detective himself engages in the construction of appearances.

When constructing an account of his investigations, the detective is involved in a process of transforming an individual event into categories which have a character of permanence and exactness. These categories are drawn from the available stock of categories stored within the police and wider legal organizations. Use of these categories allows the detective to assume that everyone else will know what this case consists of. It allows the detective, his superordinates, the prosecutor, and other court officials, to accept his account as "the facts," and therefore to act "*as if* they are in a state of perfect knowledge, and *as if* this 'perfect knowledge' has fairly stable constitutive elements . . ." (Carlen, 1976: 88, emphasis added).

"The facts" are not independent of the interpretive work that detectives use to construct them. The only question of objectivity is: how do detectives produce "facts" which come to be accepted as objective by those who receive and act upon them? Once they have decided to make something a "crime" and someone a "criminal," how do detectives "stage" it as being what they have made of it? These questions lead to the core of discovering how detectives bring order to their working environment, because "Social order depends upon the cooperative acts of men in sustaining a particular version of the truth" (Silverman, 1970: 134).

There is potential for creativity in detective work. Creativity comes about as a detective tinkers with various strategies to handle situational exigencies of a case. The kaleidoscope of people and problems the detective confronts ensures that these creative elements will enter from time to time. However, the vast majority of strategies employed and decisions made are neither creative nor original because they are derived from the available stock of recipe knowledge about rule usage and accounting practices. The range of things an event can be made into legitimately, and the number and range of things a person can be charged with legitimately, are organizationally circumscribed and constrained. The legitimate rules are not their rules, but the property of the legal and police organizations. The legitimate accounting practices—the reports on their investigations, and the number of crimes and crime clearances they report—are not their accounting practices, but the property of the legal and police organizations. In short, detectives do not just make it all up according to the whims of an informal system. Their construction of cases—the way in which they make events into crimes and people into criminals—is endemic to the organizations within which they operate.

Our contention is that things are organized in ways that allow detectives to meet their interests with minimal strain. They are provided with structural resources which allow them to engage in constructions which easily overcome others' obstructions. As a result, the potentially problematic and complex are made routine and matter-of-fact.

The matter of fact is at the heart of the matter. The range of legitimate explanations and justifications made available to detectives ensures that their work can proceed smoothly.[16] Legitimacy is accorded to their accounts, so that they become accepted as valid and take on a factual status. As Giddens (1976: 114-115) instructs,

> There are two senses in which reasons may be held by actors to be 'valid,' and the interlocking of these is of no small consequence in social life. One is how far an agent's stated reasons in fact express his monitoring of what he did; the other is how far his explanation conforms to what is generally *acknowledged* in his social milieu, as 'reasonable' conduct. The latter, in turn, depends upon more or less diffusely integrated patterns of belief which actors refer to in order to derive principled explanations of each other's conduct.

As we have considered already, it is extremely difficult for others to monitor whether detective accounts accord with what they actually did. In consequence, others give detectives "face validity" based upon trust or "blind" faith. Furthermore, detectives are supplied with a useful range of explanations which conform with what is acknowledged as reasonable conduct in the system of criminal control. This enables them to make cases based upon accurate predictions about the outcomes and whether or not someone might "blow the whistle." They can envisage whether the scene they are dealing with has the potential for a sequel in the Inspector's office, in the prosecutor's office, and in the court. Indeed, one can conceive of their decisions to move a case to the next stage—to report it to a police superordinate, and then to the prosecutor, and then to the court—as means of seeking and gaining further legitimations for their previous actions.

The legitimated constructs of detectives obviously have an authoritative element, and in this respect they are ideological (cf. Holzner, 1972: 144-147). They become part of the working ideology of detectives, serving to restrict the range of the possible while at the same time enabling detectives to do their work as they see fit. It is this working ideology in theory and practice which we wish to understand. We seek this understanding through an empirical inquiry into the general investigation detective operations of a Canadian regional police force. In the next chapter we provide an outline of how this investigation was conducted, and some insight into how our research account has been produced.

NOTES

1. The creation of the police surveillance function at this time was coincident with the increasing involvement of the State in devising and refining surveillance techniques in all areas of society, including the military, hospitals, schools, penitentiary (Foucault, 1977), and the family (Donzelot, 1979).

2. Cobb (1957: 56) reports that of the first 2,800 men enlisted in the new police, 2,238 were dismissed, including 1,790 for drunkenness on duty.

3. In 1977-78, public police expenditure (unadjusted for inflation) in Canada was approximately 19 times higher than it was in 1961-62. In 1978, the number of public police personnel was 50% higher than in 1969: the ratio of police personnel per 1,000 population was 2.04 in 1969 and 2.99 in 1978. Solicitor General of Canada (1979: 21,24). More detailed documentation of police growth is contained in Chan (1980).

4. Surveys in Canada continually show favourable public opinion and acceptance of the police (e.g., Courtis, 1970; Koenig, 1975), even when the police have been shown to have exceeded systematically their powers (Mann and Lee, 1979). Moreover, victims of crime who mobilize the police also tend to hold favourable attitudes (Hagan, 1981).

5. For example, in the Metropolitan Toronto Police Force a regulation dictates that uniformed patrol officers can only prepare cases regarding offences against provincial statutes, and *Criminal*

Code charges regarding public order (causing a disturbance) and driving offences (impaired driving; failure to remain at the scene of an accident; driving while under license suspension; and criminal negligence in the operation of a motor vehicle where no death or injury results). In all other cases, the suspect must be turned over to the criminal investigation (detective) branch for further investigation and the final decision regarding the number and nature of charges.

6. Chaiken (1975: vii), in a survey of American Municipal and County Police Departments, discovered that on average, 17.3% of police officer personnel are assigned to detective units. One-quarter of the Departments assigned less than 14% of police officer personnel to detective work, while one-quarter assigned 20% or more to detective work. In one city, 31% of the police officers were in the detective division, this being the highest proportion for any Department in the survey. In the police force we studied, 114/594 (19.2%) of police officer personnel in August 1980 were assigned to detective units, including 8.6% on general assignment and 10.6% in special services (specialized squads).

7. See Chapter Three, and in general compare the analysis in this book with the companion volume on police patrol work (Ericson, 1980).

8. For a discussion of the way in which "service is inextricably bound up with public order and law enforcement," see Reiss (1971: 63ff). Greenwood *et al.*, (1975) discuss public relations as an integral function of detective work.

9. A detailed consideration of these organizational forums as conceived in socio-legal literature on the police is presented in Ericson (1980: Ch. 1). The concept of organization as employed in this book derives from the discussion in Silverman (1970).

10. Following Giddens (1976: 104), ". . . social practices may be studied, first, from the point of view of their constitution as a series of acts, 'brought off' by actors; second, as constituting forms of *interaction,* involving the communication of meaning; and third, as constituting *structures* which pertain to 'collectivities' or 'social communities.' "

11. For example, Packer (1968: 5) introduces his treatise on the uses of the criminal sanction by describing it as "an argument about the uses of power," and then asserts that "the criminal sanction is the paradigm case of the controlled use of power within society."

12. The type of research we are reporting, and the paradigm within which it is framed can be contrasted with the work of Hogarth (1971). Hogarth related judicial attitudes and attendant philosophies of punishment to sentencing behaviour, without incorporating organizational elements in the way we have conceived them. We do not claim superiority of one approach over the other. They address different questions and therefore produce very different explanations for variability in the decisions of officials. We are concerned with generating and explaining data on the socially structured sources of detective discretion, rather than with documenting personal variations in exercising that discretion.

13. For example, prison guards have responded in similar ways when new rules have been introduced into the prison setting. (Hawkins, 1976: Ch. 5; Ellis, 1979).

14. McBarnet (1979: 29-30) makes the point in the English context: "[It is] an arrestable offence according to the 1964 *Police Act* to obstruct the police in the execution of their duty. Since this has been interpreted (Parker, L.J.) as 'the doing of any act which makes it more difficult for the police to carry out their duty' and might include simply refusing to answer questions and any sarcasm in one's manner (*Rice v. Connolly*, 1966), it is difficult to see how someone can avoid being arrested if the police have a mind to it. Furthermore, refusing to cooperate is not a far cry from resistance, which is, of course, an arrestable offence, nor is resistance far from another offence, assault. Indeed, in court, resisting arrest tends to be presented by prosecutors as indicative of guilt and therefore a justification of the arrest on the first charge anyway."

15. Similar factors which encourage discrimination are built into other procedural laws, e.g., the Canadian *Bail Reform Act*, which specifies criminal record and residential requirements as factors to determine the form of release and whether the accused can be held in custody for a bail hearing.

16. See Berger and Luckmann (1966: 110ff) for a discussion of the relationship among the concepts of explanation, justification, and legitimation.

Chapter 2

Research Strategy

As outlined in the previous chapter, our primary research interest is to understand detective discretion in terms of their use of rules and construction of accounts. We are interested in the interpretive work of detectives as this relates to the actions they take in producing case outcomes. Our research effort, based in the epistemology of symbolic interactionism, is directed at establishing valid knowledge about how detectives establish valid knowledge in their work-related transactions.

This epistemology and the attendant method have been articulated by Rock (1979, 1979a). Rock (1979: 61) states, "Valid knowledge is held to reside neither in the subject nor in the object but in the transactions that unfold between them.... It represents the emerging product of active encounters between consciousness and the materials which consciousness surveys." Sanders' (1977) and Manning's (1980) studies are the existing pieces of research on detective work which are most similar to this approach. Sanders points out how his work differs from that of many social action theorists (e.g., Goffman) in that they assume there is a real or factual state of affairs independent of interpretive work, while Sanders assumes that everything is subject to interpretation and then formulation as it is given the status of information and is presented as "factual." The point to emphasize is that there is a continuing dialectic between subject and object: they are at the same time producer and product of each other. Along with detectives and all other human beings, researchers are also involved in this process of interpretation, making inferences and ultimately deciding upon "what happened" (see generally Sanders, 1974). This process of constituting objects, of making something factual so that it comes to stand for reality, has been summarized well by Berger and Luckmann (1966) as "the social construction of reality."

In order to capture this dialectical process it is inadequate to study *separately* the subject (e.g., the interpretive thoughts and perceptions of detectives) *or* the object (e.g., the people detectives deal with; the documents they respond to and produce; the physical objects that they produce as evidence). Rather, one must observe directly the *transactions* between the two, i.e., the interpretations of detectives as they translate their thoughts into factual documents, evidence etc. in making something (literally) out of their cases. One must observe detectives at work, understanding the documents, crimes, victims, criminals, informants, etc., they produce in terms of the process by which they are produced.

In order to undertake observational work of the type demanded by our research designs, we needed to obtain a level of cooperation without precedent in Canada. This cooperation was achieved within a jurisdiction in the Canadian province of Ontario.[1] Through a series of meetings with the Chief of Police, the Chairman of the Board of Police Commissioners, the Crown attorney, and judges, a research programme was established in which a study of detectives was to be an integral part. We shall proceed to describe the procedures for the research, and then outline how the research was executed.

Research Procedures

The initial procedure for the detective study was to observe six two-person general investigation teams for at least two months each, covering both divisional stations within which criminal investigation units operated.[2] The police force had a "Special Services" branch, with separate squads dealing in homicide, fraud, morality (drugs, prostitution) and automobile related offences. However, these squads tended to engage in some long and complicated investigations involving several detectives on one case and/or investigation in very particular offence areas. By way of contrast, the general investigation officers conducted a full range of *Criminal Code* investigations, including at times the offence areas of the special squads. In order to generate a large number of cases in a wide range of offence areas, it was deemed more suitable to concentrate on studying the general investigation detective teams. As can be appreciated from a reading of subsequent chapters, a wide variety of case types were studied, representing a full range with the exception of homicide.

The strategy of working with six teams in two divisions for two months each proved to be difficult. The main problems were the uncooperativeness of some detectives, and the transfer of some detectives to special assignments or in-service courses during the period a field worker was assigned to them. Several compromises ensued. The author worked with the first team for 22 shifts, a second team for 39 shifts, and a third team for 13 shifts, over a four and one-half month period at one Division. A second field worker, who had just completed four months as an observer at the other Division on the uniform police study (Ericson, 1980), then undertook six months of field work in that divisional detective office. He worked with one team for 31 shifts, a second team for 68 shifts, and a detective operating alone for six shifts. Overall, then, the research field work period ran from May 1976 to March 1977, and involved six general investigation detective units over a total of 179 shifts.

The procedure established was for the field workers to work the same shifts as the detectives they were attached with. If these shifts changed from the usual work schedule, or the detectives were called in early, or the detectives worked overtime, the field workers normally followed the changes. This meant that during the period the field workers were attached to the detective team, they worked the same hours as detectives and therefore were with them for most activity. The only exception was when detectives were required to attend at court on their days off; if this involved a non-sample case, the field workers usually did not attend.

Field workers regularly observed detective office briefing sessions by the Detective Sergeant and/or Inspector at the beginning of the shift, as well as general office meetings held from time to time to deal with internal departmental concerns. They sat in the detective office while detectives made telephone calls regarding investigations and typed reports on investigations. They went out "on the road" with the detectives to interview complainants, victims, witnesses, and informants, to question suspects, to conduct searches on suspects, and to arrest suspects. They also went "on the road" for purposes of surveillance. The field workers did not systematically observe in-station interrogations, although they did view and/or hear many of these encounters. They also observed post-charge processing of accused persons, such as fingerprinting and photographing. They observed encounters with Justices of the Peace involving the release of accused persons, and requests for the issuance of warrants. If court time was scheduled on the shift, the field workers observed interaction between detectives and Crown attorneys, lawyers, witnesses, victims, and suspects, as well as detective testimony in court.

All cases which came to the attention of the detective teams during the period a field worker was attached to them formed the case sample for the study. This procedure produced a total of 295 cases. To argue that this constituted a random sample and that the cases are representative of all those worked on by general investigation detectives in the Force would require the following assumptions: (1) that the detective teams were randomly selected among all general investigation teams operating in both divisions; (2) that these would have been the same cases the detectives would have worked on over the same period if the researchers had not been present; and (3), that these cases are part of a wider universe of all cases coming to the attention of the general investigation units over the research period and do not differ significantly from them.

It is not possible to argue that any of these conditions were met. The detective teams were not randomly selected, but rather were variously chosen by the Divisional Detective Inspector, the Divisional Detective Inspector in consultation with the researcher, and in one case at the request of the researcher. It is impossible to determine if the detectives would have worked on the same cases if the researchers had not been present, but it is unlikely that they would have done so in all cases. For example, on a few occasions the field workers observed that a case appeared to be intentionally assigned to another detective team by a Detective Sergeant because of researcher presence with a particular team, and at other times Detective Sergeants appeared to be intentionally assigning cases to the team the researcher was with because they thought it would be "interesting" for the researcher. This type of case selection also had ramifications for the third condition noted above. For example, on a few occasions what the Detective Sergeant defined as a serious case involving more "experienced" offenders ("rounders") would appear to be purposely assigned to detectives other than those with a researcher attached to them.[3]

This situation meant that the sample was not random, and could more properly be described as a theoretical sample. That is, as the field work progressed, decisions to change detective teams and the nature of the cases being studied were taken in order to generate a wider range of cases and to examine different detective operating styles. This in turn was useful as a means of developing new information, insights, and explanations. The sampling was dictated by the paths that would be most fruitful in this connection, rather than according to the requirements of random sampling which could not in any case be met. Our primary research interest in detectives' use of rules and construction of accounts was not compromised, nor was our goal of generating verifiable knowledge (see generally Glaser and Strauss, 1967).

Three forms for systematic data collection were constructed prior to commencing the main field work period. An *Occurrence Report Investigation* form was created to document what information the detectives had at their disposal at the time the case first came to their attention, largely based on the official occurrence report originally taken by a uniform officer. This included information concerning when the occurrence took place, when it was recorded, the nature of the complaint, characteristics of the victim-complainant(s) and suspect(s), if known, a description of the damage, and the reporting officer's summary of the occurrence. It also included the dates on which the detectives received the case and completed it, their disposition of the case, whether there were other occurrences linked to it, whether the reporting uniform officer undertook any further investigation himself, whether the detectives interviewed any victim, complainant, witness or informant, and whether detectives dealt with any suspect.

Investigation forms were created to guide description of any face-to-face interviews between detectives and informants, victims, witnesses, and complainants. These dealt with status-role characteristics of interviewees; the circumstances leading to questioning; the setting of the questioning; the demeanour of the parties involved; the general line of questioning; the information obtained from questioning; detective retrospective accounts of the interview; how the detective used the information; and whether or not a formal written statement was taken.

Suspect forms were developed to guide recording of data based on any police interaction with a suspect. The topics included the status-role characteristics of the suspect; how he came to police attention; and his previous involvement with the police known at the time of dealing with him. If the person was questioned, items were included to describe the setting of questioning; the demeanour of the parties in questioning; the line of questioning and information obtained; how the person was approached; whether there were any constraints; whether the suspect confessed during questioning; retrospective accounts of the interview by detectives; and how they used any information obtained. Items were included concerning any searches undertaken. There were also items concerning the arrest process, including why an arrest was made, what was said at the time of arrest, at what stage in the proceedings the person was notified he was under arrest, and what the person said and did at the point of arrest. If the person was interrogated, items existed to record data concerning the place of the interrogation, the demeanour of the parties, the line of questioning, confessions and statements. Items were also included to cover charges and cautions; negotiation regarding charges; whether the person was apprised of his right to silence; whether access to a third party was requested and/or granted; the form of release; and, negotiations regarding bail.

Items for all three forms were open-ended, leaving room for the researcher to record details and variations that could not be anticipated in advance of field work. The items largely pertain to stages in the investigation process where specifiable decisions are taken.

Field notes were recorded for each shift. The field notes included seven main sections: a summary of times and events during a shift; notes taken by the detective himself and recorded in his own notebook; listing new cases coming to the attention of detectives on the shift; an account of all major case related activity during the shift; new information about procedures employed by detectives on the shift; explanations of significant events on the shift; and an account of the researcher's own "metamorphosis" (Sanders, 1977: 195) on the shift.

The *Investigation Interview* forms, the *Suspect* forms, and the *Field Notes*, were always written up after the shift and away from the field work setting. The *Occurrence Report Information* forms were usually written up in the office while the detectives were engaged in their "paper work." This was not problematic because this form mainly involved the copying of non-controversial material from official reports, and because this procedure allowed the researcher to be seen as "doing something" during the many hours that the detectives spent in the office.

Together, the field workers produced 167 schedules involving citizens in investigation interviews, and 96 schedules involving citizens treated by detectives as suspects, in 295 cases. The field workers also produced 871 pages of single-spaced typed field notes for the 179 shifts that were observed.

One month after the completion of each field work period, all occurrence report numbers for cases in the sample were recorded and all official documentation for them was photocopied through the records branch at headquarters. In addition, the name and date of birth of all citizens involved in the cases were checked through the police contact card file and any contact cards on them were copied.

During the course of the field work, the researchers also copied other documents that they thought might be relevant to the study. For example, copies were made of internal memoranda concerning productivity standards for detectives, and case memoranda written by detectives to senior officers and Crown attorneys.

Files were created for each of the 295 cases. Each file minimally contained the *Occurrence Report Information* giving basic details on the case, and a copy of the official occurrence report. If there were linked occurrences on the case, similar forms and official reports were included for each of them. If investigation interviews were conducted with citizens, then the appropriate *Investigation Interview* form for each citizen interview was placed on file. Similarly, when detectives interacted with persons they treated as a suspect, a *Suspect* form for each person was placed on the case file. In addition, any other relevant official documentation was filed by case, such as records of arrest, follow-up investigation reports, police contact cards, memoranda to superiors or Crown attorneys concerning the case, and written statements by victims, witnesses, and suspects.

The author created a qualitative data subject index from the field notes, and developed categories for the coding of data in quantitative form.

Four types of coding forms were established. The first dealt with basic shift activity such as when the shift took place, how time was spent on the shift, the number of new cases on the shift, the number of cases worked on during the shift, the number of contacts with persons in various role categories, arrests and charges, and case priorities. The data for this coding were exclusively derived from the field notes.

A second coding form was mainly derived from the *Occurrence Report Information* schedule. In addition to the data contained on the schedule, data from field notes were employed to create categories on what investigative activity was undertaken, the time spent on the case, the priority given to the case and the detective's reasons for doing so, the number of non-suspect persons interviewed, and the number of suspects interviewed, arrested and charged on the case.

A third coding form was mainly derived from the *Investigation Interview* schedule. In addition to data contained on the schedule, police contact cards were used to record the number of previous contacts the person had as a suspect and as a victim-complainant; and, the detective's reason for taking a written statement was recorded.

A fourth coding form was mainly derived from the *Suspect* schedule. In addition to data contained on the schedule, other items were included. As with investigation interviews, police contact cards were used to record the number of previous contacts the person had as a suspect and as a victim-complainant. The field worker was asked to record the detective's reason for *not* taking a written statement from the accused if he was charged. The "Activity" and "Detective Notes" sections of the field notes were used to obtain an estimate of the time the person was in the custody of detectives, the time in interrogation, the time spent in cells, and the time spent in routine processing after being charged.

The frequencies were examined as they informed our research interests, and they were also employed to suggest what meaningful cross-tabulations might be produced. Qualitative analysis was used where seemingly interesting or important quantitative findings begged questions that could be answered by describing particular events and providing detectives' accounts of them. Of course, heavy reliance was placed upon qualitative materials in the key areas of research interest which were not subject to meaningful quantification.

In the 295 cases included in the case sample, detectives produced 56 accused persons. These accused persons were included in a longitudinal research sample, and their cases were studied to the point of disposition in court via interviews with the accused and their lawyers, court observations, and the use of transcripts from tape-recorded discussions which transpired in offices of the Crown attorney.[4] In analyzing the detective's role in "staging" case outcomes in court, we have relied upon data from these other sources.

Research Execution

Researchers rarely give an account of their involvements in the research process and of how these involvements might influence the research product. Failure to provide an account deprives the reader of a key element needed to judge the product. As well as doing interpretive work specific to their own projects, researchers and their subjects do interpretive work in relation to each other. These transactions must be described and analyzed in order to provide a rounded research report.

In this section we provide an account of these transactions in order to sensitize the reader to data collection problems that affected the research report we have produced. This self-accusation not only provides the reader with a means of judging what we have produced, but has the additional pedological advantage of provoking others who might use other ideas and a different method into judging themselves. As Camus (1963: 113) has remarked in quite a different context:

> You see the advantage I am sure. The more I accuse myself, the more I
> have a right to judge you. Even better, I provoke you into judging
> yourself, and this relieves me of that much of the burden.

Prior to the commencement of field work the author held two meetings: one with senior officers concerning the expectations involved, and one with the detectives in the division in which the first observations would take place. General indicators of detective resistance to the research were revealed at this early stage.

The first meeting involved the Deputy Chief, the Detective Inspectors, and the Staff Sergeant in charge of the Youth Bureau. The Deputy Chief was apologetic for the tone of the meeting, which took the form of prolonged questioning of the author about his own background, attitudes, and purposes of the research. The very first indicator of problems came prior to the meeting, when the Deputy Chief said to the researcher, "We understand these things [research] at the top level, but some of the others down further just can't see it."

At the meeting, one Detective Inspector took the initiative to conduct the "interrogation." His questions reflected the concerns of his colleagues and subordinates. He asked if the research results would be used to control police discretion. He cited an FBI report which stated that nearly all criminologists in the western world are on the side of the criminal, and he sought the author's response to this "fact." He asked questions about the author's background, and attitudes towards issues such as captial punishment. As these questions become more intense, the author replied that he did not see what his attitudes had to do with the purpose of the meeting, to which the Detective Inspector responded, "You'll be asking us questions for the next eight months, so why can't we ask them now?" Another person asked about the source of funding for the project, and when the author mentioned that one source was a private foundation backed by a toothpaste and soap company, the Detective Inspectors turned to their colleague in charge of the Intelligence Unit, who smiled and stated, "They're clean."

One Detective Inspector agreed to have the researcher spend the first four months in his divisional office. The next meeting took place at this office during the shift change period, when all the detectives were present. The Inspector asked the researcher to outline his background and the nature of the project, and the detectives then asked questions which indicated similar concerns to those expressed in the meeting with Inspectors. The questions included: (1) the researcher's opinion of a journalist who had recently written an article on the criminal control system; (2) whether the research would serve the "criminal element"; (3) whether detectives could have access to research notes since researchers had access to their notes and records; (4) whether the researchers had worked out problems of evidence they might be asked to produce at *voir dire* proceedings; and (5) questions of confidentiality.

At the earliest stages both senior and line officers perceived that major problems stood in the way of complete access. Senior officers up to the level of the Deputy Chief in charge of Criminal Investigation indicated that the "subculture" that exists among working detectives would create difficulties for the researchers. The Deputy Chief noted that this "subculture" was even resistant to some other police officers, including some with years of experience, let alone a complete outsider. This statement echoes those of many police administrators and researchers. For example, Sir Robert Mark, former head of the Metropolitan London Police, stated in an address to the Institute of Journalists in London that the police have "an almost unconscious but natural bent towards reticence and secrecy in all matters" (Chibnall, 1979: 135). Bittner (1970: 65), Rubinstein (1973: 439) and Manning

(1977: 267) have all recorded that police officers are very reluctant to share information with each other, let alone with outsiders.

The Deputy Chief also expressed concern that there would be serious problems if a research observer witnessed a suspect's confession and was required to testify in court. As a result he was hesitant to allow researchers access to in-station interrogation settings, and a subsequent meeting involving the Deputy Chief, the Crown attorney, the Director of the Toronto Centre of Criminology, and the author did not resolve the matter. The result was a "wait and see" attitude that subsequently meant more waiting than seeing.

As we argue shortly, and as evidenced in the chapters that follow, these two major problems are not unrelated. Since one of the most potent rules of the detectives' occupational culture is the demand that fellow enforcers collaborate in constructing a case that secures what the police define as an acceptable outcome, conflicting definitions of "what happened" on the part of the researcher are likely to be met with immediate and permanent rejection.

In the early meetings the central concerns of detectives at all levels could be interpreted as one: whose interests would this research serve, the police or some anti-police element? Their reactions were quite understandable and predictable for a number of reasons. This was the first research of its kind in this jurisdiction, and indeed in Canada, and was therefore unprecedented. Moreover, apart from the divisional level meeting, there appeared to be little written communication within the Force about the nature of the research.[5] Any research observer is initially defined as a stranger whose loyalty and trustworthiness are suspect (Manning, 1972: 248). This "strange" aspect of our identity was compounded in our efforts at entrée into the detective world because we were a complete unknown mysteriously introduced through the top administrative level among workers whose occupation had socialized them to be persistently suspicious.

Furthermore, from the viewpoint of police interests, such suspicions are not unfounded. Detectives stake their expertise on the predictive power of their suspicions, and they are often accurate when the matter is viewed from their perspective. Detectives possess an abundance of "cynical knowledge," i.e., "information that undercuts the idealized myths or knowledge used to explain unknown events . . . and reduces altruistic explanation . . ." (Manning, 1979a: 57, referring to Gouldner, Ritti and Ferenie, 1977). They know that sustained transactions with a researcher during the course of their work will result in a transmission of this "cynical knowledge" to the researcher. They also know the uses that can be made of this "cynical knowledge": it can make questionable the public image of their organizational authority and the practices which sustain it. "[The] solid front presented to the public at large on public and ceremonial occasions, or in court for example, crumbles from the inside because of cynical knowledge" (ibid.: 57).

The astuteness of detective observations about the research

observers was translated into practice. In the author's field work experience, over four and one-half months at one division, he became viewed as a liberal sympathizer with "criminals" among other "underdogs." For example, detectives would often check what they were saying about how suspects were handled, or check racist comments, making reference to the researcher's presence. One detective, who was not on a team being observed, regularly stated that the researcher had no business being in the detective office and that he would not cooperate in any way because the research was "obviously" against police interests.

This general perception among detectives was in turn parlayed into a justification for excluding the researcher from witnessing particular events. For example, at a very early juncture in the field work the researcher asked the Divisional Inspector if there could be more access to interrogation situations. The Detective Inspector replied that access would continue to be restricted because the detectives were uncertain about the "quality" of testimony the researcher might give on their behalf. He repeatedly cited a recently completed case in which a police officer from the Force was convicted of assault and imprisoned for seven days "because" the testimony of one police officer witness conflicted with that given by the other police officers who testified. The Detective Inspector asserted that if these problems arose in the testimony of their own members, they were compounded many times over when the police had to rely on what they regarded as the more unpredictable testimony of someone who was not a member of the police fraternity.

Near the end of the first four months of field work the researcher had a dispute with a detective who refused to allow access to a routine interview with a victim. The researcher approached the Detective Inspector in an effort to rectify the situation, or to seek assignment to another detective team. The Detective Inspector replied that other than the three teams the researcher had already observed, there were no alternatives in his division because the remaining detectives all expressed a distrust of whose side the researcher was on. One explanation he gave was that the detectives were worried about researcher testimony, especially in possible civil suit situations:

> They just don't know what you're going to support in a situation like that. I'm not saying that they lie, but they want someone on their side. You're not a policeman. I don't blame them really. I would be the same way if I was in their position. I think they [the Force] went about this the wrong way. They should have had you become a policeman—even if it took two years—then you would really have understood it.

The latter response was a prevalent one made by many persons from the level of Deputy Chief to detectives subject to observation: if you want to "really" understand detective work, you must become a member of the Force. One very senior officer referred the researcher to the work of George Kirkham (1974), a criminologist who had joined a police force and who became enthusiastically pro-police in the process, suggesting that the researcher should adopt Kirkham's methods.

Translated, this meant that the researcher could only be trusted and given extensive access if he was organizationally tied in and made responsible to the detective fraternity and the wider interests they felt they represented. One detective, who said he would be willing to have the researcher as a partner on a detective team and to allow access to interrogations and all other situations, was quick to add that, "Of course, I would expect any good partner to be—you know what I mean—he would have to tell my version of what happened in court."

The researchers did not alter their observer role, and suspicion remained that different perceptions based upon different experiences meant the researchers would not collaborate in the versions of the truth the detectives wished to construct. Consequently, throughout the various ranks and units of the Criminal Investigation Branch there were active attempts to construct the research experience in very particular directions.

The researchers initially wished to select the detective teams on a random basis so that it was possible to build in related assumptions of randomness for data analysis. However, it was clear from the beginning that some detective teams might actively resist cooperation and that it would only be possible to gain access to detective teams preselected by the administration. As the field work progressed there was a little more flexibility introduced, but the effect of having organizationally-selected rather than researcher-selected teams should not be minimized.

The first team selected for observation was the "sex offence" team. Among the 12 detective teams operating in the divisional general investigation office at this particular time, only one was devoted to coordination of sex offence investigations. This assignment appeared to be made on the following grounds: (1) the sex offence area was one in which the investigation was very much victim-complainant oriented, with victim-complainant interviews conducted on a routine basis for various purposes, including "PR"; (2) compared with other offender types, sex offenders were more often viewed by the police as persons in need of "help" because their offences were "caused" by social and personal forces beyond their control; and, (3) the detectives involved were of the same age range as the field worker, one had taken university criminology courses, and they both were respected officers within the police organization. In other words compared with, for example, investigation of break and enter offences, the sex offence investigative area involved empathetic attention to victims and a more liberal-humane view of offenders worked by detectives whose training at least partially reflected this special orientation. Among the available types of investigation, this was certainly the one in closest accord with what the police might think a criminologist wanted to see, or should see.

Subsequent assignments to other detective teams occurred after fundamental problems had arisen, and/or when the field workers decided it was strategic to seek a change. There were two grounds on which the field workers sensed that they had exhausted the learning potential of being attached to a particular detective team: (1) they were being denied access to the point where their efforts were futile; (2) they had spent an extended period with a team and believed that a new assignment would enrich the quality of the data collected.

As soon as the first (sex offence) team was assigned, the researcher pointed out to the Detective Inspector that in order to obtain a rounded view it would be necessary to observe other detective teams working on property crimes. The Detective Inspector stated that he might later assign property crime reports to the sex offence team. When the researcher objected on the grounds that he did not want to interfere with the normal assignment process in the office, the Detective Inspector agreed to consider a change to a general team within two months. However, the change occurred after one month due to another set of circumstances that we shall proceed to describe.

As previously stated, the key access problem once detective teams had been assigned was the policy of exclusion from some in-station interrogation interviews with suspects. From the beginning, the researcher attempted to alter this exclusion, first by appealing to the detectives being observed, and when this failed, taking it to the administrative level. However, these attempts were unsuccessful, and in the long run they had the negative consequence of creating further problems for the research process.

The detectives and their superordinates gave various justifications for exclusion from interrogations, including: (1) referring to a particular judge who was "sticky" on statements and who might see the researcher's presence as an influence on a statement; (2) seeing an added witness to a statement as one more basis on which the detective's definition of reality might be challenged in court; (3) arguing that the presence of extra persons is not a good interrogation strategy, especially when discussing sensitive matters such as sex offences.[6] Furthermore, while they did allow access to interrogations in some situations, the detectives argued that if they were known to have allowed access to some interrogations and not others, questions would be raised about the reason for selective exclusion.

After 18 shifts with the first detective team, the field worker realized that there was a crucial shortcoming in the data brought about by lack of systematic access to interrogations. In discussions with members of the detective team, the researcher received the justifications for exclusion noted above as well as the assertion that the detectives were under orders from their Inspector not to allow access. The researcher then stated that he would proceed to seek a change in this policy at higher levels. Shortly after, one detective on the team was transferred to the citizen complaint bureau. The researcher in turn sought and obtained assignment to a general investigation team.

Soon after assignment to the second team, a meeting was held with the Deputy Chief in charge of criminal investigation in order to obtain a change in the policy regarding access to interrogations. However, citing the justifications enumerated above, the Deputy Chief continued to deny access and noted that the researcher had created problems by stepping over the heads of line officers. Not only was access denied, the entire criminal investigation branch throughout the rank structure was solidified against granting access.

The second assignment proved to be a fruitful one. It was terminated when the field worker decided to seek assignment to a third team in order to broaden his appreciation of detective styles in conducting their work. This third assignment was again problematic. After ten shifts one detective was transferred to the homicide squad, and the second detective then became very resistant to the field worker's presence. At this juncture the field work in the division was terminated, and a different field worker started at another division.

The first assignment in the new division also proved to be problematic. On the first shift, the field worker discovered that one team member had been assigned to an in-service training course for three weeks. The other detective later learned that he would go on a two week course when his partner returned, and he used this as a justification for spending a considerable period of time in the office writing reports rather than going out on active investigations. Moreover, after the first few shifts he began to arrange his activities so as to exclude the field worker. For example, on one shift the detective came into the office one hour before the scheduled beginning of the shift period and then went out on assignment with another detective. He did not return during the 1-1/2 hours the field worker waited at the detective office, and the researcher eventually returned home having wasted his time.

This pattern of arranging things without the researcher's knowlege, or simply excluding him, escalated when both detective team members returned from their courses and began working together. Over seven successive shifts, the detectives twice came on the shift early and then went out to conduct investigations without involving the researcher; excluded the researcher from interviews with informants and with a Crown attorney; went out to conduct investigations without inviting the researcher, who was in the Detective Sergeant's office; and, would not allow the researcher to join them in a "drug" raid on an apartment unit. Exasperated, the field worker approached the Detective Inspector and negotiated re-assignment to one of two detective teams suggested by the field worker.

From this point onward, the field worker managed to develop increasing rapport and attendant access to a wider range of situations. Until this point, however, the field workers in both divisions encountered considerable problems in the form of administrative transfers and detective evasive strategies that upset the field work process.

In addition to the forms of exclusion that we have discussed, there was the possibility that cases were selectively allocated or not allocated to the detective team being observed because of the presence of a field worker. It is of course impossible to estimate how pervasive this practice was because we could not determine what cases would have been allocated if a field worker was not present.

There were a few cases which seemed to be assigned because of the field worker's presence. For example, in Detective case (DC) 97 the Inspector asked the detective team to investigate a complaint from a plant manager that uniform officers had mishandled their preliminary response to a break and enter at the plant. The detectives spent the better part of a week on this investigation, which was directed more toward satisfying the plant manager than toward generating a suspect. The detectives indicated that this type of complaint was more commonly handled by the citizen complaint bureau, and they were very surprised that they had received the assignment. The field worker interpreted this as an effort by the Force to have him observe the handling of citizen complaints; senior officers had earlier suggested that the researcher spend time observing the citizen complaint bureau, a suggestion that was sidestepped by the researcher whenever it arose.

At other stages in the field work, Detective Sergeants appeared to be assigning interesting "hot suspect" cases to the detectives being observed by field workers. For example, one detective received three "hot suspect" cases over three successive shifts. This was a most unusual occurrence that was interpreted by the field worker as an attempt by the Detective Sergeant to give him some action (DS92, 93, 94).

Our cataloguing of problems in accomplishing the research would not be complete without discussion of attempts by detectives to use field workers as allies in policing tasks. We have already considered this aspect in terms of *exclusion*, e.g., not allowing field workers to systematically observe interrogations so that detectives could construct their version of reality unencumbered by the possibility of countervailing interpretations from field workers. In addition, there were many attempts at *inclusion* of field workers in policing tasks.

Some attempts by detectives to make use of field workers were not related to particular situated strategies, but rather were general efforts to alter the researcher's role. For example, one detective attempted to actively involve the researcher in investigations by handing him files to scrutinize for possible leads and by asking him to assist in questioning citizens. When the researcher stated that this was not his role, the detective revealed the key reason for wanting to involve the field worker: it was "awkward" to have the field worker sit in on lengthy interviews and simply remain silent. The detective stated that the people being interviewed during the course of investigations kept looking in the researcher's direction, and stressed that it would be appreciated if the researcher would ask questions relevant to the investigation, particularly of victims. The detective's view was also indicated in the general investigative detective office in a comment to two other detectives: "[Researcher's first name] and I were out investigating this afternoon. [Partner's first name] is off."

One could impute other motives to these actions, including the interpretation that the detective was trying to co-opt the researcher into functioning as a detective in the hope that the researcher might change his observer status and become an ally. However, our impression is that this was not the case; rather, the detective simply felt that it would ease the "unnaturalness" of the researcher's presence by involving him to some degree.

We give a similar interpretation to the detective practice of occasionally recording times and events from the researcher's notebook. This could be viewed as an attempt by detectives to officially record the same details of their activities as those possessed by the field worker in order to avoid discrepancies in accounts. However, we view this as a casual practice that occurred when detectives had simply not bothered to keep an accurate account of their activities. Detectives generally adopted a casual attitude to their notebook record, sometimes not bothering to write up shift activities until days after the shift had been worked. Since they knew field workers were keeping an ongoing account, this was an obvious way to ease their task. It was also an obvious way for researchers to show a small degree of reciprocity for the detectives' general cooperation.

Other efforts at including researchers were more strategic in character, and arose out of particular needs in specific situations. One area in which detectives fluctuated according to the circumstance was the identification of researchers to citizens. One detective team regularly identified the researcher to citizens as a researcher from the University of Toronto, except when the encounter involved a suspect who might prove troublesome. In these circumstances—e.g., during a search and attendant interrogation at a suspect's residence—the detectives would remain silent about the researcher's identity, at least until after they had obtained the evidence they desired. Similarly, when the citizen was in the role of informant, detectives led him to believe that the researcher was a detective, even when the citizen directly asked about the researcher's identity.

These situations obviously posed both pragmatic and ethical dilemmas for field workers. Ethically, citizens who believed field workers were detectives might have experienced additional intimidation in the circumstances. The experience of having three "detectives" effect apprehension for, say, indecent exposure, must have been strange indeed! Pragmatically, researchers could not have stepped in and revealed their identity without upsetting the detectives whose cooperation they struggled so hard to obtain. Moreover, if the field workers revealed their identity, the citizens might have excluded them, or alternatively, sought their assistance as "third parties" in the situation. In sum, the most pragmatic route for researchers was to go along with whatever identification the detectives produced for them in particular circumstances.

In spite of their stated wish to avoid having researchers appear as court witnesses, the detectives, through the Crown attorney, had a researcher subpoenaed as a Crown witness in relation to three separate cases. Two of these cases were settled at the Provincial Court level with guilty pleas, and the researcher was not asked to testify in court. The third case proceeded to a trial in the Supreme Court of Ontario. The researcher testified at a *voir dire* hearing on the admissibility of the accused's statement and at the trial, both of which took place before a judge and jury.

One cannot overlook the possibility that the detectives were strategically using the "halo" effect of the researcher's "professor" status to aid them in their cause. In the Provincial Court cases, the revelation to the lawyers that the Crown had a "professor" as a sub-poenaed witness to the police processing of the case, without disclosing the details of what the witness had to say, may have been an additional encouragement to a guilty plea. We do not know if this did have an ef-fect, but the potential danger was there. Researchers contemplating similar work stand forewarned of this problem.[7]

While there were numerous difficulties in accomplishing the research, there were also signs that the field workers were obtaining naturalistic data according to their original designs. This was most evidently revealed by a number of things the detectives did do in the presence of researchers, even though these things might have been viewed as highly questionable by persons who were not members of the police fraternity.

Detectives talked about and engaged in a number of legally and organizationally questionable practices in the presence of field workers. For example, they allowed field workers to become informed about legally questionable practices and possible violations of work rules. Given that we were allowed to witness various questionable ac-tivities, it is difficult to entertain the argument that our presence con-sistently led the detectives not to behave the way they "normally" did.

We argue that because we spent many shifts with each detective team, involving several hundred hours of direct interaction, we were able to overcome impression management strategies by detectives. In the observational component of their research, Greenwood and asso-ciates (1975: 46) report "that only a brief familiarization period, lasting about a day, intervenes before observed investigators return to their usual practices." This is a familiar pattern in field work experiences with any subjects; indeed, it is one of the key advantages of doing observation work over an extended period. Subjects are likely to even-tually behave "as usual" because they are unlikely, or indeed unable, to change the way they relate to the wide range of persons they deal with in their everyday occupational environment for the sole purpose of impression management vis-à-vis an observer whose role is vaguely defined (cf. Skolnick, 1966: 36-37).

Overall, the level of cooperation and the attendant access was remarkable. The major problem for the research was the lack of *systematic* access to the interrogation process, which is the obvious focal point for all transactions in the criminal process. Otherwise, we eventually accomplished the type of access initially envisaged. As mentioned elsewhere (Chan and Doob, 1977; Ericson, 1980) the level of cooperation can best be appreciated by imagining what might have happened if the roles were reversed: how would we have reacted as university staff members if detectives were given the grace of the university administration to search all our research and student files, attend committee meetings, listen to us as we interviewed students and talked on the telephone, followed us to lunch, etc.?

This outline of our research strategy informs the reader about how we entered the world of detective work. We now proceed to document what transpired in that world, beginning with an examination of the occupational environment as an important "backdrop" to the analysis of specific detective decisions that is presented in Chapters 4 to 6.

NOTES

1. A description of the jurisdiction is contained in Ericson (1980: Ch. 2).

2. In a survey of detective units within American municipal police departments, Chaiken (1975: 16) found that the "vast majority" of detectives worked singly and not in two-person teams. He also found that arrest rates and clearance rates did not significantly vary according to whether detectives operated alone or in pairs. In the police force we studied, the practice at the time of the research was to operate in two-person teams. As considered in the next section, this sometimes made it difficult for the researcher (and detectives!) because citizens who routinely deal with the police are not used to three-person teams.

3. More detail on this problem, and on other problems mentioned in this section, is provided in the next section on "Research Execution."

4. This longitudinal sample also includes 73 accused persons charged by patrol officers in our uniform police study (Ericson, 1980), and forms a core sample for a research programme entitled "A Longitudinal Study of the Cumulative Effects of Discretionary Decisions in the Criminal Justice System" conducted at the Centre of Criminology, University of Toronto. This longitudinal core sample of accused was followed in detail from the initial contact with the police through to the final court disposition as worked upon and perceived by various actors involved (police, victim, accused, lawyer, Crown attorney). Sub-studies have been conducted in relation to each of these actors in the criminal process. These sub-studies include the core sample cases as well as a much larger sample of cases unique to each sub-study (with the exception of the accused study, which is based upon the longitudinal core sample only). The reader should refer to the sub-studies on the accused (Ericson and Baranek, 1981), lawyers (Mcfarlane and Giffen, 1981), and Crown attorneys (Wilkins, 1981) in order to obtain an understanding of how data were collected for each of them. In addition, these reports document how each of the other participants perceive and transact with detectives.

5. All personnel in the police force were given a written directive from the Chief indicating that researchers would be present from "time to time" at the Chief's discretion and advising all officers to familiarize themselves with sections of the *Criminal Code* dealing with civilian assistance to police officers.

6. Skolnick (1966) reports participation in interrogations, even to the point of being a witness to signed statements of confession. However, Skolnick provides no details on the number or nature of his involvements in interrogations. Sanders (1977: 127) was excluded from interrogations. Sanders reports that this was justified to him on the grounds that interrogations are more "successful" from the detectives' viewpoint if there is only one person present in the interrogation room.

7. In the Supreme Court of Ontario case in which the researcher testified, the accused claimed that he gave a signed written statement of confession only after he was physically beaten by detectives. The researcher was interviewed by a citizen complaint bureau officer, who took a written witness statement from the researcher, and later submitted it to the Crown attorney. When the researcher was later approached by a private investigator for the defence lawyer, he agreed to give a copy of his witness statement to him. This "disclosure" angered the Crown attorney, but in the researcher's mind it was necessary in order to ensure that there was no manipulative advantage to either side.

Chapter 3

The Occupational Environment of Detective Work

The starting point for an analysis of detective work is the police organization. The police organization embodies the structural framework for detective work and includes the occupational culture of detectives through which the structural framework is filtered. In this chapter we stay *within* the police organization, examining what detectives produce in terms of internally established parameters. We initially describe detectives' work related shift activity. We then proceed to analyze how detectives as workers are tied into the organization. As Manning (1979a: 42) states, "[A]ny depiction of police work that overlooks the centrality of the integration of actors into the organization, and the form and content of that integration, will remain a partial picture." Our portrayal of detective work in this chapter provides us with necessary background for our analyses in subsequent chapters, where we examine detective transactions with those persons outside the police organization who provide grist for the mill of crime production.

An Overview of Detective Activity

Detective activity was primarily geared to the disposition of cases. A case involved one or more occurrence reports. One occurrence report was submitted for each incident that was deemed by a police officer to be worthy of reporting for organizational purposes. The occurrence reports were usually linked with a complainant, e.g., if in one act a person threw a can of paint over three cars owned by three different people, three occurrence reports would be produced. One case could have one or more occurrence reports. Whether or not there was more than one occurrence report for a case usually depended on whether occurrences could be linked on the basis of a similar *modus operandi* of the suspect(s) or other knowledge that the same suspect(s) was responsible for multiple occurrences.

As documented in Chapter Four, most cases that detectives worked on were initially mobilized on the basis of occurrence reports submitted by a patrol officer to his patrol sergeant, and from the patrol

Table 3:1

Detective Shift Activity Related to Case Clearance

Activity	Number 179 shifts	Mean 179 shifts	Number of shifts on which activity undertaken	% of 179 shifts	Mean for shifts on which activity undertaken
Case investigations worked	310	1.73	156	87.2	1.98
Non-suspect citizen contacts	405	2.26	140	78.2	2.89
Criminal Control Official Contacts	92	.51	62	34.6	1.48
Suspect Contacts	132	.74	88	49.2	1.50
Arrests	33	.18	28	15.6	1.18
Persons Charged	51	.29	37	20.7	1.38
Charges Laid	101	.56	37	20.7	2.73

sergeant through a staff sergeant to the detective sergeant, who either assigned the occurrence directly to a detective team or left it on a general file to be selected by any detective who chose to work on it. At this point the detective's task became one of deciding what investigations he could do to provide a legitimate written account of a particular case "clearance." He worked to "cover his ass" by producing a "clearance" with written reasons that fit within organizationally established criteria.

In Table 3:1 we provide data on detective shift activity as it related to the clearance of their cases over the 179 shifts of observation. The vast majority of these activities were connected with our research sample of 295 cases, although activities related to non-sample cases are also included in Table 3:1 in order to provide a complete picture of what was produced on the 179 shifts.

Over the 179 shifts of observation, the detectives studied undertook a total of 310 case-related investigations. This does not mean that they investigated 310 different cases; the same case investigated on separate shifts is counted each time. We learn from Table 3:1 that some case investigation was undertaken on 87 percent of the shifts, with an average of 1.73 cases per shift over all the shifts and almost two per shift on those shifts when this activity was undertaken. The 23 shifts where no investigative action was conducted primarily involved the detectives working on reports in the office. One detective team in particular spent several shifts on reports as they were trying to bring their "paper work" up to date prior to taking leave for an in-service training course.

The primary investigative activity was interviewing victims, complainants, witnesses and informants for information relevant to an investigation. This involved a telephone call, an interview with the citizen at the station, or a visit to the home or place of employment of the person. The non-suspect citizen contacts recorded in Table 3:1 include all those involving direct face-to-face contact with the citizen, and exclude telephone calls. Contacts of this sort were undertaken on 78 percent of the shifts, involving 405 separate encounters or an average of almost three per shift on those shifts when there was such activity and slightly more than two per shift overall.

One-third of the 179 shifts involved at least one contact related to case investigation with other criminal control agents. The vast majority of these contacts were with Justices of the Peace for warrant applications or the release of accused persons, and with Crown attorneys for advice or to discuss charges and other case related matters. Excluded from this total are telephone conversations with other criminal control agents. These contacts averaged three for every two shifts on which they occurred, and one for every two shifts overall.

Another major form of investigative activity was contacting suspects. These were face-to-face contacts typically initiated in field settings, although they also occurred at the divisional station when the person had been arrested by other police officers or when he had been asked by detectives over the telephone to come to the station for questioning. As recorded in Table 3:1, at least one contact with a suspect occurred on one-half of the shifts. The average was two such contacts for every three shifts overall, but three for every two shifts on which suspect contacts actually occurred.

Arrests were not a dominant shift activity for general investigation detectives.[1] On average the detectives arrested someone once every five or six shifts, and on those shifts where this activity did occur, there was typically only one arrest per shift. As documented in more detail in Chapters 4 and 6, detectives often took over the interrogation and subsequent processing of suspects originally arrested by uniform officers, or in a few cases by other detectives, which in part accounts for the infrequency of arrest activity by the detectives in our study. This latter point is made obvious when we consider the fact that the detectives we observed charged a total of 51 different persons even though they arrested only 33. When we take into account that some of these arrests did not result in the person being charged, we can understand the extent to which detective production in the charge category was very much an extension of activity undertaken by their colleagues, especially members of the uniform branch.[2]

Shifts when persons were charged were not frequent. The average was approximately four persons charged for every three shifts on which this activity took place, but only slightly more than one person charged for every five shifts overall.

Finally we consider the number of charges laid, noting that multiple charging appears to be the norm. A total of 101 charges were laid in relation to the 51 persons charged, resulting in an average of two charges for every person charged. While charging only occurred once every five shifts, when it did occur there were almost three charges laid per shift. It must be noted that one case included in these totals involved a person being charged with 21 separate counts over two separate shifts. If this one statistically deviant case is removed, our totals change to 80 charges over 177 shifts, and 35 shifts on which charging took place. This reduces the mean for shifts on which the activity was undertaken to 2.28. However, it could be argued that a major case of this nature, involving a large number of multiple charges related to property offences against one suspect, is likely to occur at least once over 179 shifts for any given general investigation detective team, and in that respect it is reasonable to include this case in the totals.

The portrayal of detective activity in Table 3:1 gives no indication of the fact that only one-third of the time spent on shifts by the detectives in our study was actually devoted to active case investigation. A different portrayal of the nature of detective work comes from a consideration of how time was distributed over the variety of activities that constituted the everyday work of detectives in our sample. Table 3:2 includes data pertaining to this time distribution; these data are based on field workers' recording of time spent on each activity as contained in the research field notes.

As indicated in Table 3:2, the time spent is recorded in hours. It should be noted that while the average length of each shift was exactly eight hours, this does not mean that every shift was of this duration. Detectives worked either an 8:00 a.m. to 4:00 p.m. shift or a 4:00 p.m. to midnight shift, but they also worked overtime. Overtime typically occured when an urgent case came up during the shift which required immediate extended investigation, or when a suspect was in custody and there was a need to complete the investigation in order to release him or hold him for a bail hearing. On the other hand, detectives were able to use "credits" they had obtained in working overtime in order to take time off from their regular shift schedule. Occasionally a detective would work the first few hours of a shift and then leave early. In the present study, it happened that the balance between overtime and taking leave from the regular shift schedule resulted in an eight hour average per shift.

It is important to observe from Table 3:2 that almost one half of the detectives' time was spent in the office. This does *not* include time spent in the office interviewing citizens or dealing with suspects and accused persons. Except for one shift when the detectives drove over two hundred miles to another town to arrest and return a suspect, office activity was part of the work of every shift. By far the most common activity of detectives was to sit at a desk in an open office area to type reports, review files, call citizens connected with case investigations, and to hold both formal and informal meetings about a variety of matters relating to investigation priorities and procedures, and office routine.

Among other things, the substantial amount of time spent in the office is testimony to the organizational demand placed upon the detec-

Table 3:2

Detective Time Spent on Shift Activities

Shift Activity	Time/179 Shifts (hrs.)	% of Total Time	Mean Time/ Shift (hrs.)	# of shifts on which activity undertaken	% of 179 shifts	Mean Time for shifts on which activity undertaken
Office	664.33	46.4	3.71	178	99.4	3.73
General Patrol	31.92	2.2	.18	27	15.1	1.18
Court	34.25	2.4	.19	20	11.2	1.71
Non-Police Activity	160.92	11.2	.90	121	67.6	1.33
Miscellaneous	73.20	5.1	.41	73	40.8	1.00
Case Investigation	*315.93*	*22.1*	*1.76*	—	—	—
Non-citizen Investigation	61.58	4.3	.34	60	33.5	1.03
Travelling No investigation	42.58	3.0	.24	58	32.4	.73
Travelling Investigation	103.50	7.2	.58	137	76.5	.76
Witness Interviews	14.45	1.0	.08	22	12.3	.66
Victim-Complainant Interviews	45.10	3.2	.25	75	41.9	.60
Informant Interviews	48.72	3.4	.27	79	44.1	.62
Suspect-Accused Investigation	*151.19*	*10.6*	*.84*	—	—	—
Suspect Interviews	46.28	3.2	.26	67	37.4	.69
Suspect Interrogation	64.18	4.5	.36	40	22.3	1.60
Accused Processing	40.73	2.9	.23	32	17.9	1.27
Totals	1431.74	100.0	8.00			

tive to provide extensive written accounts of his investigative activity. More time was spent providing the accounts than actually engaging in investigative activity. This is in keeping with a statement made by an ex-FBI agent (quoted by Walters and Gillers (1973)) who considers the FBI to be a "paper police" who spend more time on paper work than on the actual detection of crime. It is also supportive of the conclusion of Greenwood et al. (1975: 83) that "It is . . . not appropriate to view the investigator's role as that of solving crimes. Investigators do not spend much time on activities that lead to clearances, and most of their work in this connection could be performed by clerical personnel."[3]

Activity not related to specific case or suspect investigation accounted for a further 21 percent of detective time, including 11 percent of the total time on "non-police activity." This included activities such as conducting personal business during the shift, making personal visits to friends or relatives, and shopping. One explanation of this is that supervisors allow detectives flexibility in conducting personal business during a shift in exchange for brief periods of unclaimed overtime, shortened lunches etc. when the need arises. The "miscellaneous" category includes a variety of activities usually related to criminal cases, such as travelling to and from the location of the Justice of the Peace and spending time with him, transporting prisoners, and running errands for superior officers.

Detectives did not frequently engage in general patrol acitivity, which was thus left almost entirely to the uniform patrol branch. General patrol took place on only 27 shifts, and on those shifts the average time was slightly more than one hour per shift. When general patrol did take place, it was usually taken up as a residual activity when detectives decided there was little else to do. General patrol most frequently occurred near the end of 4:00 p.m. to midnight shifts when the detectives felt it was too late in the evening to call on non-suspect citizens for interviews. Typically it involved cruising by stores that stayed open at night, especially popular "milk stores" that closed at 11:00 p.m., keeping surveillance regarding the possibility of robberies.

It should be noted that marginally more than 10 percent of *all* detective time was spent travelling to and from investigation points. The detectives were usually "on air" to the dispatcher during this time, so that one could also regard this time as involving general patrol.

Table 3:2 also indicates that detectives spent very little shift time in court. Court was attended on only 20 shifts for an average of approximately 1-3/4 hours for each of these shifts. However, the data presented here do not include time spent in court on what would normally have been time off for the detectives; as stated in Chapter 2, detectives were not observed during these periods.

The general investigation detectives in our sample spent 22 percent of their time on activity related to case investigation other than involvement with suspects, averaging approximately 1-3/4 hours per shift in this area. However, as documented in Table 3:2, this includes time spent travelling to and from investigation points (which accounted for over 10 percent of all detective time) and an additional 4.3 percent of their total time conducting non-citizen investigation (e.g., searching for physical evidence, and surveillance). Thus, between 7 and 8 percent of the total time of detectives in our study was spent on face-to-face investigative contact with citizens in the roles of victim, complainant, witness, and informant.

A slightly greater proportion of time was spent in direct contact with citizens treated as suspects or accused persons by detectives. Approximately 3 percent of all detective time was spent questioning suspects in field settings, an additional 4.5 percent of their time involved interrogation interviews, and a further 3 percent of their time was taken up with post-charge processing of accused persons prior to their release. As we noted earlier in considering the volume of detective activity related to handling suspects and accused persons, this activity did not occur at all on the majority of shifts. From Table 3:2 we learn that only fractionally more than 10 percent of all detective time was spent dealing directly with suspects and accused persons.

Detectives frequently commented about the low level of their activity and its relationship to the kind of cases they worked on. Detectives who had previously worked in other police forces, especially the Metropolitan Toronto Police Force, claimed that they investigated matters in the police force under study that would not have been investigated in their former forces. For example, a detective reflected upon the six years he had spent in the Toronto force, stating, "There was lots to do down there. Not like here. Down there they wouldn't even deal with half the stuff we investigate here, wouldn't have time."

Another detective, also with experience on the Toronto force, claimed that not only were more trivial matters investigated in the police force under study, but the investigations were more thorough and charges were more likely to be laid. During field work observation there were occasions when matters which were minor, or could only result in summary conviction charges, were pursued with vehemence. This was particularly the case in the sex offence area; for example, summary conviction "Indecent Exposure" cases were pursued vigorously. In one case, the senior detective charged a man with having sexual intercourse with a person under 16 after a reported incident between a 22 year old boarder and the 14 year old daughter of the landlady. As one detective left the house after the suspect had been charged and released on an appearance notice, the junior detective, who had waited outside asked, "Did you charge him?"

Senior Detective: Oh, yes.

Junior Detective: Its funny, a friend of mine in 23 [Division of the Toronto police] on the same Sunday had the same circumstances. A boarder and the whole thing. But they just cautioned him.

Senior Detective: Did they?

Junior Detective: Yea, they would have done that [cautioned the present accused] in Metro. They would never have charged him there.

Detectives were also involved with many minor property offences, such as "Theft Under $200" cases involving shoplifters and the use of metal "slugs" in pinball machines. The detectives sometimes claimed they were only working on these cases because there was nothing of greater consequence to pursue.

The level of work in a detective office was not constant. It is instructive to present in ideal typical fashion examples of low, medium and high activity level shifts in order to show the variation and point to some of the reasons for it.

We have already mentioned that a few shifts were spent entirely in the office. This typically occurred when the detectives were attempting to "catch up" in writing reports, or when one member of the team was serving as an Acting Detective Sergeant. There were many more shifts in which some minor investigative activity was undertaken, but which were still relatively inactive in terms of pursuing investigations. We have selected one of these shifts as an example of a low activity shift.

DS 107 involved the detectives spending the first 5-1/2 hours of the 8:00 to 4:00 p.m. period in the office, with the major task being the preparation of a court brief for the Crown attorney. At 1:30 a visit was made to the home of a victim who had previously reported a break and enter. She was shown a photograph of a possible suspect, and identified him as the person she suspected. This victim interview lasted approximately ten minutes, and was followed by a visit to the home of an informant identified by the victim as having more information about the suspect's involvement in the case. The informant was interviewed for five minutes, but refused to supply the information the victim claimed he could offer. Following this, the detective proceeded to a pre-arranged meeting with a member of the Bomb Disposal Unit regarding a bombing of a vehicle that had occurred a month earlier and was still being investigated. This meeting lasted for three-quarters of an hour after which the detective returned to the office, where he spent the last fifty minutes before departing at 4:00 p.m.

A shift with a medium level of activity typically involved the two detectives in more investigation interviews with citizens and other activity in the field, and less time in the office on reports. On DS 161, again in the 8:00 a.m. to 4:00 p.m. time period, the detectives spent the first hour in the office working on reports. They then went out "on the road," stopping in a restaurant for breakfast before proceeding to the court building. The detectives spent fifteen minutes at the court arranging for a withdrawal of a theft charge against a suspect who was due to appear on that date. From the court, the detectives returned to their divisional office and spent the following three-quarters of an hour checking through their files for occurrences for follow-up investigations.

The detectives then proceeded to contact victim-complainants associated with these follow-up occurrences. The first of these was a fifteen minute interview with the shipper at a transport company, who had reported that an ex-employee was still using the company credit card to make purchases. The detectives took the licence number from the credit card slips, stating that they would check it to find the suspect's address. From there they drove to the airport to investigate a complaint by an airline freight manager that a large quantity of recording tapes had been stolen. This interview lasted about twenty minutes.

The detectives then stopped in at a hotel restaurant that they frequented and where they had information exchange relationships with several employees. While being treated to lunch and drinks, they were asked by the manager if they could look into a case in which a convicted person was required to pay restitution to the hotel for fraudulent cheques he had written against them, but so far had failed to do so. The detectives agreed to inquire into the matter.

The detectives then proceeded to the headquarters division of the Force to check the radio call logs for information that might confirm a witnesses' account in an "obstruct justice" and "perjury" investigation. This records search lasted three-quarters of an hour, after which the detectives returned to their divisional station and spent the remaining one hour writing reports.

High activity shifts typically involved situations where the detectives initially intended to conduct some field investigative activity, and in addition were assigned a "hot pursuit" or "suspect in custody" case that added an unanticipated workload. DS 33, scheduled for the 4:00 to midnight period on a Sunday, is illustrative.

The detectives spent the first 2-1/2 hours on the shift writing reports. During this period, one of the detectives also prepared a search warrant and took it to the Justice of the Peace for his signature. The detectives then proceeded to a residential address to execute this search warrant, which pertained to a case that had been on file for over one month. The case involved an allegation by a transport company manager that six cases of liquor were missing from a shipment and that the truck driver was the likely culprit. A search was conducted at the driver's residence, and revealed nothing.

From this location the detectives proceeded to the residence of a suspect named by an accomplice as a culprit in a series of break and enters. The suspect's father told detectives that his son was out of town but would be returning later in the evening, and the father agreed to bring his son to the divisional station the following evening. The detectives returned to the station and worked on reports for slightly less than an hour when they received a call from this suspect, who asked to come to the station to discuss the matter. He arrived shortly thereafter, and the detectives proceeded to interrogate him for one hour.

During the interrogation, a uniform officer brought in two suspects he had arrested after a CPIC check had revealed one was a parolee with a narcotics record and the other had a record for break and enter, and a subsequent vehicle search revealed "weapons" and equipment deemed by the uniform officer to be intended for use in a robbery. The Acting Detective Sergeant called the detectives out of the interrogation room and asked them to take over investigation of these apprehended suspects. The break and enter suspect being interrogated refused to confess to the offences, and was released within five minutes. The detectives then proceeded to familiarize themselves with the suspect in custody case, and within an hour commenced interrogation of one suspect, alternated to the other, and continued this for over two hours. Just before 2:00 a.m. the suspects were turned over to the uniformed Staff Sergeant to be held in the cells overnight, and the detectives then spent an additional hour writing up their notebooks and reports, completing an eleven hour shift.

On the vast majority of shifts the general investigation detectives could set their own pace of work. The field workers observed a number of patterns in this connection which illuminate the considerable occupational autonomy of the detective, especially when compared with the uniform patrol officer (Ericson, 1980).

One observed pattern was the tendency of a detective to undertake a lower level of activity near the beginning and the end of a shift series. Often the first shift after rest days, and the last shift before rest days, were characterized by little investigative contact with citizens. For example, on the last shift of one five day shift series the two detectives on the team spent about 2-1/2 hours on reports in the office, made two telephone calls in connection with investigations, and attempted to interview one witness and one victim although neither of them were at home when detectives called. The rest of the time was spent over dinner; in general patrol, which largely consisted of looking at boats in a marina; and, in a two hour discussion with other detectives in the office about various aspects of the Force, after one of the two detective team members took two hours of leave time owing to him and left early. On the first day back for the subsequent series of five shifts, the first four hours were spent in the office on reports, followed by an extended lunch. Two separate interviews of victims were conducted toward the end of the shift for a total of one-half hour, after which the detectives returned to the station and went off-duty (DS 016, 017).

Another circumstance under which activity, especially activity in the field, was kept at a low level occurred when a detective was about to go on leave for a course or to be transferred. Under these circumstances, time was mostly spent completing follow-up reports for investigations previously undertaken, and preparing court briefs, with field investigation limited to serious matters requiring immediate attention or a few interviews connected with cases already on file and deemed in need of clearance (e.g., DS 165, 166).

A shift of relatively low activity was also likely if it followed one where there had been a high level of activity, overtime, and/or a major investigation. For example, following a rape investigation which involved the detectives being called on duty at 4:00 a.m. and working 16 hours to 8:00 p.m. the following evening, and then continuing at 8:00 a.m. the following morning for eight hours, the detectives decided to spend the subsequent shift in a more "quiet" manner. The first two hours were spent in the office in general conversation and on reports, followed by a visit to the court building to listen in on the bail hearing of the accused in the rape case and to talk with a Crown attorney about another matter. This was followed by lunch and a visit to the shooting range to meet the annual proficiency requirement in pistol shooting. Upon leaving the range, the detectives heard and responded to a general radio call about an "Indecent Assault" suspect reported in a specified residential area. Detectives arrested and briefly questioned a suspect, but determined he was not the person they were looking for. They then proceeded to a 10 minute interview of a witness in another case, the only investigative activity taken on the shift on their own initiative. This was followed by another 1-3/4 hours in the office before going off duty (DS 18, 19, 20).

An impression generated from observing detective shift activity was that with very few exceptions, all case investigation was a matter of routine, and largely mundane. As we document in Chapter 4, cases were often not worked on for days or even weeks after they had been taken on by a detective. As Greenwood *et al.* (1975: 55) discovered, a detective might have dozens of occurrences on his "active" investigation file, but when there was a lull in activity these cases were not worked, often because there was little or nothing that could be done on them. The prime determinant of immediate action seemed to be whether or not a suspect was known or was readily identifiable, but even in some of these cases there was considerable delay. However, once the detectives decided to work on a case it was usually pursued to the point where some conclusion was made.

During the course of a shift, there was rarely a feeling that any particular matter was pressing. Rather, the impression was that things would fall into place in due course, and investigative work was as much waiting for relevant information as it was pursuing it. If detectives were out "on the road" and blocked in an investigation—as they frequently were, for instance, when a citizen was not at home or could not otherwise be located—they were as likely to bide their time by making "social" calls, patrolling, or taking a break for food, as they were to switch to another case. Even during the course of a significant investigation, a major break would occasionally be taken for something far less significant. For example, on DS 148 the detectives were called in at 4:00 a.m. instead of the usual 8:00 a.m. starting time in order to undertake an investigation of an alleged robbery. However, later in the morning the two detective team members received an invitation to lunch from a private investigator whom they had been involved with in connection with an employee theft case. In the middle of the robbery investigation the detectives departed for a three hour session of lunch and drinks as the guest of the private investigator, and did not do any more work on the robbery case until the following day.[4]

Alteration of work activity came about as a result of a variety of situated influences. For example, on DS 51 the detectives became involved in the investigation of a suspect who was arrested by uniform officers during a series of residential break and enters in progress. The first 4-1/2 hours of the shift were spent in interviewing the victims, interrogating the suspect and searching his apartment. The detectives then returned to the divisional station and lodged the suspect in the cells while they had lunch and checked through occurrence files. Later in the afternoon they had a compulsory two hour meeting to attend with senior police administrators, and they decided to hold the culprit in for further investigation rather than release him because they did not wish to return after the meeting to continue the investigation, which would have involved considerable overtime work.

Regardless of the influences, detectives treated nearly all of their work as routine. This is a common feature of occupations that deal with peoples' troubles and troublesome people. What is dramatic and traumatic to the citizen is part of the everyday routine of the detective's work. A situation that is potentially threatening and even dangerous is treated as all part of a day's work. For example, on DS 43, the detectives responded to a radio call regarding a report of a gun shot in a closed warehouse. The detectives drove quickly to the scene, and upon their arrival saw that several patrol officers, including the canine unit, were already there and investigating the building. As one detective rolled down the car window to speak with a uniform officer, he noticed the police dog lift a leg to a tree. The detective exclaimed to the uniform officer, "If he says piss on it, so do we," reversed his car, and sped away at the same pace that marked his arrival.

Our description of the everyday routine of detective work has touched upon aspects of detective autonomy within the police organization. We now move to a more in-depth consideration of detective autonomy through an analysis of organizational controls that operated within the general investigation detective units. This analysis provides further understanding of how detective routines are organizationally produced, and of the ways in which detectives are able to establish their own routines.

Bureaucratic Organization and Detective Autonomy

Detectives were responsive to controlling elements emanating from three basic sources: adminstrative production expectations, supervision by superordinate officers, and the occupational culture of detective colleagues.

A mark of the bureaucratic organization is the effort to measure the product of its workers' labour. This has proved to be a perplexing task in the police organization. The task is not so difficult in some areas—for example, the issuance of traffic citations (Wilson, 1968: 97)—but it becomes much more difficult for tasks that require considerable time and effort to evolve information and to produce evidence. In the area of detective work, the prime evaluative criteria have been the arrest rate and the clearance rate.[5] Some (e.g., Wilson, 1962: 112) have argued that these measures allow an accurate evaluation of detective labour, while others (e.g., Skolnick, 1966: 186ff; Greenwood et al., 1975) have shown the inadequacies of these measures for evaluation of detectives. Skolnick (1966) has argued that administrative evaluation of detectives by these criteria has a potent influence on detective actions; these criteria become the primary guide for detective actions, with negative consequences for the rule of law. All literature points to the ways in which bureaucratic production demands fundamentally influence how detectives make crime and criminals.

In the detective units we studied, individuals and two-person detective teams were required to submit monthly activity sheets pertaining to the case occurrences worked on and how they were cleared, as well as some indication of time spent on non-case related activity. However, contrary to the situation in the uniform branch (Ericson,

1980: Ch. 3), there was no apparent pressure on detectives to produce a specifiable monthly volume of arrests, charges and other clearances.[6] Therefore, within the Force as a whole, there existed a contradictory situation that detectives, whose primary assigned task was investigation geared toward arrest and charge, felt less sustained administrative pressure to produce in these terms than uniform patrol officers, who in all but minor offence areas had their investigative autonomy curtailed.

There were several indicators that the emphasis was upon collective cooperation among detectives rather than on individual productivity as a form of bureaucratic control. This does not mean that Force administrators were not oriented toward the production of clearance rates in order to impress various publics who might affect their organizational resources. Rather, the Force administration apparently viewed a cooperative effort with emphasis on quality as the means by which their work could be accomplished and displayed most adequately. With some exceptions to be noted later, this meant that detectives were not *primarily* oriented to the production of statistics that would aid their chances for organizational recognition.

One indicator came on DS 70 when the divisional Detective Inspector addressed all general investigation detectives in the regular monthly office meeting. He stated to the detectives that more credit would be given for signs of cooperation than for high levels of production that indicated an individualistic approach. During this address he stated, "I don't care who makes the pinch. I'm looking for quality not quantity, in investigation. You'll score no points with me for quantity."

Another indicator came from a series of memoranda circulated among administrators in the Force in reaction to a proposal to implement what was termed a "charge sheet" system. As expressed in one memorandum, this system was aimed at providing "the Deputy Chief [with] more control over the Monthly Output from each Office for which he is responsible. To do this, it would require each Officer to keep a record of the Charges he or she swears to, and in this way the Deputy Chief will have some knowledge as to what each Officer, and each Branch, is contributing to overall statistics." It is worth quoting at length two different memoranda written separately by two senior officers concerning why this "charge sheet" system was not a good idea.

Memo I
The general feeling, both from Supervisors and Investigators, is that this proposed Form would have a serious demoralizing effect on the Officers. First of all, it is felt that there would be a competitiveness formed which could, and eventually would, lead to a lack of cooperation between the Officers in their day to day investigations. This, in itself, could have a serious effect on the work output from the Branch, e.g., an officer has information on a possible arrest on Day shift; he will retain it himself until he is able to make the arrest, rather than turn it over to an afternoon shift worker. Second example, would be, that the Officer will become very concerned over the Occurrences

received from the Detective Sergeant and will want only those with a possible arrest, rather than the more difficult Occurrences which require considerable investigation with no actual arrest indicated.[7] This also brings out mixed feelings from the men as they have a tendency to feel that the Detective Sergeant is favouring one team of Detectives over another, again creating morale problems.

Another problem that will arise from this proposed Form, is unnecessary work being done by Officers, e.g., on arresting a subject for Theft, a Possession Charge would also be laid, just to get the second Statistic.

A far more serious example is where an arrest has been made, where several offences have been cleared. Rather than lay one Information to cover all charges, thereby reducing the paper work considerably, the Officers will lay each Charge individually, thereby raising the Statistics.

. . . . . .

Memo II

[The "charge sheet"] does not take into account the many other various duties performed by a Detective. It could also be viewed by him as some sort of a yardstick, to compare officer to officer, or uniform vs. plainclothes.

Without having a more detailed view of the reasons behind the 'charge sheet,' I cannot support its implementation, for reasons which I will be setting out.

The introduction of a 'charge sheet,' using the basis set out by the Deputy Chief, will lead to many problem areas, all of which we have personally experienced in the past.

This unit is composed of a number of individuals, all working toward a common goal, in a collective manner. Introduction of the system, for the want of a better word, will break the "all for one and one for all" attitude. Men will become individuals and work as such, not contributing to the group, but focusing their work towards the individual. The purpose being to contribute to the sheet in an effort to attain individual recognition, not concerning themselves with the group structure of recognition. I do not suggest that individualism is not present now, but if the individual is forced to justify his performance by charges laid he will forget all else and concern himself with looking good on the sheet, by the number of informations he signs.

The "charge sheet" also leads to lack of discretion, in that duplicity of charges, such as Theft and Possession are laid, out of the same circumstance, this being to be able to fill the sheet with names, for reasons of personal recognition.

It also leads to lack of communication among the group, again the reason being, "I must look after myself first," get the charge for the sheet.

A further problem of withholding charges for the next month is also a factor. Again this being, "I must have something for the sheet, maybe next month will be slack or I am going off for a few days and when I come back I'll be in to next month." This type of attitude can and has occurred within the service.

In the area of partnerships [two person detective teams], who should get the credit on the sheet. You cannot guage the value of junior officers because they have no charge on the sheet. The junior officer may be the spark plug of the team, and should have his name on the sheet, but because he is junior doesn't get credit.

In general, the "charge sheet system" attacks the morale of the men. Gives them the feeling I must produce, when do I get an easy arrest, Joe gets all the easy arrests, etc. etc.

I also feel that Detectives should not try to be categorized in the same statistical area as that of uniform officers. It is very easy to assess statistically what a uniform officer is doing, this being based on the routine type of his work. Whereas the Detective as such, has a narrower area, but has much work that cannot be shown statistically; e.g., preparing court briefs, court itself, special investigations, major investigations, the list can go on and on. Statistical output of charges laid cannot be a justification for the making of a Detective, due to the type of job he does.

Citation of these memoranda does not confirm that administrative production demands were not salient. However, arguments of this type at various levels in the organization did apparently serve to reduce the role of quantitative production criteria in the consciousness of detectives as they went about their work. The only persons in the detective office who seemed at all "production" conscious, and who engaged in practices that reflected their concern, were those who had not attained the full detective rank. One possible explanation for this was the fact that these persons, compared with their full detective colleagues, had more recently been in the uniform branch where they would have been attuned to production requirements. In this connection, they might have seen the detective activity sheet in much the same way as the uniform branch monthly activity sheet (cf. Ericson, 1980: Ch. 3), believing it to have some impact on evaluation for promotion even if more senior officers indicated otherwise.

One example of concern over production for promotion involved a constable who was working with a full detective partner. He was due to receive an evaluation based on his performance after his first six months in the detective office. He claimed that the main criterion used in the evaluation was the number of arrests one had made, and he felt he was in a good position in this respect because of the high number of arrests he had made while serving as the Divisional Warrant Officer. It is noteworthy that this person received a poor evaluation, leading to an early transfer back into the uniform branch.

Another example concerned an Acting Detective (the position attained after one full year in the detective branch) who believed "writing off" ocurrences in large volumes was the key to giving production appearances. This person translated belief into action, including the use of a practice whereby the victim would be telephoned, and then the occurrence would be written off with statements in the follow-up report indicating that a more thorough investigation had been conducted (e.g., DS 74; DC 117).[8]

Another detective, with probationary status (the position attained after two full years in the detective branch), had a reputation as the most productive detective in the office, always willing to take on cases involving overtime, especially suspect in custody cases. One reason he attributed to his activity was the desire "to obtain my rank [full detective]."

With the exception of these individualized concerns over production for promotion, and isolated cases where the administration demanded "results," there were not sustained production expectations emanating from administrative sources. Nevertheless, one might expect that supervisory officers, especially the Detective Sergeants, would effect considerable control over production during the course of their everyday review of cases worked on by their subordinates. This, however, was not the case in any clear-cut sense.

One feature of all bureaucratic organizations is that a considerable degree of power rests with the lower ranking line members (e.g., Barnard, 1968). In the police organization, this power is strengthened by difficulties in supervision of line member activity. The difficulty of close supervision of line officers has been a favourite topic among socio-legal researchers studying the police (e.g., Wilson, 1968; Cain, 1973; Bittner, 1970, 1974; Reiss, 1974; Muir 1977; Manning, 1977, 1977a, 1980). Supervisors must allow leeway because of the nature of police work, including the ways in which the bureaucracy mobilizes officers to work as information processors. One consequence is that supervisors are involved in interdependent relationships with their subordinates. Indeed, sometimes supervisors become dependent upon subordinates to the extent that they must turn a blind eye to questionable conduct in exchange for cooperation in areas that directly reflect upon the supervisor's competence in administrative eyes.

In the general investigation detective offices, the Detective Sergeants were officially regarded as advisors, evaluators and disciplinarians. In action, they were colleagues and consultants. Their input at evaluation time for those without full detective rank had some importance and was certainly a consideration among those seeking upward mobility, but it was by no means part of the everyday consciousness of these persons. Their role as disciplinarians was virtually non-existent; the occasions for discipline were rare and usually dealt with by the Detective Inspector.

Detective Sergeants were expected by detectives to collaborate in maintaining the considerable degree of autonomy they enjoyed in relation to how they spent their time, what they investigated, and how they went about investigating it. In routine circumstances, Detective Sergeants did not inquire into what a detective was doing when he stated that he was going out of the office, and in many circumstances they were not even informed when detectives left or returned. Detective Sergeants rarely told detectives to give priority to particular cases on their investigation files, and did not scrutinize investigative steps taken up to the point of the written follow-up report being submitted. The exception to this occurred when there was a major crime or suspect in custody case that required immediate attention in the eyes of the Detective Sergeant on duty, or when there was an administrative directive for special attention to a case. Even in these cases, however, the Detective Sergeant often asked for "volunteers" among the available detectives on the shift.

The rule that was reflected in the expectation that Detective Sergeants would be essentially non-directive was aimed at maintaining the autonomy of detectives, especially in relation to their control over their investigative role. The influence of this rule was perhaps most adequately demonstrated both by the fact that it was rarely violated, and that when it was violated there was an immediate remedial cycle engaged in to re-assert its prominence and the nature of the relationship it signified.

During the 179 shifts of detective field work there was only one occasion on which the rule was deemed to be blatantly violated in the eyes of detectives. This occurred on DS 116, a shift that involved 24 continuous hours because of major investigation into an "attempt rape" incident that occurred during the shift. The detectives initially became involved after they were asked to attend at the victim's residence by their Detective Sergeant. Subsequently, a suspect was arrested by the uniform branch and held at the divisional station until the detectives could commence interrogation of him. After the one-half hour initial interrogation period the suspect admitted to an offence and indicated his willingness to provide a written statement. During this period other officers were involved in various components of the investigation, including the Detective Sergeant and a policewoman who took a written statement from the victim, and the Detective Inspector who organized a thorough search for physical evidence at the location of the incident. These involvements by others were not seen as problematic by the detectives, but rather were seen as necessary because the detectives were engaged with the suspect.

Following a series of field investigation checks for physical evidence connected with this incident, the detectives decided to interrogate the suspect in relation to a series of "Indecent Assault (Female)" incidents that had previously been the subject of intensive investigative effort by several detectives in the office. After approximately 40 minutes of this second interrogation period, one of the two detective team members began doubting that this suspect was responsible for the indecent assaults. He withdrew from the interrogation, and the Detective Sergeant then joined the other detective team member, continuing the interrogation. After a period of time, the detective who withdrew returned and joined the Detective Sergeant in the interrogation, and the second member withdrew. This interrogation continued for one and one-half hours without a confession.

After a four hour period in which the accused was lodged in the cells, the interrogation continued on and off for a further six hours, involving various combinations, including one detective team member and another detective; one detective team member, the Detective Sergeant and a policewoman; one detective team member and the Detective Sergeant; and finally the two original detective team members. These subsequent interrogations did not produce a confession, but one hour after they were discontinued another Detective Sergeant reported for shift duty and insisted upon interrogating the suspect himself. He did so, but without results, and after a further hour the detectives took the accused to the Justice of the Peace to be held for a bail hearing.

The contentious issue in relation to our present discussion was the fact that the two Detective Sergeants actively moved into the interrogation of the suspect. When the first Detective Sergeant did so, there were a number of "rumblings" in the office among other detectives, with comments such as "What's [names Detective Sergeant] doing in there [the interrogation room]? If it was my investigation I'd tell him to to fuck right off." This was compounded when the second Detective Sergeant persisted in taking his turn. This evoked a direct negative comment from one of the original detective team members, and was seen as particularly uncalled for since the Detective Inspector had earlier informed a senior administrator that the suspect did not appear to be the culprit and had received other orders for pursuing the indecent assault investigations.

This violation of investigative autonomy became the subject of considerable discussion in the office, and at one stage the Detective Inspector was involved. The Detective Inspector attempted to placate the situation by emphasizing that every investigator had a tendency to think that he can be successful when others have failed, and that he himself is tempted to actively enter an investigation in this type of situation. In spite of this, the discussion served to establish with the Detective Inspector that this was viewed by detectives as an unacceptable encroachment, and the expectation was created that steps would be taken to prevent future incursions of this nature.

While the Detective Sergeant was kept in order as an advisor, he also functioned as an evaluator. The evaluation occurred as a matter of routine in that all follow-up investigation reports were passed to the Detective Sergeant's desk for review. All Detective Sergeants in the office also sat as a committee with the Detective Inspector in reviewing the progress of constables, Acting Detectives, and Probationary Detectives. The fact that the detective writing a report knew that it would be reviewed and judged by a Detective Sergeant, and possibly by the Detective Inspector, was something for him to keep in mind. As previously mentioned, it was of particular concern to those without full

Detective rank vis-à-vis the Detective Sergeant's input into decisions about their promotion or transfer back to the uniform branch. As discussed previously, sometimes this did influence the pattern of investigation and report writing among persons without the full detective rank, but the evaluative role of the Detective Sergeant was not an everyday focal concern as it was among members of the uniform branch in relation to the patrol sergeant (Ericson, 1980: Ch. 3).

The role of disciplinarian was not evident among Detective Sergeants, but rather was "moved up" to the Detective Inspector level. This itself seemed to be a recognition that the Detective-Detective Sergeant relationship was one of advisor and colleague, and that the requirement of enforcing disciplinary rules would interfere with this relationship. On balance, the Detective Inspector was identified with the administration, and his development and use of rules in relation to investigations, office routine, and the "appearances code" was seen as legitimate because of this identification. He was at a distance, the representative of the Administration within the office.

The Detective Inspector enforced disciplinary rules of two types, those relating to administrative procedures concerning the conduct of investigations (including those under the *Police Act*) and those relating to office routine. In situations where there was a violation of investigation related procedures, the divisional Detective Inspector typically reviewed the matter first and then decided whether to lay a charge against the detective concerned. If a charge was laid, a committee was formed to hear the matter; this committee was constituted by senior officers including both Divisional Detective Inspectors. In one case a detective was charged under the *Police Act* after being deemed by the Detective Inspector to have been responsible for allowing a prisoner to escape. It is interesting to note that the Detective Inspector in the other divisional office, who was required to sit on the committee hearing the case, found it necessary to address the detectives in his office on the matter. He emphasized that all assembled persons should agree that this was a major offence, and stressed that every avenue was explored before the charge was laid, thus trying to alleviate any potential conflict with his subordinates concerning the role he was required to undertake in punishing one of their colleagues (DS 130).

The Detective Inspector also functioned as an office manager who developed and enforced rules affecting the working conditions of detectives. While this was obviously not direct control over criminal production, it is important to consider because it indicates the separation of disciplinary control from the Detective Sergeants, thereby facilitating their role as advisors of, and collaborators with, detectives.

One example of this type of work routine control occurred over a period of time in one of the divisional detective offices. Detectives who wanted days off in compensation for overtime work would typically gain permission to do so when a fellow Detective was serving as an Acting Detective Sergeant; the Acting Detective Sergeant would grant the request, knowing the favour would be reciprocated when the person making the request was Acting Detective Sergeant and he himself was seeking time off. This pattern continued without interference until it was discovered by the Detective Inspector, who then created a rule that any requests of this nature must be made to himself or to a regular Detective Sergeant. Although Detective Sergeants thereby became involved in policing related to this rule, it only came about because of the Detective Inspector's interference, and enforcement could thus be legitimately displaced in the name of his authority.

The Detective Inspectors had two major sources of power in the eyes of detectives. They were experienced and knowledgeable investigators, and possessed personal authority on that basis (cf. Grosman, 1975: 35). Detective Inspectors were also key figures in the invocation of disciplinary rules that could negatively affect a detective's career, or end it. Detectives viewed these rules and their enforcement as very enabling in favour of the administration. They appreciated the irony that detective use of enabling rules against suspects was not dissimilar from the uses of internal disciplinary rules by Detective Inspectors against detectives. The Detective Inspector's power to punish was an omnipresent consideration in all detective actions (see generally Ramsay, 1972; Rubinstein, 1973; Mann and Lee, 1979).

The third internal influence on detective action were the rules and attendant practices developed within the occupational culture of detectives. Some of these rules reflected other rules emanating from the administration. For example, the administrative emphasis on cooperation in investigation was translated into rules for cooperation within the occupational culture of line officers.

In the main, general investigation detectives did not compete for cases in an effort to obtain individual credit. There were circumstances where a detective was afforded the opportunity of taking a case over from a colleague, but refused to do so. On DS 110 the Detective Sergeant re-assigned a case of theft from an airport freight warehouse involving an estimated loss of $250,000. The detective who was originally working on the case was vacationing, and there was a need to follow-up on additional information available through an informant working with an airport security officer. However, apart from talking with the airport security officer, the detective did not undertake any further follow-up even though a fence for the stolen items had been identified. He delayed any further action until the return of the vacationing detective, and did not keep the case as part of his active investigation case file.

There were some cases where one detective sought the assistance of one or more others in conducting major investigations. On DS 137, a detective investigating a series of "purse snatches," with suspects identified by an informant, requested the assistance of another detective to conduct searches and interview the suspects. It should be noted that this practice was more common when detectives were working alone rather than in two person teams.

Several other types of cooperation were observed during the field work period. On DS 171, one detective was investigating a case where drugs had been found and turned into the police; the detective later suspected that these drugs had been stolen. A suspect in this case was linked to another case of theft which was on the active investigation file of another detective. At the request of the detective investigating the "found drug" case, this detective willingly turned over the theft occurrence stating, "take as many as you like."

On DS 157, a detective became involved in a case where two suspects were apprehended shortly after a reported robbery at a milk store. The detective charged them in relation to this incident, but he did not pursue interrogation aimed at charging them for more robberies that he suspected them of. Rather, he left this interrogation for detectives coming in on the morning shift; these detectives subsequently obtained confessions to three more robberies from one of the suspects.

On DS 137, a detective used information from a suspect previously charged by another detective for "Mischief" to arrest and charge suspects wanted for "attempt robbery," "theft," and "break, enter and theft" cases. As part of the exchange for this information the detective promised the informant that he would arrange for the withdrawal of the "Mischief" charge. This detective stated to the detective involved in the earlier "Mischief" case, "I told him if this panned out we'd take care of that charge. I'm sure you and [detective team partner] wouldn't mind." The detective who had laid the "Mischief" charge agreed to the arrangement, again indicating a general rule of cooperation where it was judged reasonable. In this case it seemed reasonable both because the trade-off was for charges in relation to a more serious offence, and because it served to nurture a relationship with an informant, even if in both respects it was apparently to the advantage of one detective more than the other.

The rules of cooperation were also evidenced on occasions when detectives perceived violation. Most examples of violation came from dealings with specialized detectives outside of the general investigation units. General investigation detectives frequently complained that specialized unit detectives acted with self interest, seeking credit for all cases within their jurisdiction and ensuring that others did not encroach on their jurisdiction.[9] The homicide squad was frequently singled out in this connection, perhaps because their work represented the most haloed type of investigation in the eyes of most detectives. As an example of this, we can consider a situation where an experienced and respected investigator in the general investigation office began to use his "contacts" in developing information related to a homicide that had been difficult to solve. This officer became frustrated by what he perceived to be obstacles put up by the homicide squad, and eventually he re-directed his efforts off this case. A lunchroom conversation among three detectives about this situation is revealing:

Detective 1: He [the general investigation detective] could have the murder wrapped up now if they left him to it . . .

Detective 2: What? . . .

Detective 1: He just got pissed off with them [Homicide Squad]

Detective 3: They [Homicide Squad] want all the glory. The first thing they do in the morning when they come in is look at the papers to see if their name is there.

There were a few situations in which detectives in different units worked separately on the same case with considerable overlap of effort and little or no cooperation. This occurred in relation to DC 087, which involved Youth Bureau officers, two general investigation teams, and the sex offence team all separately seeking a person suspected of several school break-ins and one residential break-in where obscene notes were left, as well as a series of obscene telephone calls. There was no cooperation with the Youth Bureau team, even though they had previously interviewed persons the detectives later decided to interview. During one interview with a school vice principal, he said to the detectives, "You're the third or fourth group [of police officers] who have been in here" (DS 039). When detectives made a link between the break-ins and the obscene telephone calls, which had previously been investigated by the sex offence unit, they made no attempt to coordinate with this unit (DS 033). They did, however, cooperate with the other general investigation team working on the case, being kept informed about a search warrant executed in relation to one suspect and undertaking a joint interrogation of another suspect (DS 041). When the Youth Bureau finally arrested and charged a culprit, they did not involve the general investigation detectives. The general investigation detectives were extremely annoyed at this, first because they had been working on the case all along; secondly because the person was an adult; and thirdly, because the Youth Bureau officers did not charge for all offences the person admitted to and did not conduct a search of the suspect's residence for evidence of possible further offences (DS 048).

While manifest conflict of this nature existed at times between general investigation and specialized units, it was not typically evident among the general investigation detectives themselves. Occasionally some annoyance was expressed if one detective took initiative in dealing with part of an investigation which another detective clearly defined as his own. For example, in DC 078/085 one detective team charged two youths with a series of break-ins, and planned to arrest and charge a third youth who was allegedly involved in one of the break-ins. However, another detective team charged the third suspect after he had been arrested by the uniform branch on another matter, possibly because they wanted to question him about other cases they were investigating. This created some annoyance, especially because the second team did not even mention their intended actions to the first team (DS 030).

The general rule of cooperation within the general investigation detective units, where administrative production pressure was not dominant, meant that the resulting working relationships and patterns within the unit were very different from that revealed in Skolnick's (1966) analysis. On the other hand, some conflict between general investigation detectives and specialized unit detectives was evident, a phenomenon in keeping with Skolnick's analysis.

Detectives also produced their own structure of rules for use in controlling other aspects of their work, including the pace of shift activity and attendant practices. These practices were typical of those found in any large work organization. They were also in keeping with the long tradition of such activity within the police service.

The historical record documents how disciplinary control waves have always been a feature of police organizations. As noted in Chapter 1, the New Police in Metropolitan London had an annual turnover rate of one-third in the early years, due mainly to problems with drunken officers and to the fact that dismissal from the force was the only disciplinary punishment (Moylan, 1929; Cobb, 1957). Similar patterns characterized other early police forces, including the Northwest Mounted Police (Morrison, 1975: 275). The first separate detective establishment in the London police was created after an 1878 inquiry concerning the illegal gambling involvements of three senior plainclothes officers (Moylan, 1929). In Victorian times, "the popular catch-phrase, 'If you want to know the time, ask a policeman' reflected not so much the confidence of the Victorians in the reliability of the police, as their assumption that any policeman who did not quickly 'win' a watch from the pockets of a drunken reveller was unnaturally and abnormally honest, or dull" (Williams, 1961: 361). In modern times, Scotland Yard has been shaken by successive control waves against large numbers of officers involved in gambling, property offences, and pornography related graft (cf. Cox et al., 1977). This has led to arguments for re-organization of Scotland Yard, based on the contention that the separation of the CID in 1878, which was in response to detective deviance, created the enabling conditions for detective deviance![10] Contemporary American examples also abound, including many accounts by socio-legal researchers (e.g., Westley, 1951; Reiss, 1971: Rubinstein, 1973; Sherman, 1974).

In comparison with these accounts, the detective operations we observed were relatively free of disciplinary control waves. This probably reflects the fact that most detective practices were viewed by superordinates as tolerable and minor, if they were viewed at all.

Many of the detective practices related to "easing" the pace of their work (cf. Cain, 1971, 1973). For example, detectives developed strategies for covering the time that they spent on personal business.

On DS 50, the detective spent 80 minutes visiting a relative. He then undertook a five minute investigative interview with a citizen, and when this was completed he informed the dispatcher that he was "clear" at the citizen's address, thus leaving the question open as to how long he had been there. Detectives leaving early but still wanting to book off at their scheduled time required the cover of their colleagues (DS 123). Similarly, detectives who took a substantial proportion of the shift for non-police activity—such as the four hours taken by the detectives on DS 124 to attend a party—were covered by colleagues who kept informed of their whereabouts in case of a serious situation or inquiries by a senior officer.

While efforts at making work more tolerable were collectively collaborated in by all detectives, they did have their limits. Detectives who "carried it too far" because they engaged in an officially deviant activity extensively or took it to extremes were subject to attempts at control, and if necessary ostracism, by their fellow detectives. As Rubinstein (1973: 119) observes:

> The collusions that men employ provide them all with the necessary cover to protect themselves from unknown ears. Revelations of laxness are almost always the consequence of some incompetence. The punishments that follow are as much payments for failures to maintain cover as they are for violations of department regulations.
> [see also Cain, 1971: esp. 90n]

The failure to be supportive is not a result of the action being seen as intrinsically wrongful, but rather because continuation of it is deemed likely to lead to a severe administrative reaction that might affect the interests of all detectives. To illustrate this point, we can consider a development in one of the detective offices. One detective started to drink to excess both on and off duty. This was affecting his work performance to the point where he was perceived as a potential threat to himself and others. At first he was subject only to negative comments by others; later other detectives refused to cooperate with him in investigations; finally some detectives actively considered the possibility of collaborating with the administration in "forcing" him to take a leave for treatment. What is noteworthy is that these reactions were apparently a result of a shared belief that the problems of this detective were causing close administrative scrutiny of the entire detective office, and this would ultimately affect everyone. A typical comment in this vein was, "He's dragging us all down." This detective was eventually pushed outside the protective ring of his colleagues, and he was dismissed from the Force.

Detective created rules concerning specific investigative tasks were in some cases also related to working conditions. Since the degree of conformity to legal and administrative expectations concerning procedural regularity will be documented in later chapters, we shall not undertake an extensive interpretation at this stage. However, it is important to point out that while there was some tolerance among colleagues for a questionable practice that might violate procedural regularity, it too was subject to peer control for the same reason as noted above, i.e., if it was taken to excess it would lead to more serious impositions from outside. Moreover, there was likely to be more of a value-based reaction in this area compared with other activities we have described. For example, a uniform officer who avoided responding to a dispatched call that involved two murders and a suicide was reported to the administration by two officers on his platoon, and was universally condemned in the detective office (DS 108). There was considerable verbal condemnation in response to a newspaper report of officers from another police force who had been charged with break and enter offences; on the other hand, detectives were much more likely to condone violent acts by policemen, especially if these acts were in response to a threat to police authority (DS 84).

While they *contribute* to the making of crime control waves, detectives are *subject* to disciplinary control waves within the Force. Detectives established rules within their occupational culture to reduce the likelihood of disciplinary control, but the arbitrary nature of the administrative rule structure and its enforcement meant that there was always an element of unpredictability. This *potential* for being proceeded against made all detectives wary. While the majority of detective labour was directed at the use of rules against others, they always kept a small reserve of energy to combat the use of disciplinary rules against themselves.

Productivity and supervisory expectations are a key part of the police Force reality as experienced by detectives; that is, they are things that must be taken into account and accounted for as detectives go about their work. However, especially in the case of detectives as compared with uniform patrol officers (Ericson, 1980), these forces are not very restrictive. The environment created within the Force is an enabling one, allowing detectives to go about their task of making crime and producing criminals in a routine manner.

Similar to the legal framework within which they operate (see Chapter One), detectives are provided with an organizational framework that is conducive to the production of the commodities most valued by the Force. An analogy can be made with the framework of rules regulating business practices in the society at large. The legal controls are loose or non-existent as they pertain to the expansion of capital. Where the law proliferates and the controls tighten is in relation to the productivity of the masses who labour for capital. A complex system of laws, enforcement, and correction exists to put back into working order those who have thrown a spanner in the works (cf. Foucault, 1977). Comparing the police Force, we can appreciate that controls are not designed to regulate the productive expansion of the crime making business itself, but only the workers who, through minor indiscretions, threaten the productivity potential of the police economy.

In this chapter we have taken the lid off the productive machinery to scrutinize how it is put together from the inside. We now turn to an examination of how the internal operations relate to the things and people that detectives work on in order to make their crime and criminal products.

NOTES

1. For a discussion on the legal definition of arrest, and the problems this definition creates for the empirical researcher, see Chapter 6.

2. As mentioned in Chapter 1 and documented elsewhere (Ericson, 1980), patrol officers are more likely to encounter suspects at the scene of complaints. However, the vast majority of occurrences reported by patrol officers are not accompanied by an apprehended suspect. Rubinstein (1973: 345) reports on a Los Angeles Police Department survey which estimates that under optimal conditions (which never actually pertain) "the chance of each patrolman capturing a burglar occurred once every three months and a robber once every fourteen years."

3. Further documentation of this point is made in Chapter 4. In a survey of police officers, Watson and Sterling (1969: 100) asked them to state the most important single problem they faced on the job. The most frequent response (27%) was "too much paper work."

4. A similar unhurried approach to investigations has been reported elsewhere. At a hearing of the Keable Commission inquiry into police activities in Quebec, a Montreal Captain of Detectives was asked why he decided to delay the arrest of an F.L.Q. suspect who was identified after his fingerprints were found on a dismantled bomb made of 31 dynamite sticks. The Captain of Detectives replied that he did not move to make the arrest because he was about to leave on vacation. (Toronto, *Globe and Mail*, 20 February 1980).

5. Other criteria may also be of importance, including the generation of information about activities that can eventually be made into crimes, and the return of stolen property.

6. Sanders (1977) likewise opposes Skolnick's (1966) findings in this area. Based upon his observations of a general investigation detective office in a small California city, Sanders (pp. 82-83) states:

> The ratio of crimes cleared to those reported and treated as actual crimes was viewed with general cynicism. The detectives pointed out that how 'stats' were defined and manipulated was far more important than the actual number of arrests made for reported crimes ... [D]etectives are not oriented in terms of clearance rates so much as in terms of 'good rips' (arrests).

7. This is a phenomenon frequently referred to in the literature on the sociology of bureaucratic organizations (e.g., Etzioni, 1961; Silverman, 1970). There is "organizational drift" into areas that are measurable, resulting in over-production in measurable areas and neglect of the less measurable.

8. This practice is described and analyzed further in Chapter 5.

9. As Silverman (1970: 158) advises, the study of complaints made by organizational participants about each other is a useful means for understanding the expectations that guide their actions. "The role-expectations of the participants can first be established by observing the complaints that they make about each other. To complain is to imply that what one regards as a reasonable expectation of the role-obligations of another has not been fulfilled."

10. Hurd (1979: 141ff) quotes Sir Robert Mark's comments in an interview with the *Sunday Times* (13 March 1977): "Corruption within the Met is mainly the fault of the 1879 decision by the Home Office to enable the CID to become a sort of force within a force. It was disastrous, it was able to look after its own affairs. It investigated its own allegations of wrong-doing. In such circumstances corruption on a massive scale was sooner or later bound to come to light, in view of the concentration of lucrative crime and vice in central London."

Chapter 4

Detective Mobilization, Investigation, and Disposition of Cases

In Chapter One we pointed out that the police have always used their effectiveness as crime fighters as a primary basis on which to justify their operations, especially their detective operations. Within detective units, effectiveness has come to be assessed in terms of clearance-related dispositions. These dispositions include clearance by charge of a suspect; clearance otherwise (determining that a case was unfounded or cautioning a suspect); and, filing the case without clearance. Detectives work to clear cases in ways that they can legitimate organizationally, especially in their written accounts. When they have made one of the clearance dispositions, the case is completed for the purpose of police organizational records (Manning, 1971:156; Sanders, 1977: 81).

Central to our inquiry into detectives as makers of crime is an understanding of the dispositions they produce under the various clearance categories. This understanding helps us to appreciate the nature and meaning of the crime statistics which the police produce for public consumption, and the implications for questions of crime control. This is in keeping with previous thinking and research that considers how the making of crime clearance statistics reflects police organizational practices vis-à-vis behavioural events of crime (e.g., Bottomley, 1973; Skogan, 1976; Sparks *et al.*, 1977; Kelling *et al.*, 1979; Bottomley and Coleman, 1979; Ditton, 1979; Ericson, 1980).

This project commences in this chapter, and continues in Chapters 5 and 6. In this chapter, we consider how cases came to the attention of detectives (mobilization), outline various types of investigative activity and relate these to clearance outcomes, and then examine the relationship among sources of mobilization, types of investigative activity, and clearance outcomes.

Mobilization of Detectives

The vast majority of detective case mobilizations were in relation to occurrence reports initially submitted by patrol officers. Patrol officers have considerable power in influencing whether or not an occurrence report will be submitted, and what information will be transmitted in the occurrence report. In turn, patrol officers are dependent upon the citizenry to provide them with information that can be made into an organizational report. As Sanders (1977: 50) observes:

> The detectives . . . were truly 'citizen-response detectives' in that they were typically mobilized by an account supplied initially by a citizen and passed on to them by patrol. However, such accounts are interpreted and reformulated as they are processed through the organization, travelling through various points in the manner of a lump of clay that everyone molds as it goes along, 'making it information.'

The patrol officer molds the account in two critical ways. The patrol officer labels the occurrence and writes up a description to fit the label. This is done with an awareness of the likely career the occurrence will have in the police organization, including what the detectives are likely to make of it (Ericson, 1980: Ch. 5). The patrol officer also provides information about possible suspects, and on occasions actually delivers suspects to detectives. Detectives are thus heavily dependent upon the initial accounts provided by patrol officers; previous research shows there is a strong relationship between suspect identification at the time of reporting and clearance by charge or caution (Angell, 1971: 192; Greenwood et al., 1975: 82; Sanders, 1977: 81).

The patrol officer's report may be molded further before it reaches the detective. It is usually scrutinized by the patrol and staff sergeants before it is passed on to the detective unit. If it is passed on, it is reviewed by a Detective Sergeant, who decides whether to immediately assign the case to detectives (usually because a suspect is in custody or identified, the matter is viewed seriously, and/or the matter is important because of a senior officer's desire for action); whether to place the occurrence on a general file open to any detective to work on; or, whether to mark it for "Information Only" and to pass it on to particular detectives.

Among the 295 cases, 150 (51 percent) were directly assigned by a Detective Sergeant to detectives, 125 (42 percent) were selected by detectives from the general file, and 20 (7 percent) came directly to detectives, e.g., citizens initially complained directly to detectives; detectives responded to a general patrol call or dispatch and created an occurrence; detectives assisted other detectives from the Force or other Forces and at some stage took over the case.

In cases assigned by a Detective Sergeant, detectives usually felt obliged to undertake some investigative activity and to provide a conclusive account that was acceptable to their immediate supervisor. These cases had particular features which we shall proceed to identify.

In situations where a suspect was in custody as a result of a uniform patrol arrest, and there was a need for further investigation, the Detective Sergeant either assigned the case to a specific detective or asked for volunteers among the available detectives to deal with it. Sometimes these cases with apprehended suspects were assigned to a detective simply because there was no other detective available to deal with it (e.g., DS 27, DC 83). At other times particular detectives were selected from among a number of detectives available (e.g., DS 51, DC 98). As one detective noted (DS 15), this assignment did not occur in a random fashion. Rather, certain detectives in the office developed a reputation as being aggressive, willing and able to quickly obtain confessions to multiple offences and to gain other important information. Consequently, these detectives were more likely to be assigned cases with suspects in custody or with readily identifiable suspects. This selective assignment of course served to further improve the record of these few detectives, thereby enhancing their reputations in an amplifying spiral.

Detective Sergeants also assigned serious cases to selected detectives. These were typically major break and enter cases, serious assault cases, or serious sex cases. For example, on DS 93, the Detective Sergeant immediately assigned an occurrence involving an "assault occasioning bodily harm" and "possession of a dangerous weapon," and additionally instructed the detectives to take out an arrest warrant for one suspect named in the occurrence report.

There were also other types of "immediate" situations that required attention in the eyes of the Detective Sergeants and led them to quickly mobilize some or all available detectives. For example, on DS 104 an informant who was being interrogated as a suspect concerning other matters "tipped off" the investigating detective about an illegal handgun in the possession of a relative. The Detective Sergeant immediately instructed a detective team to take out and execute a search warrant concerning the residence where the gun was allegedly located.

Detective Sergeants also occasionally mobilized detectives after receiving direct calls from victims or complainants. On DS 127, the detective team was assigned a "threatening" case on this basis. According to the Detective Sergeant the victim had called him several times, and although he characterized her as a "head case" and the matter was deemed not serious, he felt the detectives should respond to her requests.

At times, the Detective Sergeant merely relayed an order from more senior officers to give investigative attention to particular matters. It was in these circumstances that supervision was the closest. This closer scrutiny was obviously related to the greater probability that senior officers would pay close attention to the way in which the investigation was conducted.

These cases were of two different types. Some were "public relations" efforts. For example, a plant manager had written a letter to the Chief of Police complaining about the way in which patrol officers had responded to a break and enter incident at his plant. The case was assigned to detectives largely in terms of investigating the initial response by the patrol officers rather than in pursuit of a suspect (DC 97). In another case (DC 291), patrol officers were alleged to have improperly handled a threatening telephone call occurrence in which the recipient of the call became hysterical and was hospitalized with a heart attack. Again, detectives were to investigate surreptitiously the patrol officers' reaction to the matter.

The other type of case that emanated from higher administrative sources related to special investigations on behalf of the "intelligence" branch. For example, DC 94 involved the investigation of a man seen taking pictures of houses in a residential area, after a senior officer became suspicious that this person was working on behalf of another person conspiring to have someone killed.

The vast majority of cases assigned by the Detective Sergeants were allocated on an individual basis under the circumstances that we have enumerated. However, Detective Sergeants were also observed giving several general occurrences at once to a particular detective team. For example, on DS 90 the Detective Sergeant simply placed six occurrence reports in the mail box of the detectives with the implicit understanding that they would investigate these occurrences. The occurrences did not seem to be distinguishable in terms of seriousness or availability of suspects, and were more of the type that detectives would draw themselves from the general file (DC 143).

Apart from cases assigned by the Detective Sergeants, the next most frequent type of case activation came through detectives selecting cases from a general file open to all detectives. In these cases, the detectives obviously had more latitude in deciding what they would work on and how they would proceed to do so. However, as we shall document shortly, sometimes there was control from superiors over this type of case selection as well.

When detectives chose to select cases from the general file they usually did so because they had recently completed a series of case investigations and/or were looking for more work. At times their selection was purely random without attention to the nature of the cases or their potential for investigative payoff. This seemed to reflect a general unarticulated obligation to keep a substantial number of cases on the active file and to eventually bring them to a conclusion.

This form of selection was evident when a detective team selected 18 new case occurrences on DS 108. One detective decided that since his partner had "written off" (disposed by clearance or filed) a number of occurrences in the past several days, it was time to select some new occurrences. His partner was upset at this idea since he felt that the number of outstanding cases had just been brought down to a manageable size. Nevertheless, the detective took out the next 18 occurrences in order from the general file. After selecting the new occurrences, the detective checked through them to determine whether there were any that could be made subject to clearance without much effort. The detective stated, "Let's see if we've got any in here with suspects on them," and he came up with two occurrences that had identification of a suspect. The detective decided to work on these cases immediately, but his partner did not join him.

In other instances, the selection of cases was not so random. Rather, in searching through the general files detectives looked for those cases which provided at least minimal investigative leads (e.g., DS 71). The general difficulty was that detectives knew cases with identified suspects, serious cases, and cases that were otherwise important to the police organization were already screened out through assignment by the Detective Sergeant. Thus, detective autonomy in the selection of cases was most often in relation to the "left overs" which had little chance for investigative payoff and were of little organizational significance.

Within this context, however, detective case selection was sometimes still geared toward "long-shot" investigative payoffs. Minor occurrences were seen in terms of their potential for generating information about possible major occurrences (Sanders, 1977: 96-97 reports a similar finding). Detectives were sometimes proactive in their use of minor occurrences in the hope of producing a major case. For example, on DS 63 the detectives spent considerable time searching through the general file, and eventually selected out just two occurrences (DC 104, 105). DC 104 was a "stolen hand gun" occurrence, involving the loss of a revolver at some point between shipping it from a warehouse and receiving it at a sporting goods store in another town. The detective commented that he selected this case because it had the potential to produce other possible investigations (e.g., if the gun was stolen and used in the commission of other crimes). In another situation the detective only selected an occurrence and created a new case (DC 95) from it because it was potentially relevant to another investigation (DC 87) that he was conducting. Two employees at the store reportedly victimized by a theft in DC 95 were listed on the occurrence report and were deemed to be potentially useful to the DC 87 investigation. One was a longstanding friend of the detective and thus someone who was likely to be very cooperative in providing information about other employees, including the second person who was a potential suspect and/or informant in relation to DC 87.

There was a development in one divisional detective office which illustrates the nature of senior officer control over these detective selected cases. The Detective Inspector in the office was attempting to document an argument to the senior administration that there was a need for more manpower in the office. Part of his argument was to be based upon the large case load carried by the existing detective staff in his office. The Inspector suggested that an appropriate case load size would be approximately 25 cases per detective, and asked those carrying less to select more cases to bring their total up to this level. In response to this, the two person detective team being observed at this time counted the cases that they were carrying and produced a figure of 28. They then selected 25 more from the general file to bring their average per man up to the total suggested by the Inspector. Other detectives in the office did likewise, and then each detective submitted a note to the senior administration indicating that each member of the office was carrying from 25-30 occurrences (DS 118).

Two months later, near the end of our research observation period, a Detective Sergeant announced that cases would henceforth be assigned to individuals rather than to detective teams. He also stated that detectives were now to work on their own as much as possible. This was directed at again increasing case load size and the conclusion of cases, rather than at increasing arrest and charge production.[1]

This situation led one detective to remark to the field worker, "See, a detective isn't evaluated on what he does. It doesn't matter how many guys he arrests. All they care about is how much fucking paper you put through." It also caused concern among one of the detectives being observed at the time, because he had only processed seven occurrences during the previous month, due in part to the fact that most of the joint investigations with his partner had been written off in his partner's name. This detective immediately selected 18 more case occurrences from the general file.

On two other shifts subsequent to the original change, detectives were observed selecting several occurrences to bring their totals up to the required number. The altered structure obviously influenced the total volume of cases selected by detectives in the later stages of the field work period. However, there appeared to be no fundamental change in investigative activity or clearance dispositions. The only apparent impact of the change was that the "no leads" cases were selected and disposed of as "filed" earlier than they would have been within the previous structure.

Among the 20 cases that were not assigned by a Detective Sergeant and not selected by detectives from the general file, the following situations pertained: eight cases where detectives were dispatched, or responded to a call dispatched to others, and decided to take on the investigation; eight cases where detectives were assisting other detectives in an investigation and eventually took over the investigation; two cases where citizens made direct complaints to detectives; one case where an informant supplied a "tip" directly to a detective; and, one case where the occurrence had originally been reported to, and investigated by, officers of the Toronto Force who eventually discovered that the occurrence had transpired in the study region.

Detectives were sometimes "on the road" to conduct an investigation or on general patrol when they were dispatched to a crime scene where uniform officers had requested detective assistance. For example, on DS 114, the detective was dispatched to a hotel where two persons were being held by patrol officers in connection with a "wounding" occurrence. The detective talked with the Patrol Sergeant and made an immediate decision to arrest and charge one suspect (DC 191).

At other times while "on the road" or at the divisional station, detectives heard dispatched calls or general alert calls which they decided to respond to. Sometimes these were judged unfounded, as on DS 34 when detectives responded to a "theft in progress" but discovered no signs of a theft or a suspect, and on DS 71 when "possible gun shots" were eventually interpreted as fireworks being let off by youths. On other occasions the matter was founded and/or suspects were present, but extensive investigation was not required and the detectives decided to let patrol officers handle the matter (e.g., DS 47; DS 54). Finally, there were situations where detectives responded to these calls and took on the occurrence for their own case load. For example, on DS 137 the detectives were in the divisional station when they heard a dispatch concerning a robbery at a milk store. They immediately telephoned the dispatch office to ascertain whether other detective units were available, learned that there were none, and then proceeded to the scene where they took over the investigation (DC 232).

Some cases were initially assigned to or selected by particular detectives, but subsequently taken over by other detectives. This sometimes occurred when detectives took over cases that had been exhausted by other detectives (e.g., DC 87); or, cases that they had which were linked to cases on the active investigation file of other detectives (e.g., DC 78, DC 85). One rape investigation (DC 47) was taken over after preliminary investigation by detectives from another police force, to whom the occurrence was originally reported but later deemed to have taken place in the study jurisdiction.

Finally, cases were occasionally generated following direct calls to detectives from victims, complainants, and informants. In some circumstances these calls led the detectives to undertake some investigation, and achieve a resolution, without any official occurrence report being created. This occurred on DS 103, when a man complained that another man was continually harassing and threatening him, mainly through written notes posted about the apartment building where the complainant was scheduled to replace the suspect as superintendent. The detectives talked with the suspect and cautioned him, but made no official record of the matter. In other circumstances, a report was taken but the detectives then turned it in for the general file rather than working on it themselves. This happened on DS 141, when a "threatening" complainant approached the detective at the police station and reported the matter to thim, leading the detective to take an occurrence report but not to keep it on his own investigation file.

The three occurrences that were reported directly to detectives and resulted in cases which the detectives took on each arose out of different circumstances. In DC 132, a restaurant manager called the detective regarding an alleged theft by an ex-employee. The reason for the direct call was apparently related to the fact that the same detective had worked on a previous similar case for the same complainant.

In DC 84, the detective originally received a call from someone with whom he had previous dealings. This person complained that his juvenile daughter was continually receiving telephone calls from someone inquiring about intimate relations she had had with her uncle.

The complainant was worried about a possible extortion attempt, and over a period of time kept the detective informed about the nature and frequency of the calls. When the complaint was first made the detective did not create an occurrence on it. It was not until three weeks later, when the complainant brought in a tape recording of one of the calls, that the detective finally created an occurrence headed "Possible Attempted Extortion" and treated it as a case on his active investigation file.

DC 82 was also kept as an "open occurrence" until the detective was more informed about the nature of the offences involved. A company manager, who suspected that some employees were involved in internal theft of expensive manufactured goods and were selling them as they made deliveries, contacted the detective. The detective had obtained information from another informant that the suspects were selling other goods as well, and decided that the case might develop into a major "theft conspiracy." The case was eventually written in occurrence form as a possible conspiracy to commit theft.

Cases mobilized in the ways we have enumerated sometimes involved more than one occurrence report. Mobilization of additional occurrence reports within a particular case file came about through linking suspects, *modus operandi*, and/or victims.

In our total sample of 295 cases, 48 or 16.3 percent contained more than one occurrence: 22 had two occurrences, 11 had three occurrences and 15 had four or more occurrences.[2] The vast majority of the occurrences that were linked to others to form one case were linked on the basis of the suspect(s), i.e., it was the same suspect(s), or the suspect(s) used the same *modus operandi* in a series of occurrences. This reason accounted for 41 out of the 48 cases where there were linked occurrences. A further six occurrences were linked because the victim(s) was the same, or both the suspect(s) and the victim(s) were the same. In one case, occurrences were linked because of a similar description of the nature of property that was stolen.

Occurrences were linked into a case at various stages in the investigative process. Some were linked prior to the arrest of a suspect because the detective noted similarities on the basis of reading occurrence reports in his own file or on the general file. Others were linked only after a suspect was apprehended and he confessed to other offences which were on file or which the detective did not even know about.

An example of the latter is provided in DC 98. This case illustrates how a suspect can be used to proactively generate occurrences that are not even reported to the police, and which are "automatically" cleared in the very act of generating them. In DC 98 the detectives took over the in-custody investigation of a suspect who was apprehended by the uniform branch after fleeing from the scene of a residential break, entry and theft incident. The suspect was in possession of several items, the value of which was only a few dollars. The items apparently came from different residences, or from cars parked in the driveways or garages of residences, but the suspect claimed he could not remember what items had been taken from which residences because he had been drinking. The detectives charged the suspect with one occurrence because they had a definite complainant and seized property for that occurrence. They then took the suspect back to the residential area and asked him to point out the other residences and/or cars he had entered. Following some additional confessions by the suspects, the detectives canvassed an entire street block to ask people if they had noticed signs of entry or were missing anything. This produced more occurrences. For example, after being approached by detectives, a young boy searched the garage attached to his house and then reported that his baseball and baseball glove were missing. The detective recorded this as a "break, enter and theft." The detectives laid charges in relation to each of these newly produced occurrences. Later, the detective searched the general file of occurrences to obtain other occurrences in the area that the suspect might admit to. Eventually, the detectives produced a total of 20 occurrences through these various procedures, all of which were cleared by charge.

Among the 48 cases with more than one occurrence, the linking of occurrences was most often provided through the detectives' own knowledge (22 cases) or through other police officers (15 cases), rather than through citizens (11 cases). In other words, police organizational knowledge of the detectives or their colleagues was much more likely to be used in adding occurrences to cases than was knowledge directly provided by suspects or other citizens acting as informants.

Types of Investigative Activity and Clearance Outcomes

In this section we consider six types of investigative activity and relate these to clearance outcomes. The nature and implications of the transactions involved are not considered in detail at this stage, but are central to the analyses in Chapters 5 and 6.

Among the 295 cases, 88 (29.8 percent) were "given priority" in that they were first worked on during the same shift on which they were received. The question of giving priority relates directly to mobilization of detectives, and it is worth considering in detail.

As discussed in the last section, detectives differentially selected cases according to the availability or identifiability of a suspect, and/or in response to directives from superordinates. These same reasons pertain when we consider why cases were given immediate priority (cf. Greenwood et al., 1975: esp. 57; Sanders, 1977: esp. 43). As recorded in Table 4: 1, 37.5 percent were given priority in terms of "investigative payoff," 52.3 percent in response to an "administrative priority," and only 10.2 percent as a result of "detective priority."[3]

Among the 33 cases given priority in terms of investigative payoff, 17 involved a suspect in custody where the detective team being observed agreed to take on the case after Detective Sergeants asked for volunteers. These cases were given priority for obvious reasons, including the legal rules restricting the time that a person can be held in

Table 4:1

Detective's Predominant Reason for Giving Cases Priority

Reason	N	%
Investigative Payoff		
Suspect in custody (detective volunteered)	17	19.3%
Suspect readily identifiable	12	13.6
More investigative leads than other cases	4	4.6
Sub-total	33	37.5
Administrative Priority		
Serious offence	22	25.0
Directive from superior	19	21.6
Public Relations	5	5.7
Sub-total	46	52.3
Detective Priority		
Sub-total	9	10.2
Total	88	100.0

custody. (cf. Greenwood et al., 1975: 152). In a further 12 cases, priority was given on the basis of the suspect being identifiable from initial occurrence report information. It is noteworthy that on some occasions, these cases took priority over other cases which the detectives agreed were more serious and which the Detective Sergeant assigned, but which did not have an identified suspect (cf. Sanders, 1977: 96-97). For example, on DS 19 the detectives were assigned an indecent assault (female) case (DC 55) that was deemed serious enough by the Detective Sergeant to discuss with all detectives during the regular briefing session on the morning shift. However, the detectives did not work on any aspect of this case during the shift; instead, they contacted a suspect in a case originally labelled "found property." This case (DC 46) involved a male apartment resident who was bothering female residents by removing their clothing from the laundry room and placing it elsewhere.

There were some anomalies to the general pattern in that some cases with identified suspects in the occurrence report were not followed-up for a considerable time even though there appeared to be no other pressing matters in the interim. For example, DC 171 involved a "break and enter into a residence" occurrence report that contained the names of two suspects, but it was not initially worked on until 20 days after it was originally received.

In four cases, priority was given because the case had more investigative leads (not including an identifiable suspect) than the others on the detectives' active investigation file at the time. This typically occurred on shifts where there was little else to do, and the detectives decided to search through their investigation file for anything that might prove to be fruitful.

Among the 46 cases first worked on during the shift on which they were received in reaction to an administrative priority, 22 were serious cases, where there was a shared definition of the situation that immediate attention was necessary. Many of these were cases assigned by superordinates, but with justification in the eyes of the detectives because of the serious matters involved. Most were recently reported complaints of violence, such as rape (DC 47) and robbery (DC 244). Other cases involved continuing offences which were creating unrest in particular locales. For example, DC 87 involved a series of residential and school break-ins where obscene notes were left, combined with obscene telephone calls being made by the same suspect. This was occurring in a middle-class residential area in which the residents were becoming increasingly concerned, and the detectives and their superordinates articulated this concern as a major reason for the special attention that they gave to the case.

Another way in which seriousness could influence case priority came about in situations where a very serious case became the concern of all detectives regardless of what they were working on at the time. During the field work period there was a particularly brutal murder that remained unsolved for several weeks. During this period all detectives were concerned about developing sources of information that would provide positive leads. This sometimes influenced priority among other existing cases available to work on. For example, DC 38 was labelled as involving an "Indecent Telephone Call" but its implications were directed toward the murder investigation. The suspect in DC 38 knew many people in the area where the murder occurred, including drug dealers and others involved in the "underlife" of the area. The suspect was at the time charged with possession of narcotics, and because of his previous record for similar offences he was fearful of receiving a prison sentence if convicted on the present charge. He was therefore willing to bargain for withdrawal of this charge and no charges in relation to the indecent telephone call occurrence, in exchange for generating information about the murder. The detectives pursued DC 38 on a priority basis because of this potential for a payoff in the murder case, not because of the intrinsic seriousness or identifiability of the suspect in DC 38.

Nineteen of the cases labelled as an "administrative priority" were primarily given priority by detectives because of a directive from the Detective Sergeants. These included those suspect in custody cases where the detective was assigned the case with orders rather than volunteering to undertake them. Also included were cases, serious and otherwise, which were deemed in need of immediate action by the Detective Sergeant and/or his superiors although the detective did not necessarily share their opinion.

A further five cases were judged to have been given priority for "public relations" reasons. These were typically of two types. Cases with high status or otherwise special victims were sometimes given immediate priority because of orders that could ultimately be traceable to the upper echelons of the police organization. In DC 140, a residential break, enter and theft occurrence, the detectives were instructed by the Inspector to treat the case as top priority; the Inspector in turn was simply relaying an order received from a more senior administrator, who apparently had particularistic reasons for wanting to create a favourable impression with the victim. The other type of case concerned those where a high status suspect complained about some aspect of police actions in relation to the case. Thus, in the already cited case DC 97, a letter of complaint to the Chief of Police from a plant manager about the way patrol officers handled a break, enter and theft, led to an assignment for detectives that essentially involved providing a suitable account of police actions to appease the complainant rather than pursuing possible suspects.

An element that is not captured by our discussion to this point is the way in which administrative decisions concerning resource allocation fundamentally influenced how particular case investigations were conducted. For example, in a "possible theft conspiracy" case (DC 82), the detectives wanted the assistance of the Intelligence Unit of the Force to set up wiretaps on the telephones of the suspects. Initially, the detectives only had evidence for "theft over $200" charges against the suspects, but they had information from informants that there was a much larger and more systematic pattern of thieving taking place. Moreover, unless the detectives could establish the conspiracy aspect, the theft over $200 charges had to be laid by officers from another police force because those particular offences occurred in their jurisdiction.

The Intelligence Unit continually delayed making a decision about the wiretaps, although the detectives made several requests. Finally, 27 days after the initial request, the Intelligence Unit turned down the request. This made the detectives very angry, leading them to lodge a complaint with their Inspector and to declare that they would not rely on the Intelligence Branch in the future. While it is not entirely clear why the Intelligence Branch refused permission, it was generally believed by the detectives to be related to a major investigation being conducted by that branch. In any case, the delays and ultimate refusal to provide assistance fundamentally affected the way in which the detectives proceeded on DC 82, the time they spent with the case on file, and its ultimate outcome of individual theft over $200 charges laid by detectives from another police force.

The final general category in Table 4:1 pertains to nine cases overall that were given priority during the shift on which they were received entirely on the detective's own initiative. These cases were generally pursued because there were no other pressing cases emanating from administrative sources or indicating investigative payoff, and no ongoing investigations that took precedence.

It is worthwhile to briefly consider cases that were not given im-

Table 4:2

Dominant Reason for not Giving Cases Priority

Reason	N	%
Investigative Payoff		
No immediate investigative leads	81	39.1%
Complete present investigation first	19	9.2
Sub-total	100	48.3
Administrative Priority		
Marked "Information Only" by Det. Sgt.	34	16.5
Non-case Duties take Priority	23	11.1
More important case(s) to work on	15	7.2
Sub-total	72	34.8
Detective Priority		
Sub-total	31	15.0
No Information		
Sub-total	4	1.9
Total	207	100.0

mediate priority in the sense that they were not worked on during the same shift on which they were received. In Table 4:2 we outline the predominant reasons for not initially treating these cases as a priority. In this categorization we maintain the same general sources of reasons as used in Table 4:1 for cases initially given priority.

Among the 207 cases not given priority, 100 (48.3 percent) were deemed to lack an immediate investigative payoff. These were in turn categorized into those which provided no immediate investigative leads (81), and those that had possible leads but which were not significant enough to warrant priority over investigations that were continuing at the same time (19).

A further 72 cases (34.8 percent) were not immediately worked on because of "administrative priority" reasons. Included in this grouping were the 34 cases marked "Information Only" by the Detective Sergeant, indicating that the detectives were simply to read them and "file" them without investigation. In relation to 23 cases (11.1 percent), non-case duties took priority. These duties included special assignments directed by superior officers, such as surveillance activity, prisoner escort, administrative errands, etc. Also included were non-police activities initiated by the detectives themselves. Finally, 15 (7.2 percent) of the cases in this grouping were not initially pursued on the same shift they were received because there were more important cases to work on, including other new cases on the shift and/or continuing investigations.

In 31 (15.0 percent) of the total cases not given priority, the detectives simply decided that the dispute was too uninteresting or inconsequential to pursue immediately. These were almost entirely the residual type cases selected by the detectives themselves from the general file. While some of these cases contained investigative leads, these were usually vague or believed unlikely to result in a substantial investigative payoff.

In summary, our analysis of cases given priority on the same shift during which they were received further strengthens an image portrayed in our consideration of the initial case selection process. Influences emanating from organizational sources—whether direct commands or requests from senior officers, or shared notions concerning what was organizationally regarded as a serious or otherwise important matter—accounted for the vast majority of cases initially mobilized and given priority. When the detectives did have some initial influence, it was typically in a residual fashion regarding cases that were not particularly significant from their viewpoint (mainly because they were not organizationally significant). Occasionally, these cases were selected because they had a potential for investigative payoff vis-à-vis other cases, even though taken in isolation they were regarded by detectives as inconsequential.

The attention given to cases was measured in other ways. Whether a case was "worked during the first week" and "completed during the first week" was measured from the day of receipt to seven days later, regardless of the detectives' shift schedule. Of course, cases could be completed during the first week without ever being worked on, e.g., those marked "Information Only" by Detective Sergeants, and those written off with only the written appearance that investigation was undertaken. Among the 295 cases, 130 (44.7 percent) were worked during the first week, and 128 (43.4 percent) were completed by the end of the first week.[4]

We also measured the amount of time devoted to case investigation, which included investigative interviews, suspect interviews, accused processing, and report writing. Only 88 cases (29.8 percent) received one hour or more of investigative time. This confirms the finding by Greenwood et al. (1975: 56) that only 1/3 of all reports receive any sustained attention by detectives. As we shall learn in Chapter 5, most cases were written off and filed after perfunctory efforts at investigation. This also reflects Sanders' (1977: 82) finding that "By reading the initial report, the detective determines whether the case has any leads. If it does not, he proceeds on the assumption that time should not be spent on it, and the case will be inactivated, sometimes after no more investigation than a phone call to the victim."[5]

Among the 295 cases, detectives directly interviewed one or more suspects in only 81 (27.5 percent), and one or more victims, complainants and/or informants in only 93 (31.5 percent). Cases with suspect interviews were very likely to also include victim, complainant and/or informant interviews; in the clear majority of cases, no direct interviews were conducted with any citizen.

In considering the disposition of cases, we exclude the 34 cases marked "Information Only" by Detective Sergeants because the disposition was pre-determined for the detective and did not require any investigative activity. We also exclude 26 cases which were completed in terms of investigation at the end of the field work period but which had not been subject to final follow-up investigation reports.

Among the 235 remaining cases, 50 (21.3 percent) were cleared by "charge", e.g., these cases included one or more suspects who were charged with criminal offences in relation to one or more occurrences that constituted the case. A further 47 cases (20.0 percent) were "cleared otherwise." This includes 16 cases where the original complaints were judged to be "unfounded" and the cases were made into "no crime,"[6] and 31 cases where suspects were "cautioned" or otherwise dealt with but not charged. These "unfounded" and "cautioned" cases were categorized together as "cleared otherwise" because they were often impossible to distinguish, i.e., many cases in which suspects were cautioned were deemed by detectives to be too weak to lay charges and at least in that sense were made into "no crimes" (cf. Steer, 1970: esp. 34-38). The remaining 138 cases (58.7 percent) were eventually written off as investigation exhausted and "filed" without clearance.[7]

In Table 4:3, we cross tabulate investigative activity and case dispositions vis-à-vis the 235 cases for which a disposition other than "information only" is known. We find that cases given priority, worked during the first week, or completed during the first week are much more likely to be cleared than their counterparts. However, this is largely explainable by the fact that many of these cases were given early attention because there were in-custody, identified or identifiable suspects. The same explanation applies to the finding that 76 percent of cases worked on for more than one hour were cleared, compared with only 41 percent for the sample as a whole. A major reason why cases were worked on for a longer period of time was the availability of suspect(s) for questioning. Obviously, cases involving interviews with suspects were particularly likely to be cleared. Clearance rates were also much higher in cases with victim, complainant, and/or informant interviews ("non-suspect interviews"). This suggests that these interviews were undertaken to collect, confirm, and/or collaborate evidence, in cases where the detectives already had a clearance via an apprehended suspect. (See Chapter 5; for supporting evidence, see Greenwood et al., 1975).

Many of the explanations for the findings in Table 4:3 relate to questions of detective mobilization, including how the cases came to their attention, the availability of suspects, and the nature of the occurrences involved. In order to pursue these questions, we must examine further the relationships among mobilization, investigative activity, and disposition.

Mobilization, Investigative Activity, and Dispositions

As outlined in the first section of this chapter, detectives initially received cases to work on directly from a Detective Sergeant, or

Table 4:3

Selected Investigative Activity Related to Case Disposition

Investigative Activities	N	Case Dispositions		
		Charge	Cleared Otherwise	Filed
Given Priority	86	47.7%	27.9%	24.4%
Worked first week	129	34.9	27.1	38.0
1 + hours investigation	87	50.6	25.3	24.1
Non-suspect interviews	91	33.0	31.9	35.2
Suspect interviews	80	57.5	31.3	11.3
Completed first week	94	35.1	25.5	39.4
Total Cases	235	21.3	20.0	58.7

selected cases themselves from a general file, or occasionally got involved in a case via other sources (radio dispatch, direct call from a citizen, take over a case from other investigators). In Table 4:4 we enumerate the relationship among these types of mobilization, selected investigative activity, and disposition of cases.

It is evident from Table 4:4 that cases selected from the general open case files by the detectives received the least investigative attention, and were most likely to be "filed." Among the 125 cases selected from the general files for investigation, only seven involved suspect interviews, only 18 included other citizen interviews, and only 12 involved more than one hour of investigation time. Furthermore, only nine of these cases were given priority, and this only arose because the case was potentially relevant to another investigative payoff or because there was nothing more pressing at the time. Among the 105 detective selected cases for which we have recorded dispositions, only two resulted in someone being charged.

On the other hand, we find that those cases assigned by the Detective Sergeant were much more likely to be given priority, to be worked on and completed during the first week, to be worked on for more than one hour, and to involve suspect and other citizen interviews. Indeed, some of these proportions are low because we have included the 34 "Information Only" cases in the total, cases which were immediately "filed" and thus not subject to any investigative effort. If we exclude these, our n = 116 and our proportions change as follows: given priority (53.5 percent); worked first week (67.2 percent); one or more hours of investigation time (50.9 percent); non-suspect citizen interviews (54.3 percent); suspect interviews (50.0 percent); completed first week (42.2 percent). Either way, cases assigned by Detective Sergeants were clearly given much more investigative attention than those selected by the detectives themselves. Moreover, Detective Sergeant assigned cases were much more likely to be cleared by charge (31 percent versus 2 percent) or otherwise (27 percent versus 16 percent), and much less likely to be filed (40 percent versus 82 percent).

Table 4:4

Detective Mobilization Related to Proportion of Cases Receiving
Selected Investigative Activity and Case Dispositions

Mobilization	N	Given Priority	Worked 1st week	Worked 1+ hrs.	Non-suspect Interviews	Suspect Interviews	Completed 1st week	N	Charge	Other Clearance	Filed
		Proportion of Cases Receiving Selected Investigative Activity						*Proportion of Cases Receiving Disposition Types*			
Assigned by Detective-Sergeant	150	41.3	52.0	39.3	42.0	38.7	55.3	112	30.3	26.8	42.9
Selected from Files	125	7.2	28.8	9.6	14.4	5.6	24.0	105	1.9	16.2	81.9
Other	20	85.0	90.0	85.0	60.0	80.0	75.0	18	77.8	0.0	22.2
Total (All Cases)	295	29.8	44.7	29.8	31.5	27.5	43.4	235*	21.7	20.0	58.3

*"Information Only" (N = 34) and "D.K." (N = 26) eliminated.

These findings are traceable to the nature of cases assigned by the Detective Sergeants. As we enumerated in the last section, cases emanating from superordinates often involved suspects in custody, identifiable suspects, and/or serious cases which were subject to demands for extra investigative attention. Therefore, it should not be surprising to discover that Detective Sergeant assigned cases more frequently received priority, entailed more investigative time and effort, and included more interviews with both suspects and other citizens.

In light of this consideration, we cannot simplistically attribute the greater investigative effort and successful clearance resolutions in Detective Sergeant assigned cases solely to the supervisory influence of Detective Sergeants. Rather, we must view the Detective Sergeant's role as a facilitator of action in cases which otherwise have elements that would lead to investigative action and a successful resolution. In other words, if there were suspects in custody or identifiable, or if a very serious crime had been alleged, one would assume that detectives would have given more immediate attention to these cases even without direction from their superiors. This is partly indicated by the fact that even in detective selected cases, they normally selected and proceeded first in relation to the most serious cases they could find and in relation to those in which the possibility of locating a suspect was greatest.

These explanations for what we have outlined in Table 4:4 are taken into account later as we examine the relationship among case characteristics, investigative activity, and outcome. However, an examination of the "other" mobilization category in Table 4:4 instructs us further about the points we have just made. The most investigative activity in relation to any mobilization type came from these "other" sources, but this again has a rather obvious explanation. As we have already recorded, these cases were either direct responses to ongoing disputes and citizen complaints (11), or cases entered into at key points after investigative leads had been developed by other police officers (9). Investigative activity was therefore highly likely, as was an investigative payoff in the form of a charge against one or more suspects. Again, we cannot discount the influence of mobilization on investigative activity and outcome, but the matter is much more complex than indicated by the provision of the simple relationships in Table 4:4.

It has become a truism for socio-legal researchers to state that detective work involves dealing with known suspects rather than pursuing clues in a "who done it?" fashion (e.g., U.S.N.C.C. 1967: 96-97; Reiss, 1971: 108-109; Sanders, 1977: 81; Bottomley and Coleman, 1979: 28ff). As Greenwood et al. (1975: 43) state in referring to six studies, there is ample support for

> ... the proposition that, to make an arrest, police investigators rarely exploit other than most direct types of evidence—apprehension at the scene, suspect named by the victim, street identification by victims or witnesses, etc. Concomitantly, the studies indicated that on-scene arrests were the most prevalent type of arrest in theft crimes, while follow-up investigations, which could involve significant proportions of investigative time, were almost entirely ineffective.[8]

As we have considered at several points in this chapter, if a suspect was in custody, identified, or identifiable, this often over-ruled every other consideration in influencing priority given to a case, investigative activity, and disposition. A general mapping of this influence is presented in Table 4:5.

Table 4:5 makes immediately apparent the importance of initial suspect identification in influencing the level of investigative activity and the way in which the case was terminated. Obviously, suspect in custody cases were more likely than the other types to be given priority, to be worked during the first week, to be worked for more than one hour, and to involve suspect interviews. Moreover, they were more likely than the other types to be completed during the first week, indicating that the investigation either involved only the matter at hand when the person was taken into custody, or was worked on intensively to the point of resolution if other offences unfolded during interrogation. Even "non-suspect" interviews with victims, complainants, informants, and witnesses were as likely in these "in custody" cases as in cases where the suspect was otherwise identified, and much more likely in these two types than in cases where the detectives were initially only provided with a description of the suspect, or where there was no suspect identification at all. This indicates that many citizen interviews were conducted during or after processing of a suspect in order to collect, confirm, and/or collaborate evidence. These uses of citizen interviews were much more frequent than interviews aimed at

Table 4:5

Initial Identification of Suspect Related to Proportion of Cases
Receiving Selected Investigative Activity and Case Dispositions

Initial Identification of Suspects	N	Given Priority	Worked 1st week	Worked 1+ hrs.	Non-suspect Interviews	Suspect Interviews	Completed 1st week	N	Charge	Other Clearance	Filed
In custody	23	95.7	100.0	82.6	52.2	91.3	87.0	23	82.6	17.4	0.0
Identified	55	37.0	49.1	43.6	52.7	40.0	38.2	47	21.3	44.7	34.0
Description Only	55	27.3	54.5	23.6	40.0	34.5	50.9	41	17.1	24.4	58.5
None	162	19.1	32.1	14.2	18.5	11.7	36.4	124	12.1	9.7	78.2
Total (All Cases)	295	29.8	44.7	29.8	31.5	27.5	43.4	235*	21.7	20.0	58.3

*"Information Only" (N = 34) and "D.K." (N = 26) eliminated

generating suspects. Indeed, as thoroughly documented in Chapter
5, many victim interviews in cases where there were no suspects
were primarily directed at placating the victim and sustaining good
police-public relations.

Comparing the 162 cases involving no initial suspect identification
with the 133 cases involving a description, identification, or suspect in
custody, we find dramatic differences. If there was no suspect identified in any form on the initial occurrence report, the case was much
less likely to be given priority, to be worked on during the first week, to
be worked on for more than one hour, to involve non-suspect citizen interviews, to involve actual contact with a suspect, and to be completed
during the first week. This indicates that without initial suspect identification in some form, detectives were likely to delay investigation of
the case and to not bother engaging in much investigative effort in relation to it. Indeed, only 19 percent of these 162 cases were given priority; less than a third of them were worked on during the first week
and only slightly more than a third were completed during the first
week (largely "Information Only" cases); only 14 percent were
given more than one hour of investigative attention; only 19 percent involved non-suspect citizen interviews; and only 12 percent involved
any contact with suspect(s).

These differences in investigative activity are in turn reflected in
the dispositions that each type received. The clearer the initial identification of the suspect, the more likely a case was cleared by charge,
although the major differences pertain to in custody cases. The vast
majority (83 percent) of in custody cases were cleared by charge and
the remainder were cleared otherwise. In contrast, only 21 percent of
the "suspect identified" cases were cleared by charge and one-third of
them were "filed"; 17 percent of "suspect description only" cases
resulted in a charged person while almost 3/5 were "filed"; and, 12

percent of no initial suspect identification cases resulted in a clearance by charge while almost 4/5 were "filed."

In a sense this is common sense. The point we wish to stress is that detectives could have spent much more time on cases with no suspect identification of any kind by starting with a victim or complainant interview and proceeding from there. A major reason for not doing so was simply a prediction by the detective based on recipe knowledge that such effort would provide little if any investigative payoff in clearance terms. This was not a case of "organizational drift" into areas that were productive and measurable (Skolnick, 1966; Reiss, 1971: 14). Rather, it was a simple realization that effort on "cold" cases was a waste of time; most often detectives did nothing on these cases even when they had nothing more pressing to do. There was a belief that an informant might eventually provide detectives with a lead, but this was seen by them to be a matter of future chance and circumstance rather than anything the detective could proactively cultivate on a case-specific basis. Most often, the "wait and see" attitude to these cases involved only waiting with no further illumination, resulting in the eventual writing off of the occurrences as "filed" following a brief telephone call to the victim-complainant or no further effort at all.

Another initial consideration for the detective upon receipt of a case occurrence report was the nature of the matter in dispute. Among the 295 cases, there was a great variety of disputes covering most conceivable offence types with the exception of violent assaults resulting in death. The initial occurrence reports on the cases involved 55 different headings, which we have collapsed into four broad types: property, violence, other interpersonal disputes, and other disputes.

"Property" disputes were the major component in 179 cases (61 percent of the sample). They included various combinations of break, enter and theft, theft over and under $200, mischief, trespass, possession of stolen property, attempts, and found property, among others. "Violence" disputes were involved in 24 cases (8 percent of the total). These were interpersonal offences involving alleged violence to others, or offences concerning prohibited weapons or illegal use of weapons, but excluded threats and sex offences. The occurrence headings included were alleged child beating, possible abduction, wounding, possession of weapons, dangerous use of a firearm, common assault, assault occasioning bodily harm, and robbery. "Other Interpersonal" occurrences totalled 77 (26 percent of the sample). These were mainly sex offences (e.g., rape, indecent assault, "possible sex offender," watch and beset, vagrancy 'E,' buggery), various forms of "threatening" including threatening telephone calls, and other "telephone call" cases involving harassment, obscene comments etc. The "other" category includes the remaining 15 cases (5 percent of the total). This is essentially a miscellaneous category including such divergent matters as "sudden death" (in a fire), "false fire alarm," a "Sunday Closing Law," and a "Breach of the Narcotic Control Act," among other matters.

As indicated in Table 4:6, property cases received less attention than any other case type, and were the most likely to be eventually "filed" as not cleared. The contrast is particularly great vis-à-vis violence cases, which were much more likely to be given priority, to be worked on and completed during the first week, to involve more than one hour investigation time, and to involve both suspect and non-suspect interviews. Moreover, compared with property cases, violence cases were much more likely to be cleared by charge or otherwise, and concomitantly much less likely to be "filed."

"Other interpersonal" disputes took an intermediate position between violence and property disputes in terms of both investigative activity and disposition. However, if we ignore the "information only" cases that are mostly in this "other interpersonal" category, we can state that the other interpersonal cases were more similar to violence cases than to property cases in terms of case priority and level of investigative activity.

The fifteen "other" cases were largely of a special character that made them different from the other types in the way they were responded to. Many involved emergency situations that required immediate response (e.g., sudden death) or suspects confronted regarding police initiated matters (e.g., DC 99, a "false pretences" case where a suspect originally charged with possession of marijuana by a patrol officer had given a false identity to the charging officer). These cases were thus particularly likely to be given priority and subject to considerable investigative attention. However, they were particularly unlikely to be cleared by "charge" because they were often victimless disputes or assistance matters without a suspect.

One reason why violence cases, followed by other interpersonal dispute cases, were more likely than property cases to involve greater investigative activity and to result in a clearance by charge or otherwise, is that these cases also were more likely to involve suspects in custody or otherwise identified. This was certainly true in relation to the 24 violence cases, as 33 percent involved suspects in custody, a further 17 percent involved identified suspects, and an additional 42 percent included a description of a suspect. In contrast, the 179 property cases included only 7 percent with a suspect in custody, 16 percent with an identified suspect, and 11 percent with a description of a suspect. Thus, two-thirds of the property cases had no initial suspect identification of any kind, whereas only 8 percent of the violence cases had no suspect identification of any kind. Among the 77 "other interpersonal" disputes, 39 percent had no suspect identification, but most of this 39 percent were "information only" cases that typically did not have any indication of possible suspects.

Among the property offences, it is noteworthy that priority was usually only given in cases where a suspect was in custody (7.3 percent) or clearly identified (15.6 percent). Otherwise, these cases were

Table 4:6

Case Type Related to Proportion of Cases Receiving Selected Investigative Activity and Case Dispositions

Case Type	N	Given Priority	Worked 1st week	Worked 1 + hrs.	Non-suspect Inter-views	Suspect Inter-views	Com-pleted 1st week	N	Charge	Other Clear-ance	Filed
		Proportion of Cases Receiving Selected Investigative Activity						**Proportion of Cases Receiving Disposition Types**			
Property	179	23.5	36.3	25.1	25.7	22.3	29.1	152	18.4	14.5	67.1
Interpersonal Violence	24	66.7	79.2	58.3	58.3	45.8	50.0	23	43.5	26.1	30.4
Other Interpersonal	77	27.3	46.7	29.0	35.0	32.5	70.1	47	25.5	27.6	47.0
Other	15	60.0	80.0	46.7	40.0	33.3	66.7	13	7.7	46.1	46.1
Total (All Cases)	295	29.8	44.7	29.8	31.5	27.5	43.4	235*	21.7	20.0	58.3

*"Information Only" (N = 34) and "D.K." (N = 26) eliminated

typically left on file for a few weeks and then written off unless additional information (usually from informants) was provided in the meantime.

In addition to the greater likelihood of the victim identifying a suspect in violence and other interpersonal cases, these cases tended to be more thoroughly screened by patrol officers. In our research on patrol officer decision-making (Ericson, 1980: Ch. 5), we found that patrol officers took a report on only 25.8 percent (n = 128) of interpersonal complaints compared with 70.8 percent (n = 137) of property complaints. If an interpersonal complaint was reported, it was likely to involve a serious allegation and therefore more likely to receive some detective attention compared with minor property disputes. As we document in Chapters 5 and 6, the major problem for detectives in interpersonal cases was the limitations on their ability to construct evidence for prosecution even if a suspect was available. In contrast, property cases involved few evidence construction problems if a suspect was available, but there were major limitations in initially obtaining a suspect.

In summary, mobilization, investigative activity and outcome were highly inter-related because mobilization decisions were most often made in terms of pragmatic considerations of investigative possibilities, efforts, and probable outcomes. The general investigation detectives we studied were not sleuths who oriented themselves to mobilization of "who done it?" cases requiring extensive investigative effort. Instead, they were reactive to organizationally produced criteria which made them bound to work on particular cases and to relatively ignore others.

Detectives were influenced by the reporting decisions of patrol officers, who in turn were influenced by the citizenry. If patrol officers were able to produce a suspect, or receive a clear identification from a citizen, detectives were most likely to undertake some investigation and to clear the case rather than file it. As we document further in Chapter 5 (see also Ericson, 1980: Ch. 5), detectives were also influenced by the way in which patrol officers constructed the information in the occurrence reports. Furthermore, there were supervisory influences on detective mobilization decisions. "Public relations" cases were given extra attention because of the special status of the victims involved, and some cases were given immediate and special attention because of the perceived seriousness of the matter in dispute. Overall, mobilization and subsequent detective work was conducted in relation to cases that would "pay off" in the currency the police organization used to legitimate itself.

The fact that the detectives did not work as sleuths meant that their work was not dependent on technology (for supporting ideas, see Skolnick, 1966; Greenwood *et al.*, 1975: 84; Kelling *et al.*, 1979: 19), nor on physical evidence clues.[9] As Moylan (1929: 180) observed half a century ago:

> If science is of great and increasing importance in the investigation of crime, 'information' . . . will continue to be the predominating factor in the great majority of cases. And next to information comes the work of those two officers who have been recognized as indispensable to every detective branch, Inspector Luck and Sergeant Chance.

In the mobilization of an investigation, in the volume of work done on a case and when it is done, and in the prospects for clearance, the detective appears to be little more than an automaton. However, it is within the transactions of the investigative process—as he seeks, selects, and uses information—that the detective has considerable autonomy and attendant ability to innovate. It is within this process that the detective can transform the third-hand account contained in the patrol officer's occurrence report into quite a different matter, "remaking" the case in a way that bears little or no relation to its original form. We now turn to an in-depth analysis of this process, first as it relates to victims, complainants and informants (Chapter 5), and then as it pertains to suspects and accused persons (Chapter 6).

NOTES

1. This change in administrative emphasis upon case clearance may have had the long term effect of putting production pressure on detectives in a way that differed markedly from the previous situation as described in Chapter 3. Since this change came about only 25 shifts short of the completion of our field work, we had inadequate opportunity to monitor its impact.

2. In the quantitative analysis of detective cases, the 48 cases with more than one occurrence report were coded in terms of the "master occurrence" as designated by the detectives themselves. This designation was used by detectives to aid their own paper work, and was usually done on the basis of the first occurrence that came to their attention, or the most serious occurrence in their estimation.

3. Obviously, one could infer more than one reason applying to the same case, e.g., detectives are ordered by a Detective Sergeant to immediately work on a potentially serious case where a suspect is identifiable. In these circumstances, the predominant reason was taken to be the one that sparked the action. In the above example, this would be the order from the Detective Sergeant. If the Detective Sergeant had merely asked for volunteers to work on the case, or simply passed the occurrence report on to a particular detective team, then the detectives' determination either in terms of the seriousness or identification of a suspect, would be taken as predominant.

4. Greenwood *et al.* (1975: 62-64) report that the vast majority of detective cases in their study were handled in a single day, by being cleared or filed, and that 86 percent of cases were suspended by the end of the first week *after the investigation commenced.*

5. Researchers and commentators, especially those concerned with patrol police work, have suggested that a lack of information makes the police officer more likely to treat a matter as a legal problem or "crime" and to proceed accordingly (e.g., Buckner, 1968; Cain, 1971: 19; Cameron, 1974: 23-24). In the case of detectives, lack of information usually means that a case will remain dormant, receive little or no investigative attention, and ultimately be "filed."

6. There have been many studies citing an "unfounded" or "no crime" rate. Pepinsky (1975: 34) states, "The Federal Bureau of Investigation annually reports that, nationally, detectives 'unfound,' or decide to treat as not stating offences, only 4% of the reports they receive." In the United States, the production of "no crime" figures has been shown to be part of an explicit political process (cf. Centre and Smith, 1973; Seidman and Couzens, 1974). In a Birmingham, England, police division in 1970, 5% of indictable property complaint reports were written off as "no crime" (Lambert, 1970: 43). Bottomley and Coleman (1979: 15ff) studied a city in Northern England and found that 11% of complaint reports were made into "no crimes," with substantial variation by complaint type.

McCabe and Sutcliffe (1978) studied police reporting practices in Oxford and in Salford, England, and concluded that the "no crime" rate will be lower in police Forces that give substantial investigative autonomy to patrol officers, because in these circumstances patrol officers are more likely to investigate and achieve a resolution where a report is deemed unnecessary. In light of this, we would expect the Force to have had a relatively high rate of "unfounded" cases because patrol officers were quite restricted in their investigative autonomy and were therefore likely to submit many cases which detectives later made into "no crimes" after undertaking a more thorough scrutiny of the complaint. The "unfounded" rate for 235 cases is 7%.

It is also noteworthy that in the vast majority of "filed" cases, detectives did not undertake sufficient investigation to determine whether the matter could be made "unfounded." Of course, this underscores the difficulty in making any meaningful assessment of crime from these figures.

7. In a study conducted in one area of Toronto for the Law Reform Commission of Canada, Becker (1974) reports a clearance rate of 39.9% for 789 cases. This is very close to the rate produced by the detectives we studied (41.3%), although Becker includes cases where the offender was known only to the complainant and cases where property was recovered although the offender remained unknown (7.9%). If we exclude these from Becker's totals, we get a clearance rate of 32%, including 13.8% by charge, 16.4% by caution of juvenile or known adult offenders not prosecuted, and 1.8% unfounded. In 1971 in New York City, the clearance rate for all reported felonies was 22% (Vera Institute, 1977: 3n).

8. As mentioned in Chapter 1, this has been the situation historically. A Montreal newspaper reports on the detection of the notorious Markham Gang in 1846: "[E]xcept in cases where the parties were recognized in the act (as in some cases of burglary) and subsequently identified; and, but for the disclosure and evidence of some accomplices of the gang, very few of them could have been discovered or brought to justice" (*The Pilot*, Montreal, 16 July 1846, quoted by Beattie, 1977: 53).

9. In the 295 cases, 253 (85.8%) involved no physical clues whatsoever, and a further 17 (5.8%) involved the identification of stolen property as the only physical evidence. Among the remaining 25 cases (8.4%), there was fingerprint evidence (4), tape recordings (3), clothing (5), forged documents (3), a handwriting sample (1), and various "other" types (9). Moreover, the physical evidence was frequently not used (18/25 cases). When it was used, it was mainly to assist in identifying a suspect, inducing a confession, and/or as evidence in court.

Chapter 5

Dealing with Victim-Complainants and Informants

Detectives are information dependent. As a result, a substantial part of their mobilization effort is directed at increasing their awareness of information (cf. Skolnick and Woodworth, 1967: 100). Unless suspects are caught in the act or are identified clearly in the reports of patrol officers, detectives can only proceed by attempting to generate information from victims, complainants, and informants. If detectives are going to work at all on a case without a suspect, it is done in the time honoured tradition enunciated by Inspector Bucket in Dickens' *Bleak House* when he told Sir Leicester Dedlock that he "had gone to work from information received."

In order to generate information from citizens, detectives must rely upon the authority of the police office. In Anglo-American legal jurisdictions this authority is not an unproblematic "given," but rather must be worked at and reproduced in the ongoing myriad of transactions between detectives and the citizenry (Bayley, 1977: 229).[1] Citizens often decide not to report matters to the police, frequently because they believe the police cannot do anything about their complaints (cf. Sparks *et al.*, 1977: 124); one task of detectives is to give appearances that something can be done. Citizens frequently present a selective account of events to serve their own interests; one task of detectives is to "read" these selective accounts for what they are and to develop strategies to go beyond them (cf. Sanders, 1977: 105ff). Citizens frequently demand dispositions that detectives are unable to achieve; one task of detectives is to deflect these demands and to incorporate them into the detectives' own framework for managing case dispositions.

In accomplishing this work, detectives are not only reactive servants of the citizenry. Detectives do not simply respond to the stimulus of citizen directives. Detectives engage in *transactions* with citizens, trying to obtain information that can be made useful in exchange for a range of commodities valued by the citizens in question. In the case of victim-complainants, the giving up of information results in a loss of power because of a loss of control over the information, and indeed, the case itself. The police as agents of the State take over the conflict, and typically exclude the victim-complainant from any subsequent transactions (cf. Reiss, 1974: esp. 695; Christie, 1977). The victim-complainant gives up his "usage rights" in the hope that he can gain "benefit rights" (cf. Coleman, 1973) via the organized power of detectives. In the case of informants, the currency of information is exchanged for other currencies, e.g., money, protection from prosecution, protection from enemies, friendship, etc.

In any case detectives, similar to other police officers and other professionals, like to "call the shots" in their transactions with citizens (cf. Shearing, 1977: 64). They are able to do so routinely because of the authority of their office and the deference that authority brings from citizens; because of their ability to employ strategic "levers" that induce compliance; and, because the one commodity detectives do not use in reciprocity is information about their own activities, so that citizens are unable to judge the detectives' product in terms of its production.[2]

It is our contention that detective dealings with victim-complainants and informants are not different in approach to their dealings with suspects and accused persons. That is, detectives coerce, manipulate and/or negotiate with (Strauss, 1978) victim-complainants and informants to achieve dispositions that meet police organizational criteria in a comparable manner to the way they coerce, manipulate and/or negotiate with suspects and accused persons to clear cases (see Chapter 6). The role of detectives in eliciting, reconstructing and using information vis-à-vis victim-complainants and informants has been a neglected area of analysis. Skolnick (1966) ignores the role of victim-complainants and mainly considers informants who were also suspects. Greenwood *et al.* (1975) do consider the role of victim-complainants in identifying suspects and discuss the public relations component of interviews with victim-complainants; however, they provide little detail on the role of informants, asserting that informants are not as significant as conversations with detectives would indicate. Even Manning (1977), who employs a negotiated order model, largely ignores detailed consideration of police interaction with victim-complainants and informants. Only Sanders (1977) has begun the task of showing how information processing vis-à-vis victim-complainants and informants is a key area of detective work, with an important bearing on case outcomes.

In this chapter we consider detective involvement in constructing versions of reality for the different audiences they must satisfy, and how detectives are instrumental in producing what knowledge comes to stand for the reality (or realities) of a case. This analysis yields a different view from those researchers who claim that the police are in the main responsive agents to citizen demands, unilaterally accepting the version of reality constructed by citizens and taking action in accordance with it. Detectives employ the authority of their office, situated strategies, and the low visibility conditions of their work to obtain, reformulate and use information provided by citizens. This process includes appearing responsive to citizen demands, but always within the framework of police organizational demands.

Of course, we are not arguing that detectives are able to go about doing whatever they wish. Their power is constrained by their organization. The power detectives have over the citizens they deal with is not personal, but organizational. The police organization along with the wider organization of crime control provide detectives with enabling power resources to accomplish tasks that are demanded by the police organization.

The main descriptions and analyses of this process must rely upon qualitative case data. However, as background information it is worthwhile to consider quantitative data on the types of detective transactions with victim-complainants and informants.

Among the 295 cases in the sample, 93 (31.5 percent) involved one or more direct interviews with citizens other than suspects. In these 93 cases, a total of 169 citizens were interviewed, yielding an average of slightly less than two citizen interviews per case.

Among the total of 169 interviews, 45.6 percent transpired in what may be regarded as private places (mainly residences); 40.8 percent took place in public areas (on the street, in stores, or work places in which others could observe or overhear the transaction); and 13.6 percent were conducted in the divisional detective office. The interviews averaged 25 minutes in duration, although they ranged from five minutes to five hours.

The longer interviews were more likely to involve the taking of written statements. Statements were taken from only 22 of the 169 citizens interviewed. Written statements were used in cases in which the detectives wished to commit the citizen to a complaint and the evidence being provided; or, because the detectives wished to protect themselves from a future complaint to the Force in situations that were ambiguous and potentially threatening in terms of internal regulations.

The citizens were in two basic role categories. There were 74 "victim-complainants" who provided information that led to an occurrence being recorded (usually by patrol officers) in the first place. There were 95 "informants," defined as citizens who provided information about a case but were not directly affected as victim-complainants in that particular case.

In Table 5:1 we provide data concerning these two basic role types, who initiated the contact for an interview, and how the information was used by detectives. Approximately 70 percent of interviews were initiated by detectives, while the remainder were undertaken after the citizen contacted the police. This is interesting as an indication that detectives still responded reactively to a significant proportion of investigative matters even though their mandate for investigation was largely a proactive one. This is partly explained by the fact that often nothing was done about a case in spite of it being on a detective's "active" investigation file (cf. Greenwood et al., 1975: 55), and it was sometimes only dealt with actively if a citizen called to provide

Table 5:1

Interviewee Role, Initiation of Questioning and
Information Use from Questioning

Interviewee Role	N	Total %	Initiation of Questioning		Total %	Information Use			
			Detective Initiated	Citizen Initiated		Discon-firming	Confirm-ing	Conclu-sive	None
Victim-Complainant	74	100.0	68.9	31.1	100.0	14.9	25.7	27.0	31.1
Informant	95	100.0	70.5	29.5	100.0	13.7	42.1	10.5	33.7
Total Sample	169	100.0	69.8	30.2	100.0	14.2	34.9	17.8	32.5

more information or to complain about inaction. As indicated in Table 5:1, informants and victim-complainants were almost equally likely to initiate the contact with detectives.

As our subsequent analysis demonstrates, detective interviews with citizens were not always related to obtaining information relevant to the pursuit of a suspect. Some provided no relevant information, and others were undertaken to provide an appearance of police effort and/or as public relations efforts. From Table 5:1 we learn that almost 1/3 of the interviews, regardless of interviewee role, were not productive in terms of information directly used for case disposition. Indeed, only 18 percent of the interviews involved the production of information that was used to conclude a case. This type of information was somewhat more likely to be produced in regard to victim-complainants, while "confirming" information (furthering the investigation but not allowing it to be terminated at that point) was more often produced in regard to informants. In 14 percent of the interviews, the information was used as "disconfirming" in the sense that it was employed to negate the investigative path being followed by detectives but was deemed insufficient to terminate the case at that point.

It is noteworthy that the majority (73 percent) of citizens interviewed had no known previous contact with the police force under study up to the time their interview was conducted (Table 5:2).[3] Among the remaining 27 percent, 18 had prior known contacts as informants, 17 as victim-complainants, and 11 as suspects. Those with previous known contacts as informants (mainly "witnesses" in the contact files) were the most likely of any group to give some information useable in confirmation of an investigative step, and in no case did they give information that was used in disconfirmation. Those with previous known contacts as victim-complainants were more likely than all other types to initiate interviews, indicating that their experience with the police in the past may have made them more persistent in their current involvement. On the other hand, this group was the most likely not to provide investigative information that was made useful. Finally, interviewees with previous known contacts as suspects were the most likely to give either information useable in disconfirmation or information

Table 5:2

Previous Known Contact with Interviewee Related to Initiation of
Questioning and Information Use from Questioning

Previous Known Contact	N	Total %	Initiation of Questioning		Total %	Information Use			
			Detective Initiated	Citizen Initiated		Discon-firming	Confirm-ing	Conclu-sive	None
None	123	100.0	70.7	29.3	100.0	15.6	35.0	17.1	32.3
As Informant	18	100.0	72.2	27.8	100.0	0.0	50.0	11.1	38.9
As Victim-Complainant	17	100.0	58.8	41.2	100.0	11.8	29.4	11.8	47.1
As Suspect	11	100.0	72.7	27.3	100.0	27.3	18.2	45.5	9.1
Total Sample	169	100.0	69.8	30.2	100.0	14.2	34.9	17.8	32.5

useable to conclude cases, and least likely to provide no useable information at all.

While data presented to this point provide a picture of the context and general nature of investigative interviews with citizens, they tell us nothing about the complexities of the tactics employed to initiate these interviews, to elicit information, and to use the information in the production of outcomes. We now focus upon these processes, first through an examination of victim-complainant interviews, and then through analysis of interviews with informants who represented organizations, and informants acting on their own behalf.

Dealings with Victim-Complainants

In their dealings with victim-complainants, detectives worked at three things. They tried to impress that as representatives of the police Force, they were concerned about the matter and doing the best job they could in a difficult situation. This was an attempt both to appease the citizens concerned and to meet organizational requirements for these appearances. Other interviews were directed at improving the detectives' informational awareness about details of the case and/or the status of the victim-complainants involved in order to assess what other investigative activity was appropriate or what disposition could be legitimated. Interviews were also undertaken to secure victim-complainant cooperation in the detectives' decision about case disposition. While some interviews with victim-complainants involved more than one of these elements, each interview was usually characterized by one element to the relative exclusion of the others. Moreover, the dominant element was typically decided *in advance* by detectives, although always subject to change as the interview transpired.

Providing a Gloss

In routine cases with no suspects and no apparent investigative leads, including especially cases in which the victim-complainant contacted detectives about the progress of investigations where there had been little or no investigative action, detectives set out to provide a gloss aimed at appeasing both victim-complainant and police organizational demands.[4] When little else could be done, the production of appearances became paramount. The detectives' job became one of "cooling the mark out" (Goffman, 1962) placating the victim in what detectives explicitly saw as a "public relations job" (Skogan, 1975: 50; Greenwood et al., 1975: 2-3). Unable to provide the victim-complainants with the satisfaction of apprehending a suspect, detectives could only offer the symbolic satisfaction that they were apparently giving attention to the case and had matters in hand.

Cases lacking both suspects and inquisitive victim-complainants were typically kept on the "active" investigation file for several weeks without any action, and then "filed" after a brief contact with the victim-complainant. Frequently, this contact was in the form of a telephone call rather than a personal visit. On DS 90, the detective set out to "file" several cases on his "active" file that were dated two months or more. He called on a residential break and enter victim, who was receiving her first interview about the matter since her original report two months earlier. After listening patiently to her account, the detective left this location and immediately commented to the researcher, "I hate doing these occurrences so much later." After looking through the remaining occurrences and noticing how dated they were, the detective commented, "I'm too embarrassed to talk to these people. These will have to be phone calls."

Detectives stated that these contacts, whether in person or by telephone, were for public relations purposes. For example, after a "file" disposition on a "threatening telephone call" occurrence that the detective handled through a single telephone interview with the victim, the detective commented to the researcher:

> You know you can't do much with them, so it's more a public relations job than anything. It is serious to the victim, so you talk with them even though we know little can be done. It's just public relations.
> [DS 63]

While everyone in the Force recognized the public relations aspect of these contacts, detectives could not officially account for their actions in these terms. Rather, detectives had to produce "necessary paper" (Manning, 1979a: 54ff) within the police organization according to criteria that made it appear that investigative efforts were expended. The written organizational account was produced to indicate that "real" detective work was done, when the only work really done was a brief PR contact and/or the paper work necessary to avoid other work. In other words, the Force requirement of providing a written justification for dispositions did not necessarily have the effect of ensuring that each case was investigated thoroughly. Instead, it ensured that an acceptable account was given even if it bore an indirect relation or no relation to what investigative activity was actually undertaken. In some cases, investigative activity was cited but not conducted. For example, in DC 125, a "theft over $200" occurrence, the detective made one telephone call to the victim, ostensibly to obtain a more detailed description of stolen property. The case was then "filed" with a follow-up investigation report stating that the "immediate neighbourhood of this occurrence has been investigated" when it was not. Similarly, in DC 117, involving a series of "theft under $200" occurrences, the detective stated in the follow-up report that "various checks in plazas in the area have proved negative" when the only check done was a casual drive around the parking lot of one plaza. In other cases, the volume and/or nature of interviews with victim-complainants was distorted. In DC 126, involving a theft over $200 from a retail store, the detective interviewed one employee in the store and one apartment superintendent from one of several apartment buildings immediately behind the store. However, the follow-up report stated that "the victim" (implying store owner or manager) was interviewed and that he was questioned about two of "his" employees. In addition, the report stated that "superintendents of the buildings were interviewed," when only one apartment superintendent was interviewed.

In DC 104, involving a theft of a handgun, there were two discrepancies in the follow-up report in comparison to the actual investigation. It was stated that it was common practice not to register packages of guns shipped in the manner they were in this incident. This was not accurate. The complainant told detectives that such packages were usually registered, and there was a sign up in the shipping room that all employees were to register all gun shipments with the post office. Furthermore, it was stated in the follow-up report that the post office "does not specifically recall the particular package containing the missing gun." The detectives did not contact the post office, assuming (but not confirming) that without registration of the parcel the post office had no way of tracing it.

These examples indicate the kind of thorough investigations that were organizationally demanded to the point that they were reproduced in written accounts by detectives, even if they were not actually carried out. In short, detectives were required to engage in the appearance of investigative thoroughness in their police organizational accounts, as well as in their dealings with victim-complainants.

Detectives maintained a reservoir of techniques to cool out victim-complainants. The particular technique employed was of course dependent upon the situation, including the nature of the complaint and the characteristics of the victim-complainant. However, the techniques were of two basic types: blaming forces beyond the detectives' control, and displaying attentiveness to the case in terms of what detectives thought the citizens thought was good detective work.

When detectives had to explain why they had not worked on a case sooner, or why they had not worked on it at all, they sometimes referred to their workload and the volume of occurrences dealt with by the Force. One detective, when confronted with inquiries about why he was only now dealing with occurrences that had been reported weeks before, would reply by showing the victim-complainant the occurrence number at the head of the report and then state, "You see, we've had [say] 25,837 occurrences to work on this year. We've just had too much to work on." This not only served to partially exonerate the detective, but also created the impression that criminal trouble was rampant, and sometimes led the victim-complainant to apologize for bothering the detective about what was now seen as a relatively insignificant problem. What was left unstated was the actual work volume of detectives vis-à-vis the way in which cases were worked on (see Chapter 3 and 4), and the fact that many occurrences involved trivial matters that were never even brought to detective attention, let alone investigated.

Another way in which detectives shifted the blame away from themselves was to indirectly blame the victim-complainant through reference to apparent security deficiencies. This was a common technique employed in relation to victim-complainants reporting property occurrences,[5] whether in an employee theft situation (DC 131), business (retail store) situation (DC 136), or a residential situation. These interviews typically took place more than a week after the original occurrence report, and they were usually entered into by the detective with the specific blaming technique in mind followed by a writing off of the case as "filed." For example, on DS 101, a wealthy victim of a residential "break, enter and theft" occurrence repeatedly telephoned the investigating detective about her case, and the detective eventually decided that he had better pay her a personal visit to ensure that she did not complain to his superordinates. The detective explicitly stated to the researcher that he intended to do a "PR job" on the victim. Addressing the victim, the detective said he had not been to see her before because he was dealing with two suspects who had admitted to a break and enter just around the corner. He explained that he had questioned them about her break and enter occurrence and he was satisfied they were not responsible. The detectives did not tell her, as he had the researcher, that at the moment he had more important cases to deal with and that he had no intention of dealing with this one any further since he had nothing to go on. The detective made a display of checking the security of the home, and carefully studied the point of entry and pry marks on two other doors, suggesting that this was an expert examination and hinting that improvements were in order.

Displays of detective expertise and the use of particular investigative methods were oriented to reproducing in the victim-complainant's mind that the detectives were doing what detectives are supposed to do. For example, in DC 283 the victim of a residential break, enter and theft occurrence insisted that the detective check for physical clues, including fingerprints. The detective complied by taking an object into the identification unit to have it analyzed for fingerprints. Following analysis, the identification officer stated to the detective, "I found some prints on it but I don't know who they belong to.

Maybe you should just tell her [the victim] that they're hers." The detective subsequently told the victim just that, although there was no way of knowing without separately taking her prints.

The books with "mug shot" photographs of suspects were another vehicle of displaying "real detective work" to victim-complainants. For example, on an otherwise "slow" Sunday evening shift (DS 2), the detectives decided to interview a twelve year old "indecent exposure" victim and her parents. Upon arrival, the parents were intially interviewed while the girl went to look for her younger sister, who apparently had also witnessed the incident. The girl returned shortly without her sister, and was shown the "sex offender" photograph identification book. When the girl picked out the photographs of two persons who allegedly looked like the culprit, the detective did not appear to take her seriously. The detective told the parents that if the daughter saw the man again, she should take down the license number of his car and notify the police. The detective then entered into a public relations "pitch," assuring the victim's mother that this was a good end of town and that the typical indecent exposure suspect does not go beyond the exhibition stage. As the detectives returned to their car, the victim came running up and stated that she had found her sister. The detective replied, "Oh, thank you, but it doesn't matter." The researcher later inquired why the detective did not have the sister look separately at the pictures. The detective replied, "We would have if [the victim] had made a definite identification, but she said it only looked like him." The necessary "face work" with the victim and her parents had been done; the case was subsequently "filed" with no further investigative activity.

In another case, on DS 13, there were three linked occurrences of indecent exposure/indecent assault that had occurred over several weeks in the elevators of an apartment complex. The same offender was believed to be responsible for all occurrences, but four months had elapsed since the first occurrence without any apprehension of a suspect. Following initial interviews with the victims, detectives did nothing in relation to these occurrences until a "rape" incident was reported in a private area of an apartment residence located two blocks from the one where the indecent exposures/indecent assaults had reportedly occurred.

The detectives seized upon this opportunity to present certain images to the victims of the indecent exposure/indecent assault occurrences. The detectives re-interviewed each of the indecent exposure/indecent assault victims separately, showing them the sex offender photograph book which included the rape accused from the recent incident. None of the three victims selected out the rape accused's photo from the photo book, and when the rape accused's photo was pointed out to them, all three said definitely that he was not the person. Each time, after the detective pointed out "the one we have in mind" in the photo book, he made a point of saying, "We picked him up for rape over the weekend. Anytime we pick someone up like this we just like to check it out and see if he has done any of the other things that are outstanding.'' The mention of picking up someone for rape had the intended shock effect. The detective created the impression that he, and his Force, were fulfilling their function regarding serious matters even if they had been unable to apprehend a suspect in relation to the indecent exposure/indecent assault occurrences. Two of the three victims said they were impressed with the fact that the occurrences they were involved in were still being investigated, as these occurrences dated back four months.

Detectives approached victim-complainant interviews with the intention of providing a gloss in cases where, based on the occurrence report information before them, they predicted they could do little, if anything, else. In other cases, detectives felt that they could not make judgements concerning possible further investigative activity and dispositions without directly eliciting information from victim-complainants.

Producing Information

When detectives set out to conduct interviews to produce further information about the victim-complainant and the complaint, they were partially motivated to do so because they did not accept at face value the occurrence reports made by patrol officers. Part of the detective's interpretation of the patrol officer's report was based on who the reporting officer was, and whether his reports had proved to be adequate in the past. The assessment was also based on the knowledge that all reports are selective accounts. The report reflects what the patrol officer wants to happen to the case rather than what the detectives might deem to be appropriate (cf. Ericson, 1980: Ch. 5), and, it may also contain elements of the patrol officer "covering his ass," reporting what he *should* have done (cf. Sanders, 1977: 65). In light of this, detectives sometimes felt it was necessary to go to the source of the complaint to produce an account and take attendant action that was of their own making.

Detectives frequently talked about the rule of checking with the victim-complainant before taking other action,[6] even if they did not always follow it. The rule was referred to and "demonstrated," for example, in the detectives' handling of DC 74. DC 74 involved a reported theft of an item valued by the victim at $700. The victim, a plant manager, reported that the item, which belonged to him personally, had been stolen from a fenced compound area adjacent to the plant. A suspect was named in the original occurrence report, and the detective's first action on the case was an attempt to contact the suspect. When this attempted contact failed, the detective decided to talk with the victim. From the victim the detective learned that the suspect was only originally named because he was the "black sheep" of the plant, a known "troublemaker" who had once smashed a plant window in an outburst of anger, and who was reputedly a heavy drinker and neglectful of his children. The victim indicated that he would be only too happy to have a good excuse to fire this employee: "If you get this guy on anything I'll buy you a drink—we just want to get rid of him." However, when asked what action he wanted taken in relation to the suspect, the victim cautioned, "Work around him but don't approach him directly. If he ever found out we were talking to you like this there would be real trouble. He could do a lot of damage in the plant. He could do ten times [pause]—you wouldn't believe the damage he could do."

Upon leaving the interview, the detective commented to his partner and the researcher that he was pleased that he had not contacted the suspect as he had earlier set out to do. The detective stated, "It just shows you should never go to the suspect until you have investigated first. This officer [the patrol officer who wrote the occurrence report] should have had more information on how this suspect was identified." The detective was particularly concerned that there was no clear evidence that the suspect was the culprit, combined with the possibility that if the suspect had been contacted it might have created problems at the plant for the victim. In working on subsequent cases the detective frequently referred back to this case, reiterating the rule that a detective should always check the victim-complainant account first because of the unreliability of patrol reports.

A major element in detective decisions about a case was their assessment of the victim-complainant in relation to his complaint. Some assessment could be made from the enumeration of victim-complainant characteristics on the occurrence report, and the description of the complaint in the patrol officer's written summary. However, detectives sometimes sought face-to-face contact with victim-complainants to produce their own assessment of who the victim-complainant was and what this indicated about the legitimacy of the complaint. As Wilson (1968: 27) states, "[I]t is essential for the police role to make judgements about victim legitimacy and ... such judgements are in many cases based on quite reasonable empirical generalizations." Given the importance of assessing victim legitimacy, detectives sometimes decided to make their judgements after their own direct empirical observations rather than rely upon the accounts of patrol officers.

Detectives developed an expertise in reading the motives of victim-complainants based on an assessment of the *context* of the complaint. In doing so, they discovered and made justifications for disposing of a case according to their imputation of motives. Contrary to the finding of Greenwood et al., (1975: 115), these motives were often included in the detective's written follow-up report to justify the action within the police organization.

The search for motives to "unfound" cases was typical in what detectives characterized as "domestic" disputes between intimates. In these cases, detectives felt that patrol officers had not made a proper reading of the events which might have led to an "unfounded" disposition at an earlier point in the process. For example, in DC 15, a "trespass" occurrence, the female victim reported that on several nights when her husband had gone out someone came to the rear and side doors of the house and started tapping. She claimed that she was afraid to check the doors because she did not wish to confront the culprit. Her husband was present at the interview with detectives, and there was considerable conflict evident in their accounts. The woman started talking about an occurrence which her husband apparently had not been informed of; she then stated that the last time the tapping continued for two hours, becoming increasingly loud so that eventually it was a banging noise. Her husband challenged the credibility of it continuing for that period of time, after which the woman replied, "It started just after you [the husband] left and continued to just before you got home."

The detectives became suspicious about the inconsistencies and the tone of the interaction between the victim and her husband, and one detective subsequently inquired, "Are you afraid to be home alone at night?" The victim replied in the affirmative, and thereby produced for the detective the interpretation that she was manufacturing these incidents and using the police as an additional lever to create an excuse to keep her husband home in the evenings. The detective proceeded to "file" the occurrence with a concluding comment in the follow-up investigation report that "It is the belief of the investigating officer that the victim has an immense fear of being left alone in the house and imagines prowlers whenever she hears a noise."

In another case (DC 9) serious allegations by the complainant were subject to similar re-interpretations by the detectives as the initial interview proceeded. A woman called the police department and spoke with a Youth Bureau Officer regarding an "alleged child beating" administered by her husband on their three year old son. The Youth Bureau officer passed the matter on to detectives, and the detectives arranged a meeting at the station with the complainant. The detectives initially entered the interview with an attempt to produce information about the alleged beating, but began altering their interpretation as the complainant proceeded with her account.

The complainant began her account by stating that she had come home the previous evening and found her three year old son without any underclothes on and with marks from a hair brush on his kidney area. She added that her son also had a skin abrasion but this was allegedly from falling off his bicycle. She said that this was a son from a previous marriage, and that her husband resented him because he resembled the previous husband. She said she had seriously considered killing herself, and that she feared for the life of the child. She stressed that her husband had guns, bows and arrows, and knives, and she expressed fear that he would use them. She reported that a year earlier the police had entered the apartment and seized her husband's weapons during a "domestic."

One detective began to interpret the matter as a "domestic," and believed that the woman was using the police as a tool. This detective said, "We'd better talk to the Detective Sergeant" and the detectives excused themselves from the office. They withdrew to the main office, where one detective said, "We certainly can't lay a charge. There's no evidence. She is pretty confused. I guess we could go out and talk with the husband." The other detective replied, "Sounds as if he's just a gun collector. My guess is he's pleasant, soft spoken. She is really confused. She just wants to get out of it all."

The detectives decided to go to the complainant's apartment to obtain further background information. Upon arrival, the complainant said to her husband, "We have some guests" and one detective immediately introduced himself as being from the police department. As soon as he heard the word "police" the husband entered into a tirade against his wife. Among his statements the husband said, "Last year she had the police in here. They got a master key and came walking in with their guns drawn! One of them said 'It's a good thing you didn't move or one of our rookies here probably would have put a hole in your head.' They took all of my guns and everything and it took me three weeks of hassle to get them back. She never talks with me. She always needs someone to back her up."

When the son put his arms around the husband's neck and said, "Daddy," the husband exclaimed, "There! Does that look like I'm dangerous?!" One detective reported that the wife had felt like killing herself, to which the husband responded that she was always saying that, that she was just like her mother who also made similar threats, and that she was "sick."

This additional information was used by detectives to confirm the matter as a "domestic." They later stated a belief that the "beating" was at most a father's attempt to spank a child as a means of discipline. The detectives advised the couple, and particularly the woman, to "seek help" although no specific suggestions were made. One detective later said that the matter would probably be recorded as a "caution," but there was no specific caution given. After leaving the apartment one detective said, "Imagine putting him down like that. Calling the police in. Threatening suicide. Saying he only earns the minimum wage. It's a wonder he doesn't take off."

Although there was never any direct statement by the woman or her husband that the complaint was based on marital discord, or that they were on the verge of separating, the formulation of the detectives in the follow-up report was entirely in these terms. The detectives' interpretation of the complaint as reflecting a conflict that was not police business led them to write off the occurrence as unfounded.

[Follow-up investigation report, DC 9]
More detailed information was obtained by the writers, disclosing many marital problems which the complainant and suspect are having. These include a bankruptcy file and a strong indication on the part of the complainant to separate from her husband. She disclosed that recently she felt like committing suicide.

The original complaint at this point seemed relatively secondary as the complainant expressed indecisive attitudes about the marriage in general.

Subsequently the writers attended at the complainant's residence and spoke with the suspect. It was ascertained that complainant is reluctant to discipline the children although when [the suspect] does so, she overreacts.

It is the opinion of the investigating officers that there was not excessive use of force by the suspect but rather a situation whereby the marriage breakdown has progressed to a point of little or no communication, resulting in the complainant seeking outside assistance [i.e., the police] to deal with the problem.

Both parties indicated a desire to seek counselling.

In cases of alleged violent assault outside of domestic circumstances, detectives sometimes obtained and used "respectability" criteria to assess the legitimacy of the victim-complainant's allegations and what action seemed appropriate. These cases frequently entailed evidence problems, but the detectives' decisions to pursue a suspect or to "write off" the case was not simply a reflection of these problems. If a victim was "respectable" and the complaint credible, the detectives went to whatever lengths they could to pursue the matter. If the victim was "unrespectable," the matter was transformed so that it could be legitimately "filed" with no further action.

For example, in DC 47, a "respectable" woman victim was brought to the detective office along with her roommate. The roommate had apparently encouraged the victim to report a "rape" incident, but the victim seemed reluctant to do so. The detectives spent five hours trying to talk the victim into following through with her complaint and giving a written statement on it. The evidence was judged problematic by the detectives because the victim said she had willingly gone to the suspect's apartment, delayed reporting the matter, and taken two baths before a physical examination. The detectives decided to apprehend and charge the suspect, and willingly worked a continous 16 hour period on this case, on behalf of a victim they characterized as "naive" and "respectable" and in need of police assistance to develop and sustain the case.

In contrast, detectives received an "Assault Occasioning Actual Bodily Harm" occurrence (DC 90) that they treated in a very different manner. The formulation of the incident in the patrol officer's report made DC 90 one of the most serious appearing cases of violence encountered in the course of the research. However, the detectives did not proceed to interview the victim until a week after they had received the occurrence report, and they did so in a very casual manner, i.e., while sitting in a restaurant on a "slow" Sunday shift, they were flipping through the occurrences in their "active" file and noticed that the victim-complainant in DC 90 lived nearby, and decided to call at his residence.

The detectives called on the victim at 11:15 a.m. The victim answered the door, appearing as if he had just arisen. He led the detectives into the apartment, which was dark, and two youths got up from the floor where they had been sleeping. There were beer bottles, a pizza box, and other "garbage" items strewn about the bachelor apartment.

The victim reported that he had been severely beaten in a fight during a private party at an apartment unit across the hall. He said he received a broken nose and was hospitalized for four days. He said he was drunk at the time and could not remember much about it. He said he knew the hostess of the party, but no other persons who might be witnesses. The victim said that the hostess' boyfriend identified the culprit as his (the boyfriend's) brother, but the victim thought it was unlikely that the boyfriend would be willing to testify against his own brother. The victim said that in his knowledge, only the hostess and her boyfriend saw the incident. He added that the hostess and her boyfriend were away for the weekend, and that they were being evicted from the apartment building because of the incident.

The detective took up the evidence problems as the means by which he could convince the victim that the case had to be written off. The detective pointed to the victim's memory difficulties and lack of witnesses, and then asked, "What do you want us to do then?" The victim replied, "Well, I would like him to be charged." The detective responded, "It's pretty difficult if you don't have anyone to say what happened" and the victim sealed the matter by saying, "That's what I figured."

At this point the detective departed. As soon as he was outside, the detective said to the researcher:

> I'll let him lay the charge [i.e., private information] He expects us to do all the work for him. Did you see the way he lives? He's probably glad he got hurt so that he had an excuse not to be working. He mentioned someone else got hit—it's probably a drunken brawl. That's why we get so angry when people criticize us. They don't realize what [kind of people] we have to deal with day in and day out.

The 15 minute interview was the total time spent investigating the case. The detective did not contact the hostess, her boyfriend or the suspect, and the case was "filed" with no further investigative activity. While evidence problems were used to justify writing it off, the explanation for this disposition lay elsewhere.

Detectives were frequently suspicious of victims and sometimes held negative attitudes about them (cf. Sanders, 1977: 202-203). This was sometimes taken to the point of treating the victim as a suspect, and using the "victim" interview to develop this angle. In particular, detectives were suspicious of victims in relation to reporting losses from theft in excess of what was taken. In some cases detectives believed that victims had inflated the loss when they learned that a suspect had been apprehended (e.g., DC 85), while in other case further direct questioning by detectives apparently led the victims to deflate the losses initially reported (e.g., DC 79).

In DC 87, a victim reported losing $5000 worth of goods in a residential break, enter and theft. A very complex investigation of this occurrence and linked occurrences ensued, continuing on and off for five months following the initial report. During this time the two detectives working on the case became very suspicious of the victim's reported loss. At one point, two months after the initial report, a detective decided to file the occurrence as exhausted by investigation because he doubted the credibility of the victim's account. Excerpts from the follow-up investigation report at the time reveal the basis of the detective's imputations:

> [Excerpts from follow-up investigation report, DC 87]
> The matter was discussed with the Insurance adjuster . . . who is also investigating the loss. He stated that the victim has had one other claim dated [4-1/2 years previous] . . .
>
> A further check on the complainant revealed that he was charged by this department for shoplifting [four months prior to reporting this break, enter and theft] . . .
>
> Although other similar break-ins have occurred in the area . . . the writer is not satisfied that this is a legitimate claim, for the following reasons:
> (1) Numerous attempts were made to get into the house, which seemed to have been obvious and unnecessary. Entry was finally made through a very small window near the front of the house. A rear basement window would have been more appropriate under the circumstances.
> (2) The complainant owns two . . . shops . . . however he is inclined to be shoplifting . . .
> (3) The jewellry stolen had been hidden in clothes and amongst dirty laundry, however it seemed to be found without ransacking the house.
> (4) Many other items were accessible to the theft or thieves to take . . .
>
> A retail credit report was obtained by [the insurance adjuster] but nothing of any value was of importance to the case.

Following this report, the case received no action for two months until new information came to the detective's attention. After the investigation spread to several linked occurrences and continued for another month, a suspect was finally apprehended. However, he reported only stealing some minor items in this particular occurrence, and the detectives who initially worked on the case and who submitted the report cited above considered the possibility of charging the victim (DS 48).

In DC 244, a woman employee of a gas station reported that she had been held up by a masked man, with whom she struggled and as a result received minor injuries. The victim suggested that the culprit might have been a former employee of the gas station, because the culprit wore a coat similar to the one the former employee wore. The detectives ignored this account, and began to treat this case as a theft committed by the victim and her sons, one of whom was an employee of the gas station and the other an ex-employee. This suspicion was apparently based on previous dealings the detectives had with members of this family. A major line of questioning in the interview with the victim concerned her family finances. When asked if she had any financial problems, the victim replied, "Oh, no, We're on credit counselling. I'd recommend it to anybody."

The suspicion of the detectives increased, and they proceeded to question the two sons of the victim. The victim and the two sons all agreed to a polygraph test, continually claiming their innocence. However, the victim later contacted her lawyer, and the lawyer called the detective to say that under no circumstances would the victim or her sons take the polygraph test. The detective became angry at this, exclaiming to other detectives in the office that this was a sure sign that the "victim" and her sons had something to hide. As a retaliatory measure, the detective called the victim's employer to inform him of the refusal to take the polygraph test; this resulted in the victim and her son being fired from their job at the gas station. The detectives then focused their attention on the suspect originally identified by the victim, and took no further action against the victim and her sons.

As these cases document, detectives could use interviews with victim-complainants to transform radically both the nature of the complaint and the patrol officer's initial report of it. These cases confirm that once the complaint was brought inside the police organization, it was clearly the property of the detectives to transform as they saw fit within police organizational criteria. "Once inside the system, enormous latitude is permitted to police participants to re-define with impunity the nature of the claims upon assistance from citizens . . . [T]he content of calls is in the possession of the police, not the citizen" (Manning, 1979: 10, 24).

In the cases we have discussed in this section, detectives used interviews with victim-complainants to increase their informational awareness beyond the patrol officer's account, and/or to assess the legitimacy of the victim-complainant vis-à-vis the context of the complaint. In other cases, detectives used interviews with victim-complainants to secure their collaboration in the investigative direction and/or disposition which the detectives had already decided upon. We now turn to an analysis of how this was accomplished.

Producing Dispositions with Victim-Complainant Collaboration

When the possibility of apprehending a suspect was part of a case, detectives still frequently prejudged the case outcome on the basis of the initial occurrence report information and/or initial contacts with the victim-complainant. Their task then became one of convincing the victim-complainant that the outcome the detectives decided upon was the appropriate one. In the case of a victim-complainant who persisted in arguing for a different outcome, the detectives had to do considerable work to ensure that they could legitimate the outcome they wanted to the victim-complainant and in their written police organizational account. The trick was to make the victim-complainant want what the detectives wanted, to ensure that the victim-complainant's "wish" was at the detectives' command.[7]

When detectives decided that they would not charge a suspect, they typically sought the victim-complainant's collaboration by initially arguing that there were evidence problems and then by having the victim-complainant agree to a "caution" of the suspect. In turn, the victim-complainant's apparent "preference" for not charging the suspect was used as a police organizational legitimation for writing off the case without charges. Skolnick and Woodworth (1967: 114) report that in one detective unit they studied, the detectives wrote off an occurrence with the justification "complainant refused to prosecute" when the victim and complainant had never been contacted. We found no instance of using this justification without any contact with the victim-complainant; however, victim-complainants were frequently contacted with the aim of securing their compliance with this formulation which was in turn used to dispose of the case without charge.

For example, in DC 76, the victim had lodged a complaint that was recorded by a patrol officer as a "common assault." The victim claimed that four youths had driven up beside him while he was walking on his own, yelled obscenities at him, and then two youths got out of the car and beat him. The victim could only identify one of the four youths, and he said that this person was not one of the two who had assaulted him.

The detectives tried several times to contact this witness but they had trouble doing so because he was working out of town on a temporary basis. The victim persisted that something be done, and his persistence continued over a three month period. The detectives then decided to develop a strategy to dispose of the matter once and for all. They decided to construct accounts from the witness, and two suspects the witness identified, in order to justify not charging the culprits. They obtained written statements from the witness and the two suspects, giving their common version of the incident. Included was reference to third party witnesses observing the incident who were not summoned by the victim, thereby suggesting that the victim was not particularly serious about the complaint. The detectives then took these statements to the victim and suggested that these accounts provided overwhelming evidence supporting the culprits' version of the incident, including the "fact" that it was a "fair fight." Faced with this kind of evidence and lacking witnesses of his own, the victim collaborated in this definition of the situation and agreed with the detective's suggestion that the culprits be cautioned only. These elements were in turn parlayed into an organizational justification for clearing the case "otherwise" through caution.

[Follow-up investigation report, DC 76]
A statement was obtained from [the witness] in which he implicated [the two suspects].

Both these suspects were interviewed and a statement taken, both admitted to the offence, but also played down the assault stating that [one suspect] was the only one involved in the actual assault. These two suspects stated it was a fair fight between [the one suspect and the victim].

[The victim] was shown the statements and agreed basically with them. He stated that only one person actually struck him and his injuries were very minor. He requested that we proceed by way of caution rather than charges being laid.

The organizational account was formulated as if the detective was merely complying with the victim's wishes, and as if the victim was the one who suggested that a caution was sufficient. It took considerable effort on the part of the detective to produce these "wishes" in the victim. The victim's ultimate collaboration in the outcome was all that appeared pragmatically possible given the way the matter was finally presented to him by the detective.

DC 102 involved a similar attempt to have the complainant comply with the detectives' prefigured justification for not laying a charge. DC 102 involved a nursing school employee who was suspected of a series of thefts. According to the occurrence report account, one member of the company management decided to set a "trap" for the employee by "planting" two one dollar bills in an area the employee was induced to work in alone. The bills disappeared and the police were called, but a search of the suspect's pockets and purse by a patrol officer revealed nothing. The bills were later found on the floor and turned over to a patrol officer, who had them sent to the identification unit to see if fingerprints could be lifted from them. On the same day, the suspect had her employment terminated.

The investigation was subsequently taken on by a detective team after being selected by them from the general files. As they drove to the place where the victim-complainant was located, the detectives looked over the occurrence report and decided that they would talk the complainant into dropping the complaint without further pursuit of the suspect. One detective commented, "She [the suspect] isn't working for them anymore anyway, so they probably don't care [if she is charged]." The other detective noted the evidence problems, referring to the fact that fingerprints had not been lifted from the bills, and he also stated that the matter was trivial.

The tactic decided upon was to refer to the evidence problem, plus the fact that the employee was no longer with the firm, as the key arguments to use in convincing the complainant to drop the complaint. The complainant initially seemed reluctant to do this, and referred to several other items that the suspect had allegedly stolen. However, the complainant did not persist, and eventually nodded agreement to the detectives' justifications for writing off the case. The matter was entirely pre-formulated by detectives, and the interview was conducted in a way that allowed them to obtain the complainant's compliance with their interpretation and desired action. The follow-up investigation report reflected the initial detective construction, with the important notion that it was on the complainant's wishes that the suspect was not being investigated further:

> [Follow-up investigation report, DC 102]
> "The identification examination of the two dollar bills in question failed to reveal any identification prints of the suspect or otherwise. In light of the foregoing the investigating officers returned to the school and spoke with the complainant. At that time she advised that the suspect has since been fired and she didn't wish the matter followed-up further by this department. The money in question was released to the complainant at that time and it is the opinion of the investigators this report could be filed as completed."

The complainant's "wish" was a reflection of the detectives preformulated strategy. In this subtle way, the complainant's "wish" was at the detectives' command.

Of course, in working to clear cases in this manner detectives were simply doing what all professionals do in processing their clients. For example, lawyers use "highly standardized legal and organizational remedies" to reconstruct what happened in a case to fit what they think should happen in terms of case outcome; and, in doing this they meet little opposition from clients because clients lack the knowledge and other elements of power to challenge their lawyer's decisions (Hosticka, 1979). In following their lawyer's advice, clients are dependent upon how the alternatives are formulated to them, and it is usually put to them in terms of "an offer you can't refuse" (Baldwin and McConville, 1977; Ericson and Baranek, 1981).

Detectives also developed justifications to convince victim-complainants that proceeding against a suspect with an eye to prosecution was the best course of action. While there were few strictly coercive elements detectives could employ to obtain victim-complainant collaboration in this regard, they did employ subtle negotiation strategies and pressures to achieve their goals.

In DC 82, the detective was trying to link occurrences of alleged systematic theft from a retail company into a larger "conspiracy" case. He wanted to make this into a "big case"; moreover, if the conspiracy angle could not be develped, the case would have to be turned over to the police Force in whose jurisdiction the thefts had allegedly occurred. The security officer complainant working on behalf of the retail company victim was reluctant to lay charges, as the company procedure was to terminate the employment of suspects without prosecution. The detective had to talk the security officer into collaboration; in doing so, he relied upon a relationship between the security officer and another detective in the office to gain the "favour."

In DC 191, a detective took a more forceful approach in producing a case that was of his own making. The detective produced a definition of who was the "victim" and who was the "suspect" and conducted the investigation accordingly.

While driving, the detective was dispatched to the scene of a tavern fight in which two persons were being held by patrol officers. Upon arrival, the detective immediately recognized one of the citizens involved (a "bouncer" for the tavern) and they exchanged greetings: "Hi [citizen's first name], How's it going?" to which the citizen replied, "Not bad [detective's first name]. Just a cut hand."

The detective proceeded to another room where the other citizen was being detained by a patrol officer. A violent exchange appeared to have taken place in this small office, since blood covered the walls and there were fresh holes in the plaster. The patrol officer handed the detective a fishing knife and said, "It's his." After asking the patrol officer about the person's identity, the detective asked, "Has he been cautioned?" The patrol officer replied, "No." The detective then stated to the citizen, "You're under arrest for wounding. You're not obliged to say anything . . ." The suspect interrupted, "*I'm* under arrest?!" The detective retorted, "Let me finish! But anything you do say may be used in evidence. Do you understand that?" The suspect stated, "No." Angered, the detective replied, "it means you're under arrest, O.K."

The suspect was severely beaten, covered in blood and with huge lumps and bruises all over his face. In contrast the victim was unmarked except for a cut on his hand. The suspect was slight while the victim was six feet in height, heavily built, and known to be employed as a karate instructor.

The researcher accompanied the suspect back to the divisional station along with the patrol officer. During the trip back the suspect complained to the patrol officer: "What's going on? Why am *I* being charged? Look what he did to me! He kicked the fucking shit right out of me! He should be charged, not me.' "

At the divisional station, the detective enlisted the help of another detective to do the paper work for the accused on a charge of "wounding." The arresting detective felt his own efforts were best directed at eliciting an appropriate account from the victim. The detective proceeded to ensure that his own definition of the situation was effectively registered in the victim's signed statement.

The mood of both the detective and the victim in the interview was jovial and friendly. The victim remarked, "It's different being on the other side for once. You know I still expect an assault charge out of this." The detective replied, "If he wants to lay an assault charge he can do it himself. You won't get it from me."

The victim began to recount what had transpired. When it became obvious that the victim had been anything but a passive participant, the detective would interject and advise, "I don't think you want to say that [victim's first name]" and would type a phrase or sentence and add, "How does that sound?" When it again became obvious that the victim had used excessive force in both apprehending and detaining the suspect, the detective again intervened and constructed a much less negative sense of what happened.

To offer a specific example of this statement construction, at one point the detective asked the victim to describe what happened when he first confronted the accused and another person, who were fighting. The victim replied, "I grabbed both of them. I was holding them apart by the hair." The detective interjected, "No, no. You better not put that down. How does this sound? 'I grabbed this guy and grabbed the other guy as he came to continue the fight with the person I had already under control.' " These exact words were put in the statement. The victim then continued his verbal description, and at a later point said, "I grabbed him in a basic karate hold, it's hard to explain. I had one hand in his pharynx and with the other hand I turned his arm back and he let go of the knife. He tried to get away again . . .". The detective again interjected, "O.K. [victim's first name], you know that it's all right to use force but only such force as is required to ensure that he doesn't escape." The detective and victim both laughed, and the detective then prepared the remainder of the statement and asked, "How does that sound?" to which the victim replied, "I couldn't have said it better myself."

The remainder of the statement read:

> I grabbed him in a basic karate hold resulting in the knife flinging free from his hand. At this time I led the person to the manager's office during which time several struggles occurred while the person tried to make good his escape. He was eventually brought into the office and police were called. I was taken to the Memorial Hospital where I received 3 stitches to a knife wound on the rear of my left hand.

After the victim left, the detective who had processed the accused commented to the detective who had taken the victim's statement, "We'd better get somebody to take the victim [indicating the accused] to the hospital. [Realizing his error the detective laughed]. He sure as hell looks like a victim to me. He sure picked the wrong guy to tangle with."

In some cases detectives pressed the victim so hard regarding identification of a suspect that the victim eventually produced a suspect who turned out to be innocent in the subsequent judgement of the detectives. For example, in DC 21 the victim was a twelve year-old girl who said she had witnessed an "indecent exposure" in a park near to her home. The girl's mother, acting as a complainant, was very concerned about the matter although she was not forceful in demanding detective action. The detectives questioned the victim at length, and developed an impression that the suspect might be someone working with a crew on a house across the street.

During the interview, the victim appeared very nervous and not entirely certain regarding the description of the suspect. At one point she said she could identify the suspect "if he wore the same clothes." However, the victim eventually admitted on further probing by one detective that she was afraid of identifying the wrong person. The other detective then explained to the victim that the culprit would not be sent to jail but would be given psychiatric help "which he needs." The victim began to cry. One detective then suggested that they take a walk outside and the victim could point out the culprit if it was indeed one of the men at the work site across the road. The detective and the victim did this, and the victim then pointed to one man as the culprit.

Without attempting to obtain prior supporting evidence from another known witness to the original incident, the detectives proceeded to arrest the identified suspect, and took him to the police station for interrogation. He was in custody for two hours before being released without charge. Upon return to the work site, the owner of the company appeared and started arguing along with the suspect that the suspect's "rights" had been violated and that they were going to call a lawyer. One detective asked, "What rights have been violated?," and then immediately followed with, "We have to pick someone up if the victim points him out."

The detectives later discussed the interpretation that the victim had probably returned home after the incident and saw the suspect she identified working across the street. Thinking there was a resemblance to the culprit, she actually described this worker in her statement to the patrol officer who took the initial occurrence report. The detectives later decided to set-up an appointment with the other witness, mentioning that it might be useful as a "cover" in case the suspect they had interrogated and released without charge carried through with his threat to obtain a lawyer and lodge a formal complaint against the detectives.

In producing resolutions that did not result in a charge being laid against an identified suspect, detectives sometimes went along with the formulations of victims. Detectives would wait for the victim to articulate the reasons for not pursuing the suspect, and then use these reasons to legitimate their actions both to the victim and within the police organization (cf. Hayduk, 1976: esp. 473-474). For example, in DC 75 the victim reported that a man with whom she had previously lived for five years had thrown a rock through a window in her apartment, causing $30 damage. Five weeks following the submission of the occurrence report by the patrol officer, the detective called on the victim and asked if she knew the whereabouts of the suspect and what further action she desired. The victim immediately responded that she had reconciled with the suspect and that the suspect had reimbursed her for the damage. She also stated that she wanted no further action taken against the suspect. The detectives made no attempt to contact the suspect and wrote off the case as "cleared otherwise," referring to the restitution and the victim's request.

In other cases the victim-complainants stated a fear of retaliation by the suspect, and this was used by the detectives to justify termination of the case without pursuit of the suspect. However, this justification was never written on follow-up investigation reports, and remained a matter of tacit agreement between the detectives and the victim-complainant. In the previously described case, DC 74 (pp. 102-3) the victim was explicit about not wanting direct contact with the suspect for fear of violent retaliation. It should be noted that there were also evidence problems in DC 74, as there were in other cases in which the victims feared retaliation (e.g., DC 116). This may have further encouraged the victim-complainants to want the investigation of the suspects curtailed, because an unsubstantiated complaint could lead to more complications. It probably also convinced the detectives that a "filed" disposition was the most appropriate course of action.

Occasionally, detectives made special concessions to a victim-complainant, agreeing to cover for them in order to maintain their own organizational cover. For example, in DC 82 the complainant became very irate at the detectives' delay in arresting two suspects who were employees at the plant he managed and who were allegedly involved in systematic theft. The delay was directly attributable to the fact that the detective wanted to broaden the investigation based on a "conspiracy" angle, as we have discussed earlier. The detective had gained the complainant's compliance in allowing him to pursue this angle, although as the weeks passed the complainant was becoming increasingly annoyed about the delay.

Immediately prior to the point at which the detectives gave up on the "conspiracy" angle, and were proceeding to arrest the suspects for "theft over $200," one of the suspects became involved in another incident for which he was fired from his job. According to the reports of the complainant and the other police department involved, this person had been drinking and became involved in an accident with a truck owned by the company. He left the scene of the accident and drove to a shopping plaza where he purposely damaged the truck further, then reported that the truck had been stolen. He was subsequently arrested and charged by another police department for failing to remain at the scene of an accident and for public mischief.

This incident made the complainant even more angry about the way the detectives had handled the entire DC 82 case. He blamed the detectives for not arresting this suspect at an earlier date, which would have allowed the employer to fire him at that time and thus have prevented the incident with the company truck. The detectives immediately proceeded to arrest this suspect and one other one from the same company for "theft over $200." However, they did not approach a third employee (who was clearly implicated by other suspects) because the complainant did not wish them to do so. This suspect had an extensive criminal record, including a term in penitentiary, but was not arrested because of the explicit request from the victim. The reasons given by the employer for keeping this person from arrest were that he had very bad health, and that he was a key employee who would not be replaced easily.

During preliminary investigations, when the "conspiracy" angle was being developed, the detective wrote a follow-up investigation report in which this third employee was mentioned, including his "criminal" status. However, he was not mentioned again in further follow-up reports, including the final one which reported the arrests of the other suspects. Thus, there was no organizational accounting of the decision not to deal with this third employee, and the complainant's request was handled entirely on a sub rosa level.

Clearly, what a case was made into and the way in which it was terminated depended upon a complex process involving detectives' prefigured justifications in terms of the occurrence report information, assessment of victim-complainant legitimacy, special requests and circumstances of victim-complainants, and the stock of police organizational legitimations useable in the writing up of case disposition reports. The finding of a "crime" and the pursuit of "criminals" were organizationally produced by detectives out of these transactions with victim-complainants. They were also organizationally produced in relation to information derived from transactions with informants.

Dealings with Informants

Producing Informants

Informants were defined as persons who provided information about a case that they were not directly involved in as a victim-complainant or as the only suspect. They were either 'organizational' informants acting in official roles on behalf of private or public formal organizations, e.g., apartment managers, factory managers, school principals, municipal officers, correctional half-way house directors; or, they were individuals acting on their own behalf who had witnessed an incident, suspects who informed on accomplices involved in the same case or other cases, or persons who had information the detectives made relevant to a case.

With the exception of suspects informing on their accomplices, most informants did not have a direct stake in the case. It was the detectives' task to ascertain some other matter in which the potential informant had a stake, and to use this to encourage co-operation. Detectives realized that informants did not typically come forward to assist the police because they were civic minded.[8] Rather, informants were usually motivated by other agendas with the police that they felt could be dealt with by co-operating in matters the detectives were concerned with at the moment. The detectives' task was to read these motives, and to use them. Alternatively, if no such motive was apparent, the detectives created one, providing the informant with a purpose that could be satisfied by meeting the detectives' demands (see generally Skolnick, 1966: 123, referring to Harney and Cross, 1960;

Klein, 1976; Sanders, 1977: 105ff). Many of the strategies employed by detectives in this connection, and the structural resources which enabled them to use these strategies, were similar to those used in other organizational spheres where informants must be created and used, e.g., bailiffs within the debt collection process (Rock, 1976; McMullen, 1980).

When informants were acting on behalf of organizations, there was a tacit basis on which detectives could expect co-operation. Both the detectives and the informants knew that there were past instances, and would be future instances, in which the organization needed police assistance. The information provided in the present case was always seen in this broader perspective. Detectives operated on the expectation that their requests for information from these organizational informants would be met routinely, and they were met routinely.

The ready provision of information on this basis came from persons in a variety of organizations, including private businesses, schools, residence complexes, civil service departments, and correctional facilities. Detectives typically approached these organizations to obtain information about possible suspects, to identify particular suspects, to find the whereabouts of a known suspect, and/or to acquire background information on a known suspect. Detectives realized that the way that they routinely tapped these sources was crucial to the way they could make their cases, both in terms of further investigative activity and dispositions (cf. Skolnick and Woodworth, 1967).

In our observations, only one potential informant in an organizational role refused to co-operate. On DS 4, the detective tried for a second time to obtain from the manager of a fast-food take-out shop the whereabouts and telephone number of an ex-employee wanted for questioning regarding a "possible sex offender" occurrence report. The refusal drew comments from the detective which illustrated his perception of the rule of co-operation with organizations of this type. The detective threatened, "O.K., if you have any breakin's up there don't call the police. I'll leave a note in headquarters that you won't co-operate with us. If you have any disorderlies, don't expect the police to be up there." This exception clearly proved the rule.

Compliance from organizational informants was routinely accomplished. Usually the informant did not inquire about anything except the nature of the trouble the suspect was wanted for. Case examples involving a range of organizations will further our point.

In DC 26, the victim complained that an identified suspect had stolen some objects from her and threatened her after deciding to cease living in the same apartment with her. The victim said she did not know where the suspect had moved to, but she did identify the company which employed the suspect. The detectives proceeded to the personnel office of this company, identified themselves to a secretary and initially asked if the person worked there. The secretary replied that the person was an employee, and then asked if the person was "in trouble." One detective replied, "No, there's just a little matter with the person he lives with actually; we just want to straighten him out, nothing serious." The secretary then provided the address from the employee file, noting that the person had just recently moved.

Routine co-operation was evident with schools, usually involving a Principal or Vice-Principal as the informant. Informants from schools tended to have regular contacts with the police, especially the Youth Bureau, and were willing to co-operate in providing school file information on named suspects or to suggest possible suspects after an incident was described to them, in exchange for discreet handling of other troubles in the school (Sanders, 1977: 148 reports a similar pattern). For example, in DC 87 the detective provided the Vice-Principal with a list of possible suspects and then asked to have items from their files so that he could check against the writing on notes left by the culprit in a series of break and enter occurrences. The Vice-Principal complied, and willingly photocopied those samples that superficially matched so that the detective could take them away with him (DS 39). In this same case, the employer of one suspect also turned over copies from the suspect's employee file for the purpose of providing the detectives with handwriting samples (DS 41).

The caretakers and superintendents of apartment buildings were similarly co-operative in providing information about their tenants. Here, the desire to keep a "clean building" and the regular use of the police to handle disputes provided the basis for reciprocity. Indeed, to the extent that persons were made more easily findable because they lived in these dwellings, and to the extent that they tended to come from a lower socio-economic group than private home dwellers, it is possible to suggest that this source of information provided one basis for a class bias in generating suspects.

On DS 3, the detectives asked an apartment superintendent and his wife to examine an "Identikit" (composite drawing) picture of an "Indecent Assault (female)" suspect. The superintendent and his wife did so, collectively agreeing that the picture resembled one of their tenants. The wife then produced the tenancy file of this person, providing the person's name, age, occupation, length of residence, car license number, and apartment number. One detective then asked whether the person kept "regular hours," and received the reply, "Well, he's around in the day and then goes out a lot at night, comes home around one or two in the morning." According to the detective's later account, this provided the necessary cue for further investigation of this person as a suspect.

Detectives also relied upon routine access to the information sources of municipal civil servants. For example, in DC 100 several bank employees reported being watched and/or followed by a person driving a taxi. The detectives labelled this as a "suspicious circumstances" occurrence, hypothesizing and later confirming that the taxi was simply using the parking lot of the shopping plaza where the bank was located as a place to pick up passengers. In order to identify the suspect, the detective proceeded to the municipal offices to talk with a person in the taxi licensing division. When the person appeared at the front counter of the office, the detective introduced himself as having been sent by a particular Detective Sergeant, who told the detective to mention his name because he was well known to this official. The licensing official immediately responded by showing the detective into his office, commenting that the Detective Sergeant had done a lot for him in the past. The detective asked if the licensing official could ascertain the identity of, and pull the file on, the person driving a taxi in the plaza area. The official made a telephone call to a taxi company, ascertained the person's identity, and then pulled the file. The official then volunteered to photocopy the file, and gave the detective a photograph of the person, which was on the file.

In relation to other criminal control organizations, detectives relied upon routine exchange of information as a normalized part of relationships with particular agents representing these organizations. For example, on DS 110 the detective was "fishing" for possible suspects in relation to a theft of an automobile. The detective had an established relationship with a staff member in a half-way house for parolees, and decided to interview him regarding possible suspects. When the detective explained the nature of his visit he asked if the staff member was aware of any possible suspects in residence at the house. The staff member's immediate response was, "Just a minute, I'll go check." He came back into the office with three files and suggested that two of these were good possibilities. The most likely suspect in his mind was one who had just done time and was on parole for break and enter and auto theft: "The guy's a loner. He doesn't talk to anybody in here. He just keeps to himself. I think he would be capable of it." The worker indicated no hesitation in showing the complete files to the detective although some parts of the files contained reports from correctional and penitentiary personnel marked "strictly confidential."

In dealings with informants who operated on their own behalf, detectives called upon a variety of strategies. The particular strategy employed was based upon other roles the informant had or could be made to adopt. As was the case with informants acting on behalf of organizations, some individual informants had ongoing relationships with detectives that involved expectations of reciprocity. These individuals were victims on whose behalf detectives had worked previously; victims on whose behalf detectives were currently working; former suspects being kept "on the line" for apparent leniency in the past; or, "marginal" persons who simply befriended particular detectives, exchanging information for advice, counsel and a sympathetic ear. Other individual informants sought or were offered specific commodities in relation to case specific information, e.g., police protection, cash. In some cases, detectives exploited specific negative aspects of the informant's relationship with a suspect to encourage co-operation. If all else failed, the threat of criminal charges against the informant was sometimes used to coerce compliance. This threat of charges was frequently employed in the cases of informants who were also judged to be accomplices, and in their cases the threat was sometimes carried out as an additional lever to gain their compliance.

In seeking information from victims with whom they had previous dealings, detectives assumed they would get co-operation on the same basis as that established with organizational victims. That is, they assumed an openness to their inquiries in exchange for past assistance and implicit willingness to give further assistance. For example, in DC 87 the detectives were attempting to identify a suspect who was linked to a number of "break and enter" occurrences and "harassing telephone call" occurrences in a small area of a residential community. The detective contacted a person he had dealt with two years before as a "break, enter and theft" victim, hoping she would provide general information about youths in the neighbourhood who might be possible suspects.

Detectives played "tit for tat" with some persons who were victims in still active occurrences unrelated to the case they were investigating. For example, on DS 150 the detectives were called for a meeting with a person who had a "mischief" (property damage) complaint on file with the detectives (DC 240). The detectives went to the meeting expecting the person to directly probe about what action was being taken on his complaint. Instead, the person opened by reminiscing about mutual acquaintances, and then proceeded to volunteer information about the identity of a suspect in another case (DC 225). The detectives then initiated the discussion about DC 240, mentioning one suspect they were unable to locate. The detectives added that they did not have enough evidence to charge this suspect on this case, but noted that they also wanted him in connection with another case (DC 241). The person then told the detectives the whereabouts of this suspect, and went on to state that the other suspect in DC 240 had threatened him. The detectives in turn asked if the person wanted "threatening" charges laid against this suspect, adding that they could in turn control the other suspect through charges in DC 241. The entire transaction evolved in a "tit-for-tat" fashion, with both parties attempting to achieve resolutions of mutual benefit.

Detectives maintained contacts with a "regular" victim, on whose behalf they would lay charges and from whom they would receive information about other occurrences. This woman regularly attended parties and other functions where youths discussed their exploits, and she passed on information about incidents and possible suspects to detectives in exchange for detective reciprocity in handling her own affairs. For example, she was one of two informants who assisted in identifying three suspects who were eventually charged for a series of break, enter and thefts in DC 78.

In spite of defining this woman as extremely troublesome, and as much to blame as the people she accused, the detectives acted against suspects she complained about. When she complained that her separated husband telephoned her and threatened her life and the life of her boyfriend, the detectives laid an indictable threatening charge even though the Detective Sergeant had advised a less serious charge via the private information route (DC 11). This charge was later withdrawn in court. On another occasion detectives laid an abduction charge against her boyfriend. The boyfriend claimed that he had called to take her out on a pre-arranged date, only to discover that she was not there and had left her young child (a toddler) alone. The boyfriend said he took the child with him, and returned later only to be confronted by his irate girlfriend, who called the police. At other times, this woman simply called for advice from detectives concerning the laying of charges in interpersonal disputes, usually involving her separated husband. The interesting feature of detective compliance with the requests of the victim in these instances was that they all involved domestic interpersonal disputes with a victim who was a regular user of the police. Cases with this type of dispute situation and with this type of victim were typically handled by means other than detectives laying a charge; indeed, most were filtered out of police organizational concern by patrol officers (cf. Ericson, 1980: Ch. 5).

Detectives also relied upon reciprocal relationships with suspects whom they had made dependent. An instance of this occurred on DS 29, when a person whom the detective had previously charged came into the divisional detective office and offered the names of two potential suspects for a homicide case. The detective later commented to the researcher that this person regularly provided information "on his own" or at the request of the detective.[9]

Other informants depended upon the friendship of detectives, and willingly exchanged information as a means of sustaining the relationship (cf. Buckner, 1968: 131). For example, a relationship was established with a young woman who lived in an apartment building populated by several known offenders, and she developed information through conversation with these persons and others in the building. She would telephone the detectives from time to time to talk about her personal life and problems, and usually invited them for a visit. On other occasions she visited the detective office, or received a visit initiated by detectives.

These visits started when detectives were investigating a case and asked an apartment superintendent if he knew a particular suspect. The superintendent replied that he did not, but thought that one of his tenants (the informant in question) would know the suspect. The detectives called on this person, she provided the information, and the relationship was initiated. A description of one subsequent contact illustrates the nature of the relationship.

The informant called the detectives on DS 35, claiming that she was going to kill herself and that she wanted a visit from them. An hour later, one detective and the researcher proceeded to her apartment, with the other detective handing his partner some "break and enter" occurrences in the hope that the informant might have some information about them. The informant answered the door in her pyjamas and invited us in. She appeared to have taken some drug and was full of "self-pity." The detective made some tea, and talked about the informant's career, which she stated she was prevented from continuing because of a serious mistake she made. She also talked about being banned from the United States because she "kicked a cop so hard he and his wife can't have any kids." She talked about going into prostitution, saying she only received $185/month unemployment insurance and that her apartment alone cost her $155/month. The detective gave her $4.00 saying, "I don't normally do this, but I looked in your fridge and you don't have much there." She complained about not being able to obtain a job, and asked if she could use the police as a reference. The detective told her that an employer could call if they wanted to know about her. The detective did not attempt to obtain any information from her, although he originally took along some "break and enter" occurrences to see if she knew anything about them. The detective spent approximately 40 minutes with her.

Some informants demanded more specific commodities in exchange for information relevant to the specific case under investigation. Protection was sometimes requested, either in the form of not divulging the informant's identity to the suspects (e.g., DC 79) or to other persons (e.g., DC 93), or in the form of promising bodyguard protection (e.g., DS 168). In only one instance (DS 153; re: DC 244) did the informant demand a cash payment. The informant, an ex-inmate from penitentiary, offered the names of two robbery suspects. The detective stated that the only basis for suspicion on these two persons was the informant's account that they were residents of a halfway house for ex-inmates and "they've had quite a bit of money lately." The detective questioned the value of the information and made no comment about the cash, although he left the possibility open as a means of sustaining the informant's commitment.

Detectives usually did not need money to capitalize on informants. Rather, as we have already documented, they could strategically rely upon other currencies of value to informants. One additional currency was the informant's desire to be vindictive against a suspect. For example, in DC 79 a suspect was identified by an accomplice as being jointly involved in three "break, enter and theft" occurrences, as well as other possible property offences. The accomplice mentioned that a former roommate had more information on these other offences and that this person would undoubtedly co-operate as an informant because she was vindictive against the suspect.

The detectives proceeded to interview this informant, hoping to obtain both personal information about the suspect that could be used in interrogation, as well as more specific details about the suspect's criminal activities. The detectives initiated the interview by inquiring about the informant's personal relationship with the suspect, drawing out the vindictive features partially through the assistance of the informant's current boyfriend, who was also present at the interview.

In the interview, the informant proceeded to tell of her involvement with the suspect, saying that she became pregnant by the suspect and had subsequently severed her involvement with him. Supported by her boyfriend, she said she was particularly anxious to retaliate against the suspect and would do whatever was necessary to have him prosecuted, even if she had to testify as a witness in court. She said the only fear she had was that the fact of her pregnancy would come to light, and this would incapacitate her as a witness because she did not want her parents to know. The detectives said that her pregnancy was not relevant and would not come to light. One detective said to her that if she gave sufficient information about the suspect's activities, she would not have to testify because the police could gather the necesary evidence, e.g., stolen property.

The informant proceeded to relate what she knew about the suspect's activities. She said he had committed many offences, including breaking into an entertainment establishment, stealing from a store he used to work in, a car theft, and a theft of collectors' coins. The informant said that she personally accompanied the suspect and his accomplice to pawn some goods obtained from one of the break-ins. The informant gave details of where the suspect hid the property in his room at home. She also talked of his "sensitive spots," such as his attitude toward the baby they had, suggesting the police could play on this when they picked up the suspect. She also mentioned the name of a third person who was involved with the suspect in some of the offences she alleged the suspect had committed.

After leaving, one detective said to the other detective and the researcher that he could use the fact that the informant became pregnant by the suspect as a lever in interrogating the suspect, i.e., use the threat of telling the suspect's parents about the pregnancy. Upon returning to the station, the detective spent the rest of the shift checking occurrences on the general file to see if any could be matched with the information obtained on the suspect.

On the rare occasions when detectives and individual informants did not share a currency for exchange, the detectives created one via the threat of criminal charges. These threats were sometimes made up in relation to the specifics of the case. For example, on DS 121 the detectives became involved in an investigation of employee theft. The investigation was based on information received from a private security officer, who said he had received the information from a company foreman, who in turn said he had learned about it from one of his workers. A detective and the security officer approached this worker directly, but he refused to co-operate. The detective replied by telling the worker he would be charged with being an "accessory." The worker then agreed to supply the information and to refrain from relating anything about the investigation to his co-workers.

On other occasions, these threats were based upon charges unrelated to the matter under investigation. For example, in DC 98 the roommate of a suspect supplied the detectives with descriptions of property and actual property that was possibly stolen by a suspect, in exchange for no charges regarding a bag of marijuana that was found in possession of the roommate during a search of the apartment, and no searches after obvious signs of marijuana being present on subsequent visits. To illustrate, on the third occasion on which the detectives called on this informant, the smell of marijuana emanated from his apartment unit. When the informant answered the door, he told the detectives he did not want them to enter because he had some friends in. One detective referred to the smell, then said, "We'll play it cool if you can help us out." Remaining in the hall outside the unit, the informant provided the detectives with an extensive list of items in possession of the suspect that the detectives believed to have been stolen. In exchange, the detectives ignored the pursuit of the marijuana.

A ready-made currency for exchange framed situations where the potential informant was also implicated as an accomplice in the same case. In these situations detectives sometimes demanded information in exchange for charge considerations, whether or not there was an actual basis for a threatened charge (cf. Skolnick, 1966: 186). They also played on the person's fears that their accomplice would deal with the detectives first and thereby gain the advantage.

Detectives routinely turned a blind eye in relation to persons who were implicated in property offences as receivers of stolen property, and who co-operated by returning the property and by implicating the person(s) who had allegedly committed the thefts of the property. For example, in DC 98 the detectives approached a person identified by the accused as being in receipt of some stolen property connected with the case. This person immediately turned over the property in question, and then provided details of his involvement with the accused and how he came to be in receipt of the property. While it is questionable that this person had knowledge that the property was stolen, the detectives played on the threat of charges in exchange for co-operation, and used a search warrant as an additional sign of their authority in the matter. In the same case, another receiver claimed that he had sold the guitar he purchased from the accused. The detective seized another guitar belonging to the receiver "to keep him honest," as well as a small quantity of marijuana discovered in the receiver's apartment during the search for the guitar. The receiver was told to have the original guitar within five days or he would be charged with possession of narcotics, but if he returned the guitar he would receive the other guitar back and there would be no proceedings on the narcotics charge nor in relation to possession of the stolen guitar. The receiver duly complied.

In a series of cases involving reported "attempted robberies," "break, enter and theft," and "theft" (DC 228-231), an informant identified one suspect. This suspect was arrested and subject to the execution of a search warrant on his residence. During interrogation, this suspect became an informant and gave a written statement implicating three accomplices in exchange for no charges being laid against him. The other suspects were subsequently apprehended. During interrogation, one of the three suspects was told who implicated him in the offences, and he in turn implicated the informant as a suspect in all the cases and provided a written statement to that effect. The other two suspects also gave explicit written statements implicating the informant as an accomplice. However, the detectives proceeded no further against the first suspect, turning a blind eye in exchange for his co-operation.

Detectives sometimes took the matter one step further, actually charging the suspect and then utilizing that as a lever in generating information with the implicit or explicit promise of a "patch" (future withdrawal of the charges) in cooperation with the Crown attorney. Contrary to what Skolnick (1966) reports,[10] this approach appeared to be less frequently used than an offer of not charging in the first place in exchange for information. One example of charging as an additional "lever" occurred in DC 220. An ongoing informant, who was known to be involved in gambling activities, was identified as the culprit in a "false fire alarm" occurrence. When the detectives contacted this person, stating that they had a warrant for his arrest on this occurrence, he immediately adapted his informant role, talking about people involved in gambling, loan-sharking and prostitution. The person was taken to the station, with the implicit understanding that there might be a patch in exchange for implicating accomplices in gambling and other activities. Altogether, the detectives questioned the person for one and one-half hours, with the conversation focusing almost entirely on the information related to possible suspects for these other activities. Ultimately, the detectives obtained information on these activities and arranged a meeting with the informant during the following week, keeping the possibility of a patch open as a lure.

When detectives charged a person with no intention of arranging a "patch," they switched to the use of other "levers" to obtain information. One lever was to threaten custody if information on accomplices was not forthcoming. For example, in DC 82 one of four suspects whom the detectives anticipated charging with "theft over $200" was arrested first and asked by the detectives to give a statement implicating the other three. As one part of the inducement, it was suggested that he would be released on a promise to appear notice rather than held in custody. Another lever employed with this same suspect was to tell him that his accomplices had already informed on him. This was a frequently used tactic in cases involving accomplices; it was explicitly aimed at generating information by creating the belief that one's accomplices might gain the advantage with detectives if one did not give an account that described their "true" involvement. Analysis of these levering tactics is furthered in Chapter 6 when we consider detective interrogation practices.

Whether dealing with informants acting on behalf of organizations or informants acting alone, detectives had little difficulty in obtaining information. Detectives could rely upon the informant's implicit need for ongoing co-operation with the police, trade a specific commodity, or create a "lever" which induced co-operation. While these strategies of manipulation, negotiation and coercion were routinely used to obtain information, the question remains how the information was made useful by detectives.

Using Informants

There have been different viewpoints on the value of informants to detective work. Westley (1951: 70) refers to the informant as "the lifeblood of the good detective," and Skolnick (1966) contents that this is particularly the case in relation to "victimless," proactive areas such as narcotics policing. On the other hand, Greenwood et al. (1975: 69) report that, "Although investigators often speak of 'their informants' as being essential to their work in solving crimes, the cases we examined did not bear this out."

To some extent, the matter is a definitional one. Taking the broad definition of informant that we have adopted, and the key role of information production in the making of detective cases, we argue that informants are central to detective work. Detectives used informants to identify suspects, i.e., to suggest possible suspects, to directly identify suspects, and to tell them the whereabouts of a known suspect. Detectives also used informants to provide useful information about suspects, including biographical data useable in interrogations and in other investigative steps, and direct evidence (e.g., stolen property) to be used against suspects. They were able to accomplish this with the strategic resources available to them (as outlined in the last section), and under the general enabling cover of low visibility conditions.

If suspects were not initially known in a case, the only significant hope available to detectives to achieve a clearance was to find and create an informant to assist them. We have already indirectly considered the assistance rendered by informants in terms of the types of information they produced, but it is worthwhile at this juncture to provide a more succinct summary of their contributions.

Informants provided suggestions about possible suspects after an initial case description by detectives. This function was particularly evident among individual informants operating on behalf of other formal organizations, including schools, resident management companies, government administrative agencies, and other criminal control organizations. Individual informants acting on their own behalf were only infrequently involved in these "fishing for suspects" expeditions, although they occasionally did provide such identification.

Individual informants operating on their own behalf were much more likely to provide identification of specific suspects. They identified culprits after explicit negotiation for concessions from detectives. These informants were either accomplices with the persons they were identifying (e.g., DC 228-231), witnesses to the occurrences for which the suspects were wanted (e.g., DC 99), or had otherwise learned that a particular individual had committed the offence (e.g., DC 98). Informants representing organizations were not typically involved in this form of direct identification of a known culprit, except in cases involving "internal" offences within organizations where the information was provided to the police by a member of the victimized organization (DC 82).

Detectives often approached informants for the sole purpose of discovering the whereabouts of an already identified suspect. This was often the function of employer, school, or public agency file-checks on persons, which were undertaken when other sources (e.g., victim-complainant information; vehicle registration checks) were unavailable or had failed. On other occasions, this information was provided along with direct identification of the suspect as the culprit.

Employer, school, and public agency file checks were also undertaken as a means of developing a biographical profile on the suspect; this in turn allowed detectives to make judgments about the suspect's "respectability," and provided cues for interrogation strategies. For example, in the previously cited case DC 100, the detective used a taxi license office file check on the suspect to ascertain that the person was also employed as a teacher, owned a house, and had a family, all of which were subsequently used in the follow-up report as indicators of respectability to partially justify writing off the case as "unfounded."

Similarly, individual informants operating on their own behalf were used to provide biographical detail on suspects. As we considered in relation to DC 79, an informant provided considerable detail on the personal life of one suspect, who was the informant's ex-boyfriend. This information was deemed valuable by the detectives for use in interrogation, allowing them the possibility of threatening to reveal specific personal information about the suspect as a lever to induce a confession from him; and, allowing them to create a general impession that they knew "everything" about the suspect, providing them with a psychological edge in interrogation.

Another component of biographical information gathering on known suspects was contacting other criminal control organizations about the criminal status of suspects. In the case of persons on probation or parole, this was usually a matter of finding out if an agent had any general information concerning unusual habits or circumstances involving the suspect. In addition, the detectives attempted to ascertain the specific conditions of the probation or parole orders pertaining to the suspects. For example, in DC 3 the detectives designated a particular individual as "dangerous" and in need of being subject to some legal controls that would keep him from his alleged sexual attraction to younger boys. The detectives had this person charged with "Vagrancy 'E' " and they were searching for some additional charge that might be useful as a "lever" at the point the case reached trial.[11] The detectives learned from the police information system that the accused was subject to a probation order, and decided to contact the probation officer to ascertain the conditions and possibly discover grounds for a "breach of probation" charge. The detectives ultimately obtained a copy of the probation order, which had as one condition that the probationer was not to associate with or communicate with any male person under the age of 21. When arrested on the Vagrancy 'E' charge the accused had been playing tennis with boys under the age of 21 and this provided the detectives with grounds for laying a "breach of probation" charge as a back-up "kicker" to the original charge.

Informants were also engaged to provide detectives with specific evidence in relation to an identified suspect. Informants offering this type of information were typically individuals implicated as accomplices in a case. They provided either direct physical evidence, such as stolen property (e.g., DC 98), or gave statements to detectives providing explicit allegations against named suspects (e.g., DC 99; DC 151; DC 228-231).

Persons representing organizations were much less likely to have access to conclusive evidence against a suspect. If they did, they were more likely to operate in the role of complainant on behalf of the organization. Occasionally, however, they did act as informants regarding evidence. They were sometimes enlisted to look out for transactions involving stolen property (e.g., a pool hall operator concerning DC 169), or provided a form of evidence that could be used by detectives to justify the arrest of a suspect (e.g., photocopying employer files for handwriting samples to compare with notes left by the culprit, DC 87).

Except where informants supplied stolen property, their evidence was generally of the type used by detectives to justify an arrest for the purpose of seeking a suspect confession and other evidence, rather than to directly provide evidence that could or would be used in court. As Buckner (1967: 133) observes, "Intelligence information which has been gathered from a number of sources which would not be admissible in court may be useful in dealing with any marginal activity either as trading material or as a threat. The more a police officer knows, regardless of source, the better able he is to cope with the problems of his environment and to develop admissible evidence." Informants were useful as building blocks in the construction of a case, but did not usually provide the mortar to solidify or seal it.

While substance was provided by the information of informants, what that substance was shaped into in constructing a case remained in the hands of detectives. Detectives were able to mold information according to organizational designs because of the enabling low visibility conditions under which they operated. Informants were typically kept "secret" to others in the organization of criminal control and within the police organization. In applications for search warrants and arrest warrants, the name of informants typically would not be given and the Justices of the Peace typically would not make an inquiry to find out. Informants identity or use rarely appeared on any investigative reports submitted by the detectives. There were even occasions when detectives partners did not reveal to each other a source of information, or an informant's identity.

The low visibility aspect was the most general enabling resource available to detectives. It allowed them to take action within their own set of organizational priorities, and to cover their actions via selective accounts to the various parties concerned. Typically, detectives only did one type of undercover work: "covering their ass" through selective accounts to interested parties. Typically, detectives only did one type of patrol work: "patrolling the facts" so that they produced the outcome they wanted in a way that would not be questioned. A detailed discussion of DC 38 will illustrate the processes involved.

In DC 38, a victim had reported that she was the recipient of repeated "obscene telephone calls" from a suspect whom she identified. The detectives proceeded to assist the victim by having the telephone company put tracing equipment on her line so that the number of the caller could be identified. When the detectives were satisfied that they had sufficient evidence, they proceeded to apprehend the suspect. However, once apprehended the suspect attempted to deal for no charges being laid on the "obscene telephone call" occurrences, and for a withdrawal of an outstanding possession of marijuana charge, in exchange for the return of a dangerous gun. The detectives initially baulked at this, but then agreed to the arrangement if the suspect provided them with information about a murder that had remained unsolved. The suspect agreed, and he was transformed into an informant rather than an accused person.

The next piece of work required of the detectives was to account for the disposition of DC 38 in terms of the organizational record, and to the victim.[12] This task was problematic because the victim had been vehement about wanting the suspect apprehended and prosecuted, and because the official record could not legitimately indicate that the case was disposed of without charge because it was traded for what the detectives regarded as a more important matter.

The detectives decided to clear the occurrence by "caution" of the suspect. In order to justify this to the victim, the detective first tried to argue diminished responsibility on behalf of the suspect, saying this was one of "the crazy things he does when he's high on speed." The detective added that the suspect was already facing drug charges and that he was sure to be penalized anyway. The victim refused to buy into these justifications, and the detective then tried another one. He said that there was poor evidence because the telephone tracing equipment had not worked properly, and therefore only a caution of the suspect was possible. The victim was not entirely satisfied with this, claiming that the matter had caused her considerable strife over a six month period. She said she was going to contact her lawyer and find out what he thought about the matter, i.e., the caution as opposed to charges. The detective stressed that he would lay a charge if the culprit did it again, and the victim repeated that she would call her lawyer. Following the interview, the detective said to his partner and the researcher, "Call her lawyer about her rights. Hah. A murder is more important than that."

At this point the detectives were uncertain about whether or not they had cooled out the victim. However, they decided to dispose of the case by "caution" of the suspect, formulating their report within the well established justifications of evidence problems and victim's wishes.

[Excerpts from follow-up investigation report, DC 38].
On [date specified] the writers contacted the ... Telephone Security Department and they advised that they had a Pen Register on the suspect's phone during the time of the call on [date specified]. Security advised that they had checked the tape that was on the [suspect's] phone and had not found the victim's phone number. Apparently there had been a malfunction with the Pen Register and there was one phone number on the tape that was similar to [the victim's] but the fourth digit was different. Security advised that they could not give evidence in court regarding the tape.

The writers contacted [the victim] and explained the situation to her. She advised at this time that she was not interested in [the suspect] being charged but that she wanted the phone calls to stop. The writers advised her that [the suspect] would be spoken to and cautioned.

There were many features of this case construction which were "apparent" to some and unknown to others. Apparently, the detectives achieved the outcome they wanted vis-à-vis organizational criteria of importance. The suspect's role as an informant was nowhere indicated in this report. The entire formulation of the case for organizational purposes ignored the wider role of the suspect as an informant. The matter was localized to this one case by creating the impression that the conflict was worked out by detectives through the willing co-operation of the victim.

The lesson of this case example is coincident with the lesson of this chapter. Detectives dealt with victims and other citizens who may have had useful information in order to produce case outcomes that met their own police organizational agenda. Detectives had the power to produce these outcomes in the context of the authoritative aura of their office, specific commodities of exchange at their disposal, and the low visibility conditions of their work. These elements allowed them to selectively provide legitimate accounts for their actions that predictably went unchallenged. Through this process detectives transformed victim troubles into police property (Christie, 1977).

This process was typically *transactional,* rather than unilateral. Detectives and citizens had a use for each other. Detectives used citizens in the construction of case outcomes that could at once serve detective interests and be made to appear organizationally appropriate. Citizens used detectives to handle their own complaints and to produce for themselves other commodities they valued and wished to traffic in.

What was finally made of a case partially reflected the informational materials obtained from victim-complainants and informants. When suspects and accused persons were involved, many additional elements were made relevant to the case. We now turn to an examination of detective dealings with suspects and accused persons, providing more substance to our arguments about how crime and criminals are made in the course of detective work.

NOTES

1. Bayley (1977: 223) contrasts the American situation with his analysis of Japan: "[J]apanese policemen make twice-yearly visits to every residence in order to obtain information about inhabitants, addresses, and problems of neighborhoods and to give advice about crime prevention. Japanese do not consider this extraordinary, still less a threat to individual liberty; it is a routine accepted as essential in order to detect crime and provide security."

2. In referring to their research in Kansas City, Kelling *et al.* (1979: 12-13) state that "... citizens surveyed on a random household basis cannot even distinguish changes in the quantity of police services, let alone their quality."

3. "Previous known contact" was ascertained through a check of all citizens' names in the contact file kept at headquarters. It should be noted that this file cannot be regarded as complete in terms of contacts, thus the inclusion of the word "known" contacts. The practice of record-keeping in the Force meant that some cards were missing or misfiled (cf. Chan and Doob, 1977). Some informants used regularly by a detective might not appear on this file because of the detective's desire to keep their identity secret from others in the Force.

4. Sanders (1977: 97-98) reports a similar finding: "If the victim of a crime complained that nothing was being done about his or her case, a detective would be dispatched to PR (public relations) the case. . . . It is understandable that the victims become upset when they are told that the investigation has been inactivated, and it is also understandable why the detectives put on a 'make-believe' investigation in these situations."

5. As researchers have pointed out (e.g., Greenwood *et al.*, 1975: esp. 79; Vera Institute, 1977), property occurrences are particularly likely to be "filed" without clearance if a suspect is not apprehended at the scene or the suspect is not an 'intimate' of the victim and thus not previously known to him.

6. This rule was part of the recipe knowledge of detectives in the general investigation units we studied. It is also articulated in texts on detective procedures (cf. Inbau and Reid, 1967: 108ff).

7. Historically, there have been less subtle ways of discouraging victim-complainants from pursuing prosecution. For example, in 19th century England indigent complainants were committed to prison as material witnesses, while the accused could be set free on bail. Ignatieff (1978: 133) describes the case in 1800 of Mary Rich, who alleged she had been raped by a lawyer and who was held in prison for over a month while the accused was freed on bail:

When the case came before the grand jury, Mary Rich showed signs of starvation and fainted on the witness stand. The jury immediately inspected the prison and discovered that material witnesses like Mary Rich were held in solitary confinement on a bread and water diet while waiting for their cases to come to trial. Sir Francis Burdett procured a copy of the grand jury's report and demanded another commission of inquiry. William Mainwairing, chairman of the Middlesex justices and MP for Middlesex, replied to Burdett's charges of cruelty by claiming that Mary Rich was an untrustworthy whore. She had been discovered 'with several boys on the stairs in a way not proper to mention and had received half pence from them.' To the charge that she had been starved, Mainwairing replied that she was better fed in prison than at home.

8. This contrasts with an often quoted statement by J. Edgar Hoover: "Unlike the totalitarian practice, the informant in America serves of his own free will, fulfilling one of the citizenship obligations of our democratic form of government" (quotation in Skolnick, 1966: 122; Harney and Cross, 1960:18; Klein, 1974: 96).

9. In a similar manner, debtors are "kept on a string" by bailiffs (McMullan, 1980), and "bums, drunks, junkies and prostitutes" are "exploited for information" by patrol officers (Rubinstein, 1973: 388).

10. Skolnick (1966: 125, 138) observes, "It is true that the policeman needs the informer, but it is equally true that he can often control the informer only by invoking the law . . . [T]he main payment is legal authority, and it is handed out at a later stage in the process than is usually assumed. . . . Penalties thus are the capital assets of the informer system."

11. The *Criminal Code* paragraph 175(1)(e) provides that "Everyone commits vagrancy who having at any time been convicted of an offence under a provision mentioned in paragraph 689(1)(a) or (b), is found loitering or wandering in or near a school ground, playground, public park, or bathing area." Paragraph 689(1)(a) lists offences for which a person might be considered a "dangerous sex offender," including attempted or completed rape; sexual intercourse with female under 14; indecent assault on female; buggery or bestiality; indecent assault on male; acts of gross indecency. In DC 3, the suspect had a record for indecent assault (male), including a term in prison after being convicted on three counts involving child victims. The case of this suspect is considered in detail in Chapter 6.

12. LaFave (1965: 135) contends that police officers will not offer immunity to informants who want to avoid charges on crimes with victims, and will only deal in relation to crimes without victims. We contend that detectives will deal crimes with victims for information about what they regard as more serious matters. They are able to do this because they have a range of credible accounts which allow them to cool out the victim and to legitimate the case disposition within the police organization. This is a neglected area of analysis in the study of detective work.

Chapter 6

Detective Dealings with Suspects and Accused Persons

The pragmatic aspect of detective dealings with victims, complainants and informants carried over into their work with suspects and accused persons. Detectives employed the organizational resources available to them to secure the compliance of suspects, to develop useful information from them, and to make acceptable "crime" and "criminal" outcomes to their cases. This work was accomplished under the protective cover of low visibility conditions. It was also done with the assistance of police organizational and legal rules, which allowed detectives to justify their actions as they moved their dealings from low visibility conditions (e.g., the interrogation room) to high visibility conditions (e.g., appearing in court).

We argue that detectives had ample organizational resources to accomplish the outcomes demanded of them in their work. They were able to secure suspect compliance routinely because of the authoritative aura of their office, backed up by enabling laws pertaining to the full range of their actions (i.e., arrest, search, suspect's right to silence, suspect's access to a third party, evidence needed to use substantive laws). This means that the process was not characterized by adversary conflict and struggle as depicted in some scholarly versions of the criminal process (e.g., Packer, 1968). Detectives were able to use skillfully the resources available to them to accomplish the making of cases against suspects in a routine and unproblematic manner. Far from serving as an arbiter of conflict, the rules were used by detectives to defuse any potential conflict and thereby to ease their task.

In sum, the rules of due process did not restrict crime control efforts (*ibid.*); instead, the rules of due process were used by detectives *for* their crime control efforts (cf. McBarnet, 1976, 1979). Detectives used these rules as frameworks for justification and ultimately legitimation of their actions when moving their cases from the low visibility of transactions with suspects to the high visibility of providing accounts to police superordinates, Justices of the Peace, Crown attorneys, lawyers, and judges. Of course, these rules were also used to predict that it would be better to use discretion and not transform the suspect into an accused person, thereby keeping things under the protective cover of low visibility.

In any case, *the* work of detectives in dealing with suspects was keeping their work under the organizational covers available to them. This "undercover" work characterized detective actions, as we shall proceed to document. We initially review how suspects came to the attention of detectives. We then consider how detectives gained control over, and compliance from, suspects. This is followed by an analysis of how suspects were used in the production of information deemed relevant to the disposition of their cases. Finally, we examine court outcomes in the making, considering detective construction of criminal charges and detective involvement in plea discussions aimed at transforming accused persons into convicted "criminal" persons.

Producing Suspects

Prior to the analysis of how detectives dealt with suspects, it is important to review how suspects were produced. We can recall from Chapters 4 and 5 that detectives did not pursue endless physical clues, undertake "stake outs," or do what is popularly known as undercover work to produce someone they could thereby ascribe as a suspect. To the contrary, detectives were dependent upon other persons to initially define someone in the role of suspect. This is not to say that detectives did not actively pursue persons who would produce these definitions of others as suspects. As we considered in Chapter 5, there were many detective strategies for doing just that. Detectives relied upon patrol officers, or coerced, manipulated, and negotiated with citizens, to produce suspects for them. It was then the detectives' task to employ strategies aimed at confirming the suspect status and to take action in relation to it.

In the sample of 295 cases, only 76 (26 percent) involved dealings with suspects. In these 76 cases, 61 had one suspect only, 11 had two suspects, 3 had three suspects, and 1 had four suspects, making a total of 96 suspects. As enumerated in Table 6:1, one-half of these suspects were initially identified in their roles through the work of patrol officers. Patrol officers either apprehended persons they thought could be legitimately designated as suspects (29.2 percent of the total), or recorded information about identified suspects on occurrence reports after receiving information from victims, complainants, or informants, or after doing proactively mobilized investigations (21.9 percent). A further 22 percent were produced from detective involvements with informants, including informants not also implicated as accomplices (16.7 percent), and informants who were judged to be accomplices (5.2 percent). An additional 18 percent were identified by victim-complainants via detective interviews. The remaining 9 percent were identified in other ways, i.e., in outstanding arrest warrants; by being present at an incident initially responded to by detectives; through arrest by officers from another police department; and by turning themselves in to the detectives.

Table 6:1

How Suspects were Identified to Detectives

Source of Suspect Identification	N	%
Patrol Officer—suspect in custody	28	29.2
Patrol Officer—occurrence report	21	21.9
Informant—non-suspect	16	16.7
Informant—suspect's accomplice	5	5.2
Victim-complainant	17	17.7
Other	9	9.3
Totals	96	100.0

In sum, the detectives' task was to process readily available suspects (cf. Greenwood, *et al.*, 1975; Sanders, 1977). The detectives' work was to deal with suspects delivered to them or otherwise identified through the work of others. However, once suspects were confronted by detectives, it was up to detectives to decide what could and would be done. Their first job was to indicate the nature of their power relationship, to ensure that the suspect was under their control.

Controlling Suspects

Detectives could immediately take power over suspects by putting them under arrest. The definition of arrest is problematic from an empirical research standpoint, and it is necessary to address definitional problems before commencing our analysis of the decision to arrest.[1]

In Canada, an arrest legally occurs when a police officer places his hand on the suspect and states that the person is under arrest; or, if the person submits to the police officer's directions whether or not he is told he is under arrest or is touched by the police officer. The general test is whether the suspect perceives he is at liberty to depart from the presence of the police officer if he wishes to do so.[2] Arrest involves detention, and it can be effected with or without an arrest warrant issued by a justice. A police officer can arrest a person without warrant if he finds him committing any criminal offence, or if the police officer has reasonable and probable grounds to believe that he has committed, or is about to commit a specified indictable offence; or, if the police officer has reasonable and probable grounds to believe that the suspect cannot meet specified release conditions for less serious offences.[3]

As several commentators have documented (e.g., LaFave, 1965; Reiss and Black, 1967; McBarnett, 1976, 1979; Freedman and Stenning, 1977), the law of arrest is enabling for the police.

First, apparent restrictions in the law of arrest can be circumvented by gaining the "consent" of the suspect to help the police with their inquiries. Of course, the nature of "consent" is highly problematic because, at least in our observations, suspects were never provided with a clear statement indicating that they had any option but to follow the detectives' orders and answer their questions.

Second, the definition of "reasonable and probable grounds" for arrest is open to wide interpretive latitude, and allows courts who support the police to easily justify decisions in their favour. Indeed, because "reasonable and probable grounds" are usually debated in terms of the "facts" constructed by the police officer, there is little leeway for arguing that they are unreasonable. The closest the courts can get to the "real" matter is by reference to the ideal man facing the same "facts" the police officer has constructed: "The real test is whether the facts relied upon would create a reasonable suspicion in the mind of a reasonable man."[4]

Third, the interpretive latitude available to the courts to support the police is evident in relation to other elements. For example, the Supreme Court of Canada has broadened further the provisions of *Criminal Code* paragraph 450(1)(b) by stating that the words "finds committing" an offence must be interpreted as "finds *apparently* committing," thus enabling an arrest of a person allegedly engaging in a criminal act to be deemed lawful even if the person is subsequently not convicted.[5] In another case, an accused was subject to the forcible search of his mouth by police officers who were looking for narcotics. Later the accused's car was searched, narcotics were found, and the accused was subsequently charged in relation to the narcotics and for assaulting the police (biting the officer's finger). The accused appealed his conviction on assaulting the police, arguing the police officer had not been acting within his legal powers in searching the person of the accused and that the accused was therefore justified in resisting the arrest. In deciding against the accused, an Ontario Court of Appeal judge stated:

> It is important to observe that the search that was made is justifiable as an incident of the arrest i.e., the search of the accused's mouth. . . . In my opinion there was an arrest here when the constables seized the person of the appellant. The evidence would indicate that they did not inform him immediately that he was arrested and the cause of the arrest.[6]

In subsequent reference to *Criminal Code* sub-section 29(2), which requires that persons be informed of both their arrest and the reason for their arrest, the judge stated that police officers should not be "encumbered by technicalities" in cases of this type since "those who carry on the traffic of drugs are cunning, crafty and unscrupulous almost beyond belief."

Fourth, the *Criminal Code* provides enabling laws to use against persons who challenge police efforts at arrest, and to protect the police officer from criminal and civil liability. Resisting or wilfully obstructing a police officer in the performance of his duties carries a maximum penalty of two years imprisonment if proceeded on as an indictable offence (*Criminal Code* section 118). In a recent ruling of the Supreme

Court of Canada (*Moore v. R.* (1979), 5 C.R. (3d) 289), the majority held that failure of a suspect to identify himself to a police officer attempting identification for the purpose of issuing a summons without arrest amounts to an obstruction of the police officer. There was no law requiring the accused to identify himself in the circumstances; however, the obstruct police conviction was upheld because the accused had factually obstructed the officer in the execution of his duty by not identifying himself. As E. W. Ewaschuk (Director, Criminal Law Amendments, Federal Department of Justice) comments in an annotation, ". . . the *Moore* case seems a further step in the law enforcement approach the Supreme Court has adopted in cases involving police powers."

Assaulting a police officer with intent to resist or prevent arrest carries a maximum penalty of five years imprisonment if proceeded on as an indictable offence (*Criminal Code* section 246(2)); use of a firearm to prevent arrest carries a maximum penalty of fourteen years imprisonment; and escaping lawful custody carries a maximum penalty of two years imprisonment (*Criminal Code* section 133(1)). Furthermore, a police officer, as someone "who is required or authorized by law to do anything in the administration or enforcement of the law . . . is, if he acts on reasonable and probable grounds, justified in doing what he is required or authorized to do and in using as much force as is necessary for that purpose" (*Criminal Code* section 25(1)). As Freedman and Stenning (1977: 95) record, this provision has been applied to protect arresting persons from criminal and civil liability, and to remove from accused persons in some cases the defence that the arresting person was acting unlawfully. *Criminal Code* section 25(4) authorizes "as much force as is necessary to prevent the escape by flight, unless the escape can be prevented by reasonable means in a less violent manner" in situations where a police officer "is proceeding lawfully to arrest, with or without a warrant, any person for an offence for which that person may be arrested without warrant." In short, this section justifies deadly force against escaping suspects.

In light of this arsenal of means available to police officers to effect an arrest, it should not be surprising to discover that most suspects unquestioningly submit to police orders. Citizens do not have a good working knowledge of the criminal law (cf. Griffiths and Ayres, 1967; Friedland, 1978; Ericson and Baranek, 1981), and they are typically in no position to judge whether the police officer is acting in a way that he can later make organizationally and legally legitimate. Deference to the authority of the detective's office is called for, and it is of little wonder that it is routinely forthcoming.

Among the 96 suspects dealt with by detectives, 66 appeared to have been under arrest in the sense that if they had attempted to leave the presence of detectives they would probably have been prevented from doing so, while 30 were subject to preliminary questioning without any indications of being in custody at any point. Among the 66 arrested, 32 were originally in custody of patrol officers before detectives took over their cases; 20 were taken into custody by detectives without being told they were under arrest or the reasons for their arrest; 10 were taken into custody by detectives after being told they were under arrest and given reasons; and 4 were taken into custody by detectives who executed arrest warrants.

When confronting suspects, detectives prospectively decided how to deal with them. If they set out to question a suspect with no intention of laying a charge, they did not bother seeking a justifying cover for their actions. On the other hand, when arrests were planned, detectives sought to cover their actions within the legal and police organizational legitimations available to them.

In the same way that detectives decided in advance to contact a victim to justify writing off an occurrence (see Chapter 5), they sometimes contacted suspects with a pre-established outcome in mind. They approached the suspect with a view to writing off the case without charge, rather than with the intention of taking custody of the suspect and pursuing the investigation. For example, DC 103 involved a "Mischief" complaint from a company representative who stated that cable wires serving an apartment had been cut. The manager of the apartment building listed six possible suspects in the building, including one person who was already charged for alleged damage he had done in the same building. The detectives decided to interview this suspect only, and approached the interview entirely in terms of exonerating the suspect without any deep probing, followed by a "filed" disposition. The detective quickly outlined the occurrence and asked the suspect if he was involved. The suspect replied, "No, it weren't me." The detective then asked the suspect if he knew a girl he named, and the suspect replied, "Yes." The detective asked, "Would she do a thing like this?" and the suspect replied, "No." The detective then asked the suspect where he was from, and the suspect replied he was from a town in the Maritimes. The detective said, "It's better down there than up here, except I guess it's hard to get a job." The suspect replied that there was a new plant open there paying better than $5.00 an hour and that he was considering a return to the town. The detective said, "That would be a good idea" and then, departing, added, "If you see anyone breaking up the place let us know."

When the decision was made to take the suspect into custody, detectives developed strategies to "manage" arrests (Sanders, 1977: 149) in the sense of controlling the suspect and ensuring that a suitable organizational justification was available. The most common strategy (used in 20/34 instances) was to have the suspect apparently "consent" to being questioned in controlled circumstances (cf. LaFave, 1965: esp. 28-30, 229) e.g., in an interrogation room in the detectives' office; in the rear of the detectives' car (which had no door handles on the inside to allow the suspect to get out). This was done in cases where the arrest was primarily for investigative purposes. Arrests for investigative purposes are not legal, but this could be covered by the "consent" aspect; by the prediction that the suspect would not be likely to complain if released without charge; and, by the fact that the arrest would usually be organizationally recorded only if there was also a charge, which in turn could be retrospectively used to justify the arrest.[7] In this connection it is noteworthy that the detectives released without charge 9/34 suspects they arrested, and 8 out of these 9 were never explicitly told they were under arrest or the reasons for their arrest.

In accomplishing arrests without explicitly indicating to the persons that they were under arrest, detectives used a variety of techniques. One technique was a "rear of car" arrest. The suspect would be told that the detectives wished to talk with him, and would be asked to sit in the rear of the detective car so that discussion could take place in private. Once the suspect entered the car, the door would be closed and questioning commenced. Since the rear doors had no handles by which the suspect could open the door, the suspect was in a confined situation. A period of questioning would sometimes be followed by the detectives simply starting the car and driving the suspect to the divisional station with comments such as, "Let's take a drive" or "We'd better go down and get this matter cleared up." Another technique was to "dial-an-arrest." Suspects were telephoned to come to the detective office for questioning, with few details of the inquiry given until they arrived at the station. Upon arrival at the station these suspects were interrogated without any mention being made of their arrest status. Regardless of the technique employed, all 20 suspects who could be made to appear as "volunteers" offered no resistance to being brought under the control of detectives.

In planning arrests for investigative "fishing" purposes, detectives sometimes did more than create the cover of apparent suspect compliance without formal announcement of arrest. They also looked for other covers to ensure that in the unlikely event their actions were called into question, they had a readily available justification. For example, in DC 87, the detective was investigating a series of linked "break, enter and theft," "break and enter," and "obscene telephone call" occurrences. Lacking other investigative leads, one detective decided to explore the possibility that the suspect was someone whose first name was the same as the name given by the culprit when he made the telephone calls and when he left obscene notes at the scenes of the break-ins. After considerable effort at canvassing persons in the neighbourhood, the detective learned from an informant that there was a youth in an adjacent area with the same first name as that used by the culprit in the telephone calls and notes. On this basis, this youth became a suspect.

The detective decided to contact the employer of this suspect to obtain the suspect's employment file, from which he could extract handwriting samples that could be compared with those on the notes left by the culprit at some break-ins. The employer readily complied with the detective's request. Apparently anticipating the need for a cover, the detective had the employer collaborate in stating that there was indeed similarity between the handwriting in the suspect's employment file and that contained in the notes.

The employer then took the detective over to the plant. The detective had initially considered interviewing the suspect in the plant, but there was no private office or space for the interview, and the detective suggested to the suspect that the best place for the interview was the detective's car. The suspect entered the rear of the car and was shut in before being told anything about the investigation. He was not told that he was under arrest at any point. The detective told the suspect about the break-ins and the obscene pictures and notes left, and that the writing on the notes was similar to that of the suspect. The suspect denied the offences, and asked where they were supposed to have occurred. The detective told him that it was at an identified school. The suspect said he never spent time at this school, and added that his friends could testify to this. The suspect twice asked to see the handwriting sample on which the detective was making his assessment, but the detective refused to show it to him. After approximately ten minutes the detective said, "I think we had better go to the station and get this cleared up. We should have you back here by lunch—maybe." The suspect did not reply.[8]

In justifying the control they were taking over suspects, detectives most often relied upon a statement that they were under a duty to act upon information provided by citizens. Information constructed through victim-complainants and informants (see Chapter Five) could be used to justify the detective's actions both to the suspect and with reference to the law.[9]

Arrest warrants were involved in only 4/34 arrests made by detectives, confirming the findings of others that warrants are rarely used (LaFave, 1965: 8). The problem was not one of obstacles erected by Justices of the Peace in granting warrants; as we document in considering searches and release conditions for the accused, and as other researchers have documented (ibid., 8, 34; McBarnet, 1979: 31), Justices of the Peace routinely grant whatever detectives request of them. Rather, detectives engaged in a pragmatic consideration of whether it was worth the effort to obtain the warrant when the person was not likely to resist anyway, vis-à-vis the tactics for compliance available to detectives and the enabling framework within which they could accomplish arrests (cf. Renton and Brown, 1972: 28). Moreover, if the detectives were engaged in a "fishing" investigation, it was obviously better to state that the person voluntarily co-operated with the detectives rather than have it documented through a warrant that he was arrested for a specified offence which he may not have committed, thus opening the detectives' actions to possible challenge.

Detectives could occasionally use warrants to their strategic advantage (cf. LaFave, 1965: 35-51), and obtained one where they saw such advantage. The primary advantages of the arrest warrant included the added authority it could provide at the point of arrest; the cover it could provide if the detectives' actions were called into question; and, its use as a sign to court officials that the case was serious enough, and/or the suspect "dangerous" enough, to invoke the rare practice of obtaining a warrant.

In DC 11, a detective took out an arrest warrant prior to contacting the suspect at his place of residence. The suspect was accused by his separated wife of threatening her life (*Criminal Code* section 331(1)(a)), and he was well known to several detectives for previous alleged violent offences involving his separated wife. The detective told the researcher that an arrest warrant was being used as a sign of authority because the suspect was "violent" and might do unpredictable things at the point of arrest. This view was backed up by the fact that this detective enlisted the assistance of another detective to effect the arrest; the assisting detective had a reputation for being strong and forceful with suspects. The detective added that the arrest warrant would cover the detectives' actions should the suspect decide to challenge their attempts to detain them. In this case, the point of arrest was made very explicit. The detectives were met at the apartment door by a woman, who called out, "It's the police." One detective asked for the suspect by name, and the suspect appeared saying, "What is it this time?" The detective stated, "Threatening your wife's life by telephone." The suspect exclaimed, "What? That fuckin' bitch," at which point the detective interjected, "We have a warrant, so you might as well just come along. You can consider yourself technically under arrest." The suspect was returned to the divisional station without resistance.

Detectives routinely managed arrests without resistance from suspects. None of the 34 suspects they arrested resisted physically. Three suspects resisted verbally; all three were told explicitly that they were under arrest, and they then raised objections. The degree of compliance achieved is testimony to the authority of the detectives' office, and to the legal powers which enhance that authority.

In securing compliance at the point of arrest and thereafter, detectives rarely gave suspects an opportunity to do anything but comply with what the detectives wanted. In this connection, it is noteworthy that most suspects were not given right to silence cautions, and few suspects demanded, let alone received, access to a third party as a means of countering detective actions.

In legal doctrine, citizens have a right to remain silent in the face of police questioning because the police do not have any right to legally compel an answer to their questions (Law Reform Commission, 1973: 6). Indeed, at one point in nineteenth century England judges excluded evidence obtained by any questioning of suspects in custody (Williams, 1960: 338). In contemporary times, verbal or written statements by suspects can be used as evidence against them if they are judged to be voluntary statements (Kaufman, 1974). One consideration in this judgement is whether the police made the suspect aware of his right to silence and of the fact that anything he says may be used in court as evidence against him.

In Canada, the English view is accepted that right to silence cautions given by the police are but "one of the circumstances which must be taken into consideration [and it cannot be said] as a matter of law, that the absence of a caution makes the statement inadmissible."[10] According to the English Judges' Rules, the right to silence cautions should be given when the "police officer has made up his mind to charge a person with a crime" (#2). Moreover, "persons in custody should not be questioned without the usual caution being first administered" (#3). When a suspect offers to "volunteer" a statement, the police officer should again state the caution (#4).

In practice, there are many elements which make the Rules of little use as a control over police actions, and useful only as a retrospective justification for police actions. For example, the Rules do not have legal status, and apparent nonconformity with the Rules does not render the statement inadmissible. Any possible restrictions imposed by the rules can be circumvented on the same basis as "consent" arrests and searches: the police can say that the suspect is not in custody but merely helping them with their inquiries (Gooderson, 1970: 274; Greenawalt, 1974: 248-249). Furthermore, the English courts have ruled that the right to silence caution need only be given when the police already have enough other admissible evidence to justify reasonable suspicion (Zander, 1978: 356, referring to *R. v. Osbourne, R. v. Virtue*, [1973] 1 All ER 649). This is an explicit recognition that the caution serves only as an *apparent* protection for the suspect, applied retrospectively after the police have already got what they want.

From the suspects' perspective, there are other aspects of the law which should be taken into account in deciding upon silence (see generally Ericson and Baranek, 1981). In Canada, "a court may . . . take the accused's pre-trial silence into consideration in determining what weight (credibility) to attach to some explanation or defence which has subsequently been put forward by him (e.g., at his trial) and which he could have put forward at the time he remained silent: *R. v. Itwaru* (1970), 10 C.R.N.S. 184; *R. v. Robertson* (1975), 29 C.R.N.S. 141" (Freedman and Stenning, 1977: 153-154; see also Doob and Kirshenbaum, 1972). The English courts have gone further in ruling that silence can be taken as an indication of guilt if the parties speak on even terms. In one case, (*Parkes v. The Queen*, [1976] 3 All E.R. 380), the accused and his landlady (whose daughter had been murdered) were said to have been speaking on even terms; therefore, according to the Judicial Committee of the Privy Council, the judge was entitled to instruct the jury to take silence into account, along with other matters, in deciding the accused's guilt. In another case (*R. v. Chandler*, [1976] 1 W.L.R. 585), "the court (per Lawton L.J., and a prominent member, and now Chairman, of the Criminal Law Revision Committee) ruled that the parties were on even terms for this purpose even where the suspect was being questioned by a police officer—because he had his solicitor with him." (Zander, 1978: 356). In these circumstances, it may be a disadvantage to follow the advice of a solicitor to remain silent.

In addition to the legal rules as facilitators of detective efforts at obtaining answers to their questions, the low visibility of detective transactions with suspects creates further enabling conditions. Detectives can choose not to give cautions with little likelihood of the suspect or anyone else raising objections at a later stage. Even with the legal force of the *Miranda* decision in the United States, which required the police officer to give cautions at the point of arrest at risk of having any statements without warnings ruled inadmissible, the majority of suspects were not warned or were given incomplete warnings (cf. Wald *et al.*, 1967; Ayres, 1970). Moreover, even when cautions are given, they can be presented in a way that they are not fully understood (Wald *et al.*, 1967: 276; Ramsay, 1972: 65; Sanders, 1977: 162). This may not only involve active attempts at distortion by the detective issuing the cautions; the way the right to silence caution is worded is ambiguous and appears to assume that the person will talk (Morris, 1978: 39-40).[11]

In view of these considerations, commentators have repeatedly concluded that rules relating to right to silence cautions do not inhibit the police from getting what they want from suspects via questioning (e.g., Greenawalt, 1974; Morris, 1978; Zander, 1978). Cautioning only becomes an issue if the suspect is charged, and even then it is very easy for the police officer to manipulate the caution so that it does not inhibit his construction of the case. Indeed, at this point giving the caution may be useful to the police officer in constructing the appearance that everything proceeded with procedural regularity and that the accused acted voluntarily in condemning himself.

In our observations, detectives did not often state the right to silence cautions up to the point that suspects provided written statements. Only 13 suspects were known to have received right to silence cautions at any point prior to the commencement of interrogation. However, if detectives decided that they were going to charge a suspect and use a written statement of confession as part of their evidence, they invariably had a means of showing that the accused had been cautioned because the caution was typed in at the head of the statement form. Thus, all 35 suspects who provided written statements of confession were given the right to silence caution before they *signed* the statement, although not necessarily before they had given the statement orally.

The most common practice was not to provide a right to silence caution up to the point the suspect agreed to give a written statement. Interrogation was geared toward generating a verbal confession, and if this verbal confession was forthcoming, the detectives would then ask the suspect to "volunteer" a written statement which included the caution.[12] If the detective could not obtain the accused's signature, he could still use the "verbal" as evidence. If he did obtain the accused's signature, the detective could "show" procedural regularity to the Crown attorney and others in court; regardless of when the detective decided to charge the accused, he could always indicate that it was at the point the suspect "volunteered" a statement and point out that the statement was duly recorded with the rights caution written in.

In maintaining control over suspects, detectives also strategically regulated the suspects' access to a third party. According to the *Cana-*

dian *Bill of Rights* (1960, section 2), "no law of Canada shall be construed or applied so as to . . . deprive a person who has been arrested or detained . . . of the right to retain and instruct counsel without delay." However, the police in Canada are under no legal obligation to inform a person that he has a right to counsel before he makes a statement (*R. v. DeCleriq*, [1966] 2 C.C.C. 190 (Ont. C.A.)). In our observations detectives certainly did not treat this as an obligation, as they were only known to have informed one out of the 96 suspects in the sample of a right to counsel.[13]

On the other hand, suspects apparently did not often ask for access to a third party. Among the 96 suspects, only 19 were known to have asked for access to a third party.

This finding compares with other studies which report a similar low proportion of requests. For example, Medalie *et al.* (1968: 1351-1352) report on a scheme in Washington, D.C. where legal aid lawyers were available to help suspects in custody, yet only 7 percent of suspects who could have used these lawyers did so. Some suspects believed the lawyers were associated with the police, some felt that the promise of a lawyer did not apply in their case, and some did not appreciate the point of having a lawyer.[14]

In an interview study with accused persons in the Birmingham, England Crown Court, Baldwin and McConville (1977: 69) report that only 30 percent of accused said they asked for access to a third party, and only 1/7 of these said they were granted access. The English law is enabling for the police in denying access, because the courts "have wholly failed to impose any restraints on the way the police exercise their discretion to refuse access to a solicitor" (Zander, 1978: 362). As Zander (1972: 1238) states elsewhere, "In the absence of any ruling by the courts it would not be surprising to find that it was being given a broad interpretation by the police in their own favour." (See also Leigh, 1975).

The fact that most suspects do not ask for access to a third party indicates their docility in response to what detectives demand (cf. Ericson and Baranek, 1981). The suspects' docility is further indicated by the fact that even when suspects were known to have asked for access to a third party, most of them did not ask for a lawyer. Only six persons requested access to a lawyer, while six wished to contact a friend, five wished to contact a family member, one wished to contact a clergyman and one wished to contact a worker at a half-way house for parolees. Furthermore, the requests were most often made after interrogation had commenced. Seven persons made the request prior to interrogation, five made the request during interrogation, and seven made the request after the interrogation was completed. Among the six requests for lawyers, four were requested after interrogation was in progress. Among the 13 requests for persons other than lawyers, eight were requested after the interrogation was in progress.

Detectives were known to have granted 17/19 requests by suspects for access to a third party. The point in investigation at which these requests were granted, and the way in which they were granted, demonstrated their strategic use by detectives.

When suspects requested access to lawyers, the detectives granted three at the time the request was made, two at a later point, and refused one. When suspects requested access to third parties other than lawyers, the detectives granted eight at the time the requests were made, four at a later time, and refused one.

In the entire sample there was only one suspect who apparently used access to a third party to his advantage vis-à-vis the decision not to give a statement. In this instance the suspect's lawyer called the police station after he learned from the suspect's girlfriend that the suspect had been arrested (DC 11). At the time of the call the suspect was being interrogated. The detective allowed the suspect to leave the interrogation room to talk with his lawyer over the telephone, and following the conversation the suspect returned to the interrogation room but did not give any verbal or written confession.

Where access was granted to parties other than lawyers, it was typically granted in exchange for co-operation from the suspect. For example, in DC 89 the suspect had already confessed to "theft under $200" (shoplifting) incidents when he asked to call his mother. The detective readily granted the request, and also talked with the mother himself in order to explain her son's situation. In DC 233, the suspect was granted access to his girlfriend (who was waiting at the divisional station while he was being interrogated), only after he had confessed to one of several offences he was being investigated for, and after his girl friend had agreed to assist detectives in a consent search of the apartment she shared with the suspect.

Detectives sometimes constructed the course of interaction in a way that deflected the suspect's request, or led the suspect to change the nature of his request. For example, in DC 98 the detectives were conducting an ongoing interrogation of the accused that had started at the divisional station, continued at the scenes of some of the offences he had confessed to, and was concluding with a search of the accused's apartment.

> As the detectives were about to leave the apartment, the accused's friend said to the accused, "You've got to keep quiet man. You should call a lawyer. Don't say anything to these turkeys until you get a lawyer with you."
> Detective: You've been watching too much T.V.
> Accused: Can I make a phone call?
> Detective: In your position you should probably get legal aid. They're up at the court. You can see one of them up there.
> Accused: How many calls can I make?
> Detective: As many as you like. You should call your minister friend. [The accused had previously mentioned a minister as his only "respectable" friend in the area] Do you have a phone here?

Accused: No
Detective: You can call him from the station.

The detectives eventually did allow the accused to call his minister friend, although this was at a point when he had already confessed and had turned over stolen property. He had no contact with a lawyer prior to his release, as the detectives effectively skirted his request for one.

Overall, suspects who received access to a third party after a request for access were no less likely to confess than those who did not request access, or requested but did not receive access. Among the former group, 47 percent confessed, while among the latter group 41 percent confessed. This is not surprising given that requests were most often made in relation to third parties other than lawyers; and were sometimes granted only after the person had confessed or otherwise consented to something that would further the detectives' case.

In summary, detectives had ample legal resources (enabling laws or the absence of any legal controls), organizational resources (especially low visibility conditions of work), and the necessary tactical skills to accomplish control of suspects from the point of contact onward. This control was necessary as a first step toward generating the information required to dispose of the suspect, and the case, by charge or otherwise. We now turn to an examination of the process of generating information from suspects, including property searches and interrogation.

Using Suspects

The use of suspects during in-custody investigations is to have them supply the information needed to dispose of the case in terms of the official clearance categories. If the disposition involves a criminal charge laid against the suspect, the suspect is asked to assist in providing the evidence that will secure the legitimacy of the charge and the predictability of a conviction. In short, detectives use suspects to generate the information necessary to condemn them, or to decide that an alternative dispostion is both justified and justifiable.

One method of generating information is to search the suspect and the places where he keeps property. According to Salhany (1972: 45-46), "It is the fundamental right of every citizen of Canada to be secure against unreasonable and arbitrary searches by the police and the seizure of his property for use as evidence. This right, firmly rooted in the common law from the earliest times, was able to withstand even the practice initiated by the Star Chamber at the beginning of the 18th century. . . ." In light of this, the pragmatic task of detectives is to ensure that their searches are not seen to be "unreasonable and arbitrary."

Detectives are greatly aided in this task by the law pertaining to searches. Police officers have a common-law right to search arrested persons.[15] They can also search "a building receptacle or place" with a search warrant obtained from a Justice. As researchers and commentators have argued (LaFave, 1965; Menzies, 1978; McBarnet, 1979), this is rarely problematic because Justices routinely issue warrants without question, having little or no means to independently investigate the grounds on which the police officer seeks the warrant. Moreover, there is a common law right allowing police officers making an arrest without warrant to enter private property to effect the arrest (*Criminal Code* section 7; see also Dickson, J. in *Eccles v. Bourque, Simmonds and Wise* (1975), 1 W.W.R. 609 (S.C.C.)). Furthermore, the legal rules can be circumvented by obtaining the expressed or implied consent of the suspect. And, in terms of their goal of obtaining evidence to sustain charges and obtain a conviction, detectives are able to have evidence obtained from illegal searches used as legitimate evidence against the accused in court (Fontana, 1974: 61).[16]

Among the 96 suspects, 27 were subject to one or more searches of their property by detectives. Seventeen of these suspects were subject to at least one search where the detectives had obtained a search warrant, and 10 submitted to searches when detectives were not equipped with a search warrant. These searches were typically conducted with persons who were also arrested; 13 of the 17 persons subject to search warrants were arrested, and 8 of the 10 persons subject to non-warrant searches were arrested.

Searches were conducted at any stage of the processing of suspects or accused persons. In some cases they were undertaken after a suspect confessed and was co-operating in the return of stolen property (e.g., DC 78); in other cases, searches were undertaken as part of the interrogation questioning (e.g., DC 79); and in other cases they were undertaken on an exploratory basis at the preliminary questioning stage (e.g., DC 73). In total, 18 searched persons were charged, five were cautioned and four were not subject to a charge or caution.

Twenty-one of the 27 persons searched were involved in "property" cases. In these cases, two primary purposes of the searches were to obtain physical evidence that could be used to assist in the prosecution of suspects, and to retrieve allegedly stolen property on behalf of the victims.

Searches had other functions, especially when they were executed as part of the interrogation process in relation to suspects who were under arrest. The identification of allegedly stolen property during a search could be used as a "lever" to gain a confession. The discovery of other contraband (e.g., illicit drugs) was useable as a "lever" to gain a confession on the matter under investigation and/or to gain information on other criminal activity in exchange for the detectives' agreement not to lay a charge. The discovery of items not directly related to the original matter under investigation was also useable in constructing a more broadly based case against the accused, e.g., as a "dangerous" person.

Searches were frequently part of the interrogation process. When used in this way, they produced both physical evidence and accused statement evidence. The detectives typically selected items and asked the suspect to admit that they had been stolen. A common strategy was to start with items the detectives had already identified as being stolen in order to give the impression to the suspect that they "knew everything"; the hope was that the suspect would in turn produce items and confess in relation to matters the detectives had no knowledge about.

An example of this practice was evident in DC 98. The detectives released the accused after charging him with a series of residential "break, enter and theft" occurrences, but continued to investigate other occurrences in the same residential area in the hope that they might also be able to charge the same person on these occurrences. This investigation centred on the identification of property the detectives still believed to be in the accused's possession and which they had mentally recorded in a previous search of the accused's apartment. The detectives used the accused's former roommate as an informant to assist in naming property in possession of the accused, and canvassed victims for identifying marks on property that had been stolen.

The detectives then proceeded to the accused's residence, equipped with a search warrant and a new series of possible charges to lay. Upon meeting the suspect outside his home, one detective stated, "We're back [suspect's first name], for stolen property. We're going to get it all this time." The suspect replied, "Come on in, look anywhere you want."

The suspect led detectives to his room. One detective picked up a rug identified by a victim as having been made in a foreign country and having a distinguishing mark on the reverse side, checked the identification signs, then said: "Where did you get this?"

Suspect:	I bought it at a store.
Detective:	Where?
Suspect:	I can't remember.
Detective:	It's stolen. Where did you get this stereo?
Suspect:	I told you, [names store].
Second Detective:	Bull shit. We checked and they don't even sell this make.
Suspect:	[more specific in naming store]
Detective:	That's where we checked. They don't sell it. Don't lie to us. We gave you one chance and you blew it. We're not going to give you another chance, this time we get everything. I want everything you've stolen out. Everything! What about these records?

[This detective then picked up records, putting them on the bed and telling the suspect to select out those that were stolen]

Second Detective:	We told you we would come back if you didn't tell us the truth. Now you're in twice as much shit. If you don't give us everything this time we'll come back again and you'll be in three times as much shit.
Detective:	Where did you get the stereo?
Suspect:	Out of the townhouse.

After the items that detectives were specifically looking for had been selected out, the detective said to the suspect, "Now what else in here is stolen? I want everything. I have a good memory. If there is one thing in here that I find out later is stolen, I'll come back up here and tear this whole house apart. Your parents won't like that will they?" The detective pointed to a book shelf and asked the suspect to pick out those books that were stolen property. The suspect said, "None, they're my mother's," then pulled out one book and said it was stolen. The detective picked up a flag from a dresser and said, "Where did this come from?"

Suspect: An employer.
Detective: Was it stolen?
Suspect: No.
Detective: What employer?
Suspect: A gas station I used to work at.
Detective: Up here or down there?
Suspect: Down there.
Detective: Was it stolen?
Suspect: No, well, I guess you could say it was.

At this point the detective told the suspect he could talk privately with his father for a few minutes. The detective then said to the father:

"Tell your son that it is in his own best interests to tell us everything. The courts already have more than enough now to do with him what they please—to give him time or anything else. More charges at this point aren't going to make any difference to what the court does . . . We're going to get everything he's done and clear this all up once and for all."

At this point the suspect remembered that there was another item that was also stolen property, and he immediately went to retrieve it.

Searches also enabled detectives to uncover evidence for criminal charges in relation to matters that were not part of the primary matter under investigation. One detective team in particular looked for drugs made illegal under the *Narcotics Control Act* while they were undertaking searches connected with property crimes. If drugs (in all cases marijuana) were found, they were typically used as a lever to obtain confessions to the property offenses, and/or to encourage assistance in the return of stolen property, and/or to elicit information about other crimes. Thus, in DC 79 the detectives discovered marijuana during a search for stolen property at the suspect's residence. Following the search, one detective told the suspect that if he named a person he was involved with in a suspected auto theft, he would not be charged with possession of the marijuana. The suspect had not confessed to this auto theft himself; the detective's hope was that the suspect would identify his accomplice who could in turn be interrogated and who might possibly reveal more about the suspect's involvement.

Searches also enabled detectives to generate evidence that would back-up the image of the accused they wanted to construct on the main charge against him. For example, in DC 193 a suspect under investigation for an alleged attempt rape and a series of indecent assaults had a search warrant executed by detectives on his residence. The detectives searched not only for physical evidence concerning the offences, but also for "pornographic" material that might prove useful in constructing an account of the suspect that would make him appear to be the kind of person who would engage in offences of this type. In DC 47, the detectives admitted that they did not have "tight" evidence for the rape charge they planned to lay, and they explicitly searched for possible "back up" or "kicker" charges against the suspect that would contribute to an image of him as a "dangerous" person with the potential of being a "rapist." In searching the suspect's apartment, one detective noticed a gun on a shelf that contained a large number of other ornaments. This gun was seized and later measured to confirm the detective's suspicion that it was too short and thus a restricted weapon as defined in *Criminal Code section* 82(1)(c). The suspect was subsequently charged with this offence (*Criminal Code section* 91(1)(a)), allowing the detectives to traffic in an image of "dangerousness" at the suspect's bail hearing and subsequent trials that could in turn potentially influence how the rape charge was perceived and dealt with.[17]

As pragmatic actors ever ready to use whatever resources they could to accomplish their tasks, detectives displayed considerable resourcefulness in using searches. In a non-sample "attempted murder" case on DS 176, the detectives went to a residence and brought three persons from there back to the divisional station for questioning. During the occupants' absence, a wiretap was placed on the telephone in the residence. Four separate detective teams then executed four search warrants on other residences belonging to suspected associates of the victim. In the words of one detective, the strategy of this investigation was "to kick in a few doors and stir up a lot of shit to get the wires humming."

In accomplishing searches detectives could choose to obtain a search warrant, or hope to obtain the consent of the suspect for a search without a warrant. The decision to obtain a search warrant was related to the wider strategy of the detectives in making their case.

Search warrants provided the strength of a Justice backed legal justification for a search, and could be referred to if there were any legally based challenges to a search. Usually "reasonable and probable grounds" for a search were constituted by a victim-complainant's allegation that a particular suspect had committed an offence and that this suspect might be in possession of evidence that would substantiate this claim.

Search warrants also provided detectives with added authority in taking power over the suspect. Detectives sometimes explicitly decided to take out a search warrant on a suspect they predicted might resist their efforts to conduct a search. For example, in DC 296, the detectives charged four suspects after a series of "shoplifting" incidents. After charging the suspects based on property found in their possession at the time of their apprehension, the detectives decided to search each of their residences. Three of these suspects had their residences "consent" searched without a warrant, while detectives took out a warrant in relation to the fourth suspect's residence because they anticipated resistance.

If detectives were equipped with a search warrant when they initially contacted a suspect, it allowed them to circumvent the possibility of being refused admission and then having the suspect dispose of the evidence while the detectives went to obtain a warrant. On DS 104, a detective used this reasoning in deciding to obtain a search warrant to assist in a search for a handgun reported by an informant to be illegally in possession of the suspect. There was discussion between the Detective Sergeant and the detective about the advisability of taking out a search warrant. The Detective Sergeant suggested that a warrant would not be required since people of the suspect's ethnic background would not know one was required. As a compromise to the detective, who wanted to take out a search warrant, the Detective Sergeant suggested that the detective "just take a blue piece of paper (an unprocessed warrant) and wave it at them. They won't know the fucking difference." The detective insisted on a proper warrant, stating, "What if we get half way through searching the place and he tells us to get out? Then we have to go get a warrant anyway and when we're gone he'll just get rid of the piece [gun]." The detective's view prevailed, and he proceeded to process the warrant.

Obtaining a search warrant never proved to be difficult. It could be argued that detectives were expert at predicting when a Justice would issue a warrant, and only applied for a warrant when they were confident that they would obtain one. An equally likely explanation is that Justices acted on trust when a detective, whom they had known for a long time, applied for a search warrant. This element, plus the impracticality of the Justice undertaking his own independent investigation to establish the grounds for the warrant, resulted in "automatic" compliance with the detectives' requests.

If we consider all detective attempts to obtain search warrants during the course of our observations, we find that 39/41 requests were granted by Justices of the Peace without any question, and 2/41 were granted after some questioning (Menzies, 1978: 17).[18] An examination of the two exceptional cases "proves the rule" that Justices of the Peace were seen and used by detectives to "rubber stamp" search warrants.

In DC 172, the application for the warrant was made to a Justice of the Peace who had been appointed recently. The detective approached this Justice of the Peace because he was in the court building and this person happened to be available. The detective was astonished when the Justice of the Peace asked on what grounds he was applying for the warrant. The detective became visibly upset and stated that he simply had reasonable and probable grounds to believe that stolen items were located at the address indicated. The Justice of the Peace then signed the warrant, but the detective continued to be annoyed and later commented to the researcher, "The stupid bitch asked *me* what my grounds were. They're right there on the fucking information. I wouldn't take out the warrant if I didn't know the grounds. [The J.P. should] just sign the fucking warrant. I don't need this shit!"

In relation to DC 98, the detectives proceeded to arrest a suspect in another jurisdiction. They had intended to have a Justice of the Peace in their own jurisdiction sign the search warrant before they departed, but forgot to do so and consequently approached a Justice of the Peace in the other jurisdiction. This Justice of the Peace questioned the detectives about their grounds for the search, and he was also very "picky" about the wording they had used. However, he eventually signed the warrant. This Justice of the Peace was a very close friend of the suspect's family, as indicated by the character testimony he later gave at the suspect's sentencing hearing.

It was obvious that although the Justices of the Peace were supposedly functioning in a judicial capacity (e.g., see *Schumacter v. Attorney General of Saskatchewan and Satterio, J.P.* (1960), 33 W.W.R. 132), in practice their function was usurped by detectives, who invariably obtained search warrants, usually without question. In this connection the detectives effectively controlled all facets of their searching actions in spite of legal ideals to the contrary.[19]

It is arguable that Justices of the Peace could do little else in any case because they had no independent means of validating the information presented to them by detectives. *Criminal Code* section 243 states that police officers may be required to bring any seized material before a Justice of the Peace, but this was not a regular practice during our observations. However, the detectives were selective in choosing the Justices of the Peace they routinely did business with. The detectives had developed longstanding relationships with particular Justices of the Peace and relied on their routine co-operation to ease their tasks. Thus, one detective said he regularly used two out of four possible Justices of the Peace available in his divisional area because he had a "good relationship" with them, which translated meant a "co-operative" relationship. Occasionally this co-operation went well beyond the point of signing warrants without question. On one occasion, two detectives went to five addresses, mainly for the purpose of locating a suspect. Anticipating resistance from the various occupants, they took along some unsigned search warrants and "left handed" them (signed a J.P.'s name) as they went. These warrants were later logged in the divisional records, and the two Justices of the Peace whose names were used were subsequently contacted and their collaboration gained. In another situation the detectives arrived at an address to undertake a property search only to discover that the Justice of the Peace had dated the search warrant but had mistakenly not signed it. Commenting, "Just like the old days, left-handing a warrant," one detective signed the name of the Justice of the Peace and proceeded to effect the search.[20]

Given the advantages of having search warrants, and the ease with which they were obtained from Justices, the obvious question to ask is why they were not obtained in all circumstances. One explanation is that from a pragmatic viewpoint, it was easier to not bother taking out a search warrant if the suspect's compliance could be reasonably predicted. Gaining the suspect's compliance without a search warrant was simply a less bothersome procedure that could save the time of all parties concerned.

A more complex set of reasons for not obtaining a search warrant concerned the tactical and legal advantages in not doing so. If a suspect consented to a search, it gave the enterprise a character of voluntariness similar to that we discussed in relation to some forms of arrest. The detectives had a psychological edge because suspects were then obeying on the basis of the detectives' pervasive authority as police officers rather than on the displaced authority of another legal agent. Moreover, the voluntariness component could be employed in arguing at the court stage that any evidence seized was provided with the apparently uncoerced co-operation of the suspect. In relation to these considerations it is interesting to note that even when detectives obtained a search warrant in advance, they sometimes never produced it to the suspect but rather proceeded by "consent" (DC 73; DC 98). In these circumstances, the search warrant was obviously a back-up in case the suspect objected, but the situational strategy was to gain the presumed advantages of suspect compliance based on the detective's "own" police authority.

Undertaking a consent search where a search warrant was not obtained in advance could also be strategic in situations involving suspects who were apprehended on very "shakey" grounds of suspicion rather than on more "reasonable and probable" grounds. While our observations would suggest that reasonable and probable grounds sufficient to satisfy a Justice of the Peace could usually have been constructed, in some situations it may have been a better cover to keep the entire transaction at a low level of visibility. For example, a person in DC 87 was designated a suspect entirely on the detectives' own suspicions rather than because of a citizen identification (see pp. 140-1). While the suspect was arrested, interrogated for two hours, and subject to an extensive search of his residence and his car, all of these actions were undertaken on a "voluntary" basis. This suspect was eventually released without charge, and was subject to no further investigation. From the detective's viewpoint it may have been advantageous that there was no written record of any of these transactions other than a brief internal investigation report which read:

> [The suspect] denied any knowledge of the offence and voluntarily supplied the department with a copy of his fingerprints, as well as a sam-

ple of his handwriting. Although there are similarities in the handwriting, it is felt that [the suspect] may not be responsible for the occurrence. The suspect also allowed the investigating officer to search his residence, which was done, with negative result.

A more detailed report, or a registered legal document such as a warrant, might have disadvantaged the detective if his actions were formally called into question by the suspect at a later stage.

Only one suspect raised strong objections to a consent search. In DC 296, the suspect was apprehended by a store security officer for an alleged "theft under $200" (shoplifting). A patrol officer searched the suspect's vehicle and discovered other items he believed to be stolen. He took the suspect to the station and turned him over to a detective for interrogation. During the interrogation, the suspect refused to confess that the other items in his possession were stolen. The detective repeatedly threatened to search the suspect's home, which would embarrass him in front of his wife, if he did not confess. The suspect repeatedly said that he did not want his house to be searched, and that he would confess to avoid this even though he did not steal the items. The detective eventually took the suspect to his residence and thoroughly searched it in the presence of the suspect and his wife, selecting out dozens of items and asking if they were stolen. This process did not result in additional charges being laid.

In some cases, searches were conducted in relation to suspects on the consent of a third party. In DC 233, the girlfriend of the accused consented to a detective search of the apartment that she shared with the accused after she was allowed to speak with the accused in the interrogation room at the divisional station. Officials in organizations also gave consent for searches in relation to suspected members; for example, an employer permitted the search of employee lockers (DS 172), and a hospital permitted the search of patient lockers (DC 144).

In only one instance did a third party object to a search (DC 98). In this situation, the accused allowed the consent search of the apartment he was living in after being charged for a series of "break, enter and thefts." Upon entering the apartment the detectives immediately seized some marijuana. The accused's room-mate, who had been sleeping in the main room, then awoke and demanded a search warrant, saying "This is my place, he [the accused] just stays here. This is all my stuff." The detective, holding up the seized marijuana, asked, "Can we search it?" and after some hesitation the room-mate stated, "Sure, go ahead." The detective later told the researcher that if the room-mate had refused to allow the search, he would have arrested the room-mate for joint possession of marijuana and taken both the room-mate and the accused back to the station while a search warrant was obtained. This would have allowed the detectives to search the apartment before the room-mate could remove any of the stolen property they were searching for.

Detectives routinely obtained search warrants from Justices and effected compliance with citizens, providing all the legal coverage they needed to generate information through searches. Justices of the Peace were nothing more than "automaton[s] in the hands of the constable," and citizens did nothing but "consent" to searches in face of detective tactics for gaining "voluntary" compliance. This degree of compliance is testimony to the authoritative apparatus of detectives and the power resources they have available to accomplish their tasks.

In our analysis of searches, we have already considered some aspects of questioning and interrogation as vehicles for generating information from suspects. Along with searches, probing for information and statements of confession from suspects in interrogations was central to the detectives' work of making cases aimed at particular outcomes.

There has been a debate in the socio-legal literature on the value to the police of interrogation and confessions. The debate has centred upon the question of whether interrogation is necessary to "solve crimes" and produce convictions. Blumberg (1970: 280n, 289) notes that his research and a study by a New York judge indicate that the large majority of cases were "predicated upon evidence independent of any confession of the accused." In a study in Pittsburgh, Seeburger and Wettick (1967) estimated that confessions were necessary to gain a conviction approximately 1/5 of the time. Other studies on the impact of *Miranda* also report that interrogation and confession played a major role in only a minority of cases. Wald *et al.*, (1967) say that interrogation was essential or important in 13 percent of the cases in their New Haven study, and Witt (1973) produces a figure of 24 percent. Wald *et al.*, (1967: 1641) report on other studies which confirm their view. An unpublished study by the Detroit police department indicates that investigators considered confessions "essential" in only 1/5 of cases, and Younger (1966) reports that deputy district attorneys deemed 67 admissions "necessary" among 487 cases under study at the trial stage.

As Wald *et al.* (1967: 1641-1642) state, studies of this type have concentrated upon *one* function of the interrogation and confession process. They question whether cases could be constructed using information other than from suspect confessions, and conclude that in most cases they could. However, from the police viewpoint there are a number of other functions of the interrogation and confession process.

First of all, confessions commit the accused to a view of himself as a guilty person, and may be useful in encouraging guilty plea settlements at the court stage. Several studies have documented how some accused persons perceive the confession to the police as tantamount to a guilty plea, making any challenge in court seem empty or even impossible (Dell, 1971; Bottoms and McClean, 1976; Baldwin and McConville, 1977; Ericson and Baranek, 1981). Wald *et al.*, (1967: 1608-1609) document that in the perception of lawyers, and in their own analysis of cases with and without confessions, the defence is much more able to obtain a bargain from plea discussions when there has been no confession.

⚡While a confession is a major goal of interrogation, the failure to get a confession does not mean that the interrogation was unsuccessful from the police viewpoint. Incriminating evidence useable in court can be obtained even if there is not a full confession. Sufficient evidence to convince a police superordinate and/or prosecutor of the need for further investigation can be produced. Other cases can be cleared up, either by having the suspect agree to accept responsibility for them without being charged (Bottomley and Coleman, 1979: 30), or by having the suspect inform on other people and about other activities (Skolnick, 1966: esp. 186). Moreover, all of these things may save the detectives time and effort. Without a confession, the detective would have to spend more time independently gathering physical evidence, talking with witnesses, and so on.

As we discussed in our analysis of how detectives effect control over suspects, the police have no right to compel suspects to answer their questions. However, it should be evident that detectives can be compelling in their tactics for gaining co-operation. Moreover, many of the tactics they use are tacitly supported by the law of confessions.

In Canada the law pertaining to confessions is entirely judge-made. Questions of voluntariness of statements and their admissibility are decided subjectively by each judge in each individual case.[21] This means that various manipulative strategies employed by the police to obtain a confession may be taken into account by a trial judge in assessing the voluntariness of a statement and whether or not it is admissible. Thus, various forms of trickery and deceit, refusal to allow access to a third party, and failure to give right to silence cautions may be taken into account in the judicial assessment but they do not necessarily render the statement involuntary and inadmissible. On the other hand, promises of bail, offences taken into consideration, pardon, lighter penalties, better treatment or financial inducements have rendered a statement inadmissible. Unwarranted detention and constant interrogation may also create doubt about the voluntariness of a confession and lead the judge to render it inadmissible. According to Kaufman (1974: 158), the test is whether the statement can be deemed trustworthy:

> The theory for the rejection of confessions is that if they are obtained under certain conditions, they are untrustworthy. It follows that the use of a trick or artifice, however reprehensible, will not by itself suffice to reject a statement so induced, provided that the circumstances do not cast doubt on the truth of its contents.

Freedman and Stenning (1977: 132ff) suggest that the law has developed very much in support of police interrogation tactics. For example, if the police pose themselves to the suspect as a person who would not be regarded as a person in authority, they are not deemed to be persons in authority and can therefore expand their repertoire of tactics. "Clearly, the law in this respect appears to be supportive of some of the 'interrogation techniques' recommended in a number of well-known manuals . . ." (*ibid.*: 146). The judicial opinion on how "unfairness" can be used to exclude otherwise admissible confessions also supports a wide range of police means to achieve their goal of a confession.[22] Another enabling element is the doctrine of confirmation by subsequently discovered facts, which means that statements that are inadmissible do not affect the admissibility of other evidence obtained as a result of the statements. Moreover, if this other evidence confirms the confession, that part of the confession which is confirmed is admissible as evidence even though it was obtained in an otherwise improper manner.[23]

The enabling elements of the law of confession which allow a variety of police tactics; the doctrine of confirmation by subsequently discovered facts; the fact that most accused plead guilty so that the interrogation and confession process is not often questioned in court; and, the many functions of interrogation beyond confessions admissible as evidence in court, all create a license for detectives to use interrogations to their advantage. Indeed, training manuals instruct police officers to use their creative ingenuity in generating information from suspects, since there are likely to be advantages even if, on rare occasions, someone challenges the propriety or legality of their methods. Even after the *Miranda* decision, which was partly decided in reaction to their manual, Inbau and Reid (1967: 163) argue that the only rule of thumb for interrogators is to ask the question, "Is what I am about to do, or say, apt to make an innocent person confess?" Otherwise, the matter is wide open, and not always to the exclusion of possibly innocent persons: "In dealing with criminal offenders, and consequently also with criminal suspects who may actually be innocent, the interrogator must of necessity employ less refined methods than are considered appropriate for the transaction of ordinary, everyday affairs by and between law-abiding citizens" (p. 217).

Freedman and Stenning (1977: 152-153) quote an RCMP issued training manual entitled *Interrogation Techniques*, written by a Calgary City Police Inspector, which states in the Introduction:

[T]here is a point which is reached in every interrogation when you still may not have that statement and you know if you go any further in the specific technique that you are employing that your statement will be ruled inadmissible. It is at this point that the interrogator must make a decision: does he now leave the interrogation room without the statement or does he now proceed with other techniques which he knows will not allow the statement in but may give him information which will lead to the securing of other evidence which itself may be admissible. I suggest at this point that the Marquis of Queensbury Rules go out the window and the interrogator must open up his bag of tricks and go for the recovery of the weapon or the stolen property or the names of accomplices or any evidence which may be presented in court regardless of the method employed to secure that evidence.

At this stage of dealing with suspects, in keeping with the other stages we have examined, both the law and the rules of police practice direct the detective to use suspects to whatever degree they can be exploited. Moreover, some argue that this exploitation is fullest against the weakest, i.e., the naive, cooperative individual who is least able to defend himself (Law Reform Commission, 1973: 11; Greenwalt, 1974: 262). Again, it is not that detectives are acting surreptitiously, doing things which violate rules in order to get the job done. Rather, they are directed to do the things they do to make their cases.

Among the 96 suspects in our research sample, 62 were subject to interrogations (defined as questioning of suspects who were in police custody). Forty-eight of these interrogations primarily took place in the divisional detective office interrogation rooms; five in an identification office interrogation room; one in a Detective Inspector's office; one in a general detective office; four in interrogation rooms at police stations of other police departments; and, three in detective cars.[24] If detectives made the arrest, the typical pattern was to ask general background information of the suspect as they drove back to the divisional station, then to undertake specific offence-related questioning at the station. In relation to 51 suspects for whom the researchers were able to record time in interrogation, the average time was 71 minutes and the median time 45 minutes, with a range of 5 to 470 minutes.

Among the 62 interrogated suspects, 39 (63 percent) were known to have confessed to offences.[25] This is a higher proportion than that reported in most other studies (see pp. 156-7). Among the 39 who confessed, 29 confessed to the offence(s) they were originally suspected of, 8 confessed to the offence(s) they were originally suspected of plus other offence(s) revealed during the course of interrogation, and two confessed to only some offence(s) they were suspected of. Written statements were obtained from 35/39 accused who confessed. Among the 23 persons who did not confess to any offence(s) during interrogation, eight received an unconditional release, four were cautioned, and 11 were charged.

In the interrogations we were able to witness or overhear, detectives did not use physical force. They proceeded by way of the carrot rather than the stick, although threats with coercive consequences were prevalent. It is arguable that the stick was unnecessary since suspects could be otherwise made to bite at the carrot because of the wide range of legitimated tactics for gaining confessions and other information from suspects. As several socio-legal scholars have pointed out, the rules which enable detectives to employ their "bag of tricks" function to minimize the use of physical force in obtaining information and confessions from suspects (Skolnick, 1966: 174; Wald et al., 1967: 1549; Reiss, 1968; Clark and Sykes, 1974; Katz, 1974; Sanders, 1977:

127). Indeed, regular use of violence would undermine police legitimacy, while regular use of the "bag of tricks" relies upon existing sources of police legitimacy to secure routinely all that is necessary to make a case.

The particular tactics employed by detectives depended very much on the situated features of the case, and the detectives' best guess as to what would work. However, some generally shared rules did apply. For example, if more than one suspect was involved in a case, detectives would typically interrogate the "weakest" first, with weakness being measured primarily by the person's criminal record, along with some assessment of education and intelligence. This rule is fostered by those instructing the police on approaches to interrogation (e.g., Hatherill, 1964: 171), and is supported in the observations of some researchers, (e.g., Wald, *et al.*, 1967: 1644).

This rule was evident in a variety of cases. In DC 78, one of two suspects had no previous criminal record and the detectives explicitly set out to arrest and interrogate this suspect first. One detective commented to the researcher, "It is better to pick up a person who hasn't been through it before—he is more likely to break down." When the two suspects in this case were eventually apprehended at the same time, the detective first interrogated the suspect with no record. In DC 88, a suspect who was a parolee from penitentiary was interrogated after the interrogation of a suspect who had a less serious criminal record. In DC 190, a female suspect with no known previous police contacts was interrogated before her male accomplice, who had previous contacts. In DC 245, a suspect who was known from previous contacts to be unco-operative was left in the cells after arrest until one of his accomplices, who had a criminal record but was judged to be co-operative, was interrogated.

In DC 222, the detectives did not initially follow the rule but quickly reverted to it when they ran into difficulty. The detectives were assigned this case after three suspects had been apprehended the previous night by patrol officers and held in custody for detective interrogation on the morning shift. The detectives did not choose among the three based on "sophistication," but rather started with the first suspect listed on the report. This suspect refused to cooperate and demanded a telephone call to his wife or lawyer. This suspect was granted his request and then placed back in the cells. Before getting the next suspect from the cells the detectives discussed who would be most likely to "crack." A second suspect had a lengthy criminal record and was known as a "real asshole" by several detectives. The detectives decided against interviewing him, and selected a third suspect who was considered less sophisticated because he was five years younger than the other two and not previously known to the detectives. This suspect confessed within ten minutes. In one detective's words, "He's serving it up for us. He's fingering the other two."

In our observations, detectives employed a variety of tricks and threats to obtain information from suspects. The tricks all involved playing upon the suspects' lack of knowledge about some aspect of the case and/or about police procedures. They included attempts to get "the truth" from suspects by suggesting that the victim's account was inaccurate; giving the appearance of having foolproof means of obtaining evidence, e.g., through fingerprint analysis and polygraph tests; and, giving the appearance of having evidence by creating the impression that the detectives "know everything" about the suspect's personal life and activities.

In order to overcome the deceit of suspects, detectives deceived them into believing that they were being deceived by victims. For example, suspects were advised to identify specifically what they had stolen from a particular victim in order to avoid being blamed for more than was stolen.[26] Thus, during an interrogation of the suspect in DC 98, the suspect continually stated that he had a poor memory of what residential break-ins he had committed and what items he had stolen because he was drunk at the time of the alleged offences. One detective's response to this was to make the following statement to the suspect:

> It's better for you to make sure you point all the places out now, so we can go and talk to each person and find out exactly what happened, what they're missing. We don't want more victims to come to us later and say they're missing things—some of them do it for insurance claims, to make some money out of it.

In this situation, the detective had no knowledge that victims were doing this, but he obviously wanted the suspect to believe it might happen in order that the suspect might consider it better to give a detailed confession than to face possible false allegations.

Another technique was to make the suspect believe that the detectives had or could obtain physical evidence to implicate the suspect when they had no such evidence (cf. Wald, *et al.*, 1967: 1546). On DS 64, a detective arrested and interrogated a juvenile who was near the scene of a car the detective believed to have been recently stolen. One tactic used by the detective in this interrogation was to say that he would take the suspect's fingerprints and check them against fingerprints on the car. In the later stages of the observational period, an officer trained in polygraph examinations became available, and detectives began using him as a means of inducing confessions, usually without going through the examination ritual. Given the limitations on the admissibility of expert evidence from polygraph examinations in court (Freedman and Stenning, 1977: 213), this device was used mainly for the purpose of inducing information from suspects that could be developed into admissible evidence by other means, or otherwise made useful to detectives. Refusal to take the test was taken as suggestive of guilt (Inbau and Reid, 1967: 106-108).[27]

Another trick of the trade was to create the impression that detectives were omniscient about the suspect's personal life and criminal activity, and by implication had enough evidence to charge the suspect (for supporting observations, see Skolnick, 1966: 177; Buckner, 1967:

293; Sanders, 1977: 126). For example, in DC 79 the detectives obtained detailed biographical data on the suspect, and information about his criminal activity, from his female accomplice and an ex-girlfriend serving as an informant (see Chapter 5, pp. 123-4). They then approached the suspect with the air of omniscience, or, as one detective put it directly to the suspect, "We know more about you than your fucking mother does."

When more than one suspect was involved, this display was sometimes augmented by using written statements from one suspect to show the other suspect(s) that the detectives had "hard" information. The hope was that the other suspect(s) would want to tell the detectives their account of what happened in order to avoid more serious allegations against them. This was similar to the strategy used in dealing with allegedly distorted accounts by victims. The ultimate goal was to have the other suspect(s) in turn provide written statements implicating the suspect who had originally provided the statement (DC 78, 222, 228).

In addition to these manipulative tactics, detectives employed threats as a means of generating information and confessions. These threats included stigmatization of the suspect by revealing his activities to family and employers; continued police custody; more charges, or charges in a more serious category; and, the possibility of a harder sentence.

In using threats, detectives tried successive ones until the suspect confessed or the repertoire ran out. For example, in DC 29, labelled "possible sex offender," a female complainant reported that a man approached her and her girlfriend and offered them some money "for a good time." The girls said they kept walking, and the man then stated that he was a police detective and produced identification from his wallet. They said the man then drove away, but the girls obtained a license number from his car and this was used by the detectives to trace his address.

The detectives parked outside the suspect's residence and waited for him to return home from work. As the suspect approached, one detective called out his first name and asked him to enter the detective car for a talk. The man did so, and he was locked into the rear of the car. The other detective opened by asking the suspect if he was in a particular geographical area on the date in question, and after receiving an affirmative answer, asked what he was doing there. After the suspect stated that he had been job hunting and then visited a girlfriend, the detective asked him for a description of "the incident" without specifying what "the incident" was. As the suspect continually pleaded ignorance, the detective drew upon successive threats. One detective threatened that if the suspect did not "tell the truth," he would be taken to the police station and held overnight.

The detective obviously held a particular truth in mind, because the suspect continued to deny knowledge and the detective continued his efforts to get the answer he wanted. The detective stated that if the suspect did not tell the truth the police would contact his employer and cause him to lose his job. This evoked a response from the suspect that he may have talked with some girls, but he refused to state precisely what he had said to the girls. The detective then asked for the name and telephone number of the suspect's employer. The suspect gave the name of his employer. At this point, apparently recalling the suspect's statement that he was visiting a girlfriend, the other detective asked the suspect if he was having trouble with his wife and if she knew that he was visiting a woman on the date in question, thus hinting that the wife might be informed about this if the suspect did not provide more information. The suspect persisted in refusing to provide the type of information the detectives wanted. The detectives finally warned the suspect and cleared the case by "caution."

Threats regarding continued custody were also promises of early release in exchange for co-operation in the generation of information that would make the detectives' case. For example, in DC 82 one out of three suspects was arrested by detectives and taken to the police station of another police department for a joint interrogation with detectives from that department. Immediately upon arrival at this police station, the following transaction took place:

Other P.D. Detective: I'll give you five minutes of my time, no more. Either you tell us about it or I'll throw you in the cells. You're already up on something. I'll fucking show cause and keep you in.

Suspect: I'll co-operate, but I'm not going to admit to something I didn't do.

Other P.D. Detective: I treated the other two like humans and they are out on a piece of paper. You tell me the fucking truth and I'll treat you the same; otherwise you're in the cells.

Research Detective: We're not talking about one or two days in jail either.

In DC 98, one detective formulated the prospects for release in less threatening terms. The suspect had been interrogated extensively on a series of property crimes, and had co-operated in making confessions. The detective promised the suspect that if he co-operated in assisting with the return of stolen property from receivers he identified, he would be released; the suspect readily complied (DS 58).

In using the threat of charges as an interrogation lever, detectives typically relied upon the presumed ignorance of suspects about the basis for substantive charges. One approach was to suggest that "perjury" charges could be laid on the basis of lying during the course of interrogations, or because the accused would have to take the stand in court and "lie" if he pleaded not guilty. For example, in DC 23, the detective stated, "The offence you have committed [indecent exposure—summary conviction maximum of six months imprisonment] isn't serious, but perjury is. I don't want you getting up in court and perjuring yourself. There's a five year sentence for that, whereas what you have [in this occurrence] is a minor thing."

The presumed ignorance of suspects was also used by detectives to ease the Force out of situations where patrol officers had made what detectives considered to be questionable arrests. In this situation, the suspect was made to believe that he could be charged but that he was being given a "break." This "break" could in turn be parlayed into other possible investigative payoffs. For example, in DC 91 the suspect was arrested by a patrol officer on suspicion of being in possession of stolen property. While searching the suspect's vehicle during a "routine check," the officer discovered a radio tape deck under the seat. According to the patrol officer, the suspect's girlfriend said the suspect asked her to hide the tape deck under the seat, and the suspect reported that he had bought the tape deck for $20.00.

A Detective Sergeant told the detective that this suspect was in the cells and asked him to interrogate the suspect. After brief questioning of the arresting officer and the suspect, the detective decided that he could not lay charges because he could not prove it was stolen. The detective's partner took down the serial number on the item and ran a property check, but the item was not listed.

The detective then asked his junior partner to interrogate the suspect. "We can't prove it's stolen, but he says he knows about some stolen property. See what you can get off him." The tactic was to let the suspect believe he could be charged, then to set up an exchange relationship with him by saying he would not be charged if he supplied information about others with stolen property and about other criminal activity.

> Detective: You've just been down in the cells, eh?
> Suspect: Yeah.
> Detective: How would you like to spend two months there?
> Suspect: Oh, no, I wouldn't want to go back there at all.
> Detective: O.K. then [suspect's first name], you'll have to co-operate with us. You know, you scratch our back and we'll scratch yours. We could charge you with this, you know that. You know what the penalty is for this? Five years minimum. Possession. An indictable offence. You could do five years for it. Ignorance of the law is no excuse. We could charge you even if you didn't know it was stolen.[28]

The suspect proceeded to identify the person who sold him the tape deck, identified a particular article in the person's possession that was allegedly stolen, and said the person used drugs. The suspect also agreed to become a general informant (DS 35).

Threats were also evident when detectives mentioned the possibility of leniency in sentencing in exchange for confessions from suspects. In DC 98, the detective told the suspect and his father that confessions to more offences would not make any difference to the judge's sentence: "The courts already have more than enough now to do with him what they please—to give him time or anything else. More charges at this point aren't going to make any difference to what the court does." In this situation, the assumed judicial practice of concurrent sentencing was used to encourage the suspect to confess to all offences. On the other hand, the implied threat was that if more offences were uncovered later they could result in separate proceedings that would ultimately be more detrimental to the suspect.

In DC 79, one suspect was interrogated during the course of a property search at his place of residence. After being told that he was under arrest and after the search had commenced, the suspect asked about the sentence he could expect. One detective initially stated, "That's nothing to do with us. It's up to the judge." This detective then added, "He'll [the judge] take into account how co-operative you have been with us. He'll look at how much property we have recovered, whether you co-operated in telling us about the offences you did, things like that." During the search similar comments were repeated twice.

The process of gathering information from suspects was directed toward the possibility of making a criminal case against the suspect through the laying of charges. We now turn to an examination of how detectives got their charges, transforming suspects into accused persons.

Charging Accused

Detective charging decisions were a culmination of the information production process we have described to this point, and were directed at the release and conviction outcomes we describe in subsequent sections of this chapter. When detectives decided to charge a suspect they did so with careful consideration of what bail related controls they wanted placed upon the person up to the point of his conviction, and with strategic planning as to how the construction of charges would maximize the chance that the accused would be convicted and receive a sentence within a predictable range.

The charge decision is crucial to producing the outcome of the case because it frames the relevant issues (McBarnet, 1976: 190). Since most cases are effectively concluded in out of court discussions among the detective, the defence attorney, the Crown attorney, and sometimes the judge, resulting in a guilty plea by the accused with no trial, the charge decision is particularly crucial for framing the limits of the possible in plea negotiations. As Alschuler (1968) states, "The charge is the asking price in plea bargaining, and the drafting of accusations is therefore an integral part of the negotiating process."

Detectives decided upon what the suspect deserved and proceeded to make the appropriate criminal charges. They attempted to "seal" the case through their charges and supporting evidence so that the outcomes were predictable vis-à-vis what they thought the suspect deserved. This orientation to the criminal process was astutely recognized by Lewis Carroll in *Alice in Wonderland* when he stated that justice consists of the sentence, then the trial, then the charge. It is also recognized in contemporary television shows about detectives, in which the complete cycle of justice occurs on the street between police and criminal: "It is not in the courts that convictions are obtained but in the face-to-face world of police and villains" (Hurd, 1979: 122). Detectives had no qualms about charging on this basis because they believed that the people they charged were guilty of something and therefore deserving of some punishment, even if it was just the embarrassment and annoyance of being subject to prosecution.[29]

As outlined in Chapter 1, the law, the court organization and the police organization collectively provide an enabling environment for detectives to charge in this manner.

The substantive law is enabling in the way some offences are vaguely described to encompass a range of behaviour, especially in public order situations (e.g., causing a disturbance, obstructing police). However, this feature is probably of greater use to patrol officers than detectives (cf. Ericson, 1980). The substantive law is also enabling because it provides such a wide range of offences that some charge can usually be found to deal with a suspect. As Goldstein (1970: 152) observes, this is one reason why police feel "that the law should be left on the books; it may come in handy sometime." The research literature contains many examples of how police officers use the law in a "handy" way to get the outcome they want by choosing among a wide range of possible substantive charges (e.g., Steer, 1970; Sanders, 1977; Vera Institute, 1977; Heumann, 1978; McCabe and Sutcliffe, 1978).[30]

The court and police organizations are explicitly set up to process routine cases in a way that will routinely produce convictions. As Black (1976: 96) states, "A modern state is more organized than any of its adversaries, and so it has an advantage at every step of the legal process. This is especially striking in criminal cases, as in modern America, where the typical defendant ultimately pleads guilty, giving the state a victory by default." Court agents share the presumption that those not guilty have already been screened out, and that those standing before the court are typically guilty of something. In consequence, they collaborate in the out-of-court transactions which lead the accused to plead guilty, and then cloak it in a "legitimacy veil" by partaking in a court ceremony "which appears the very model of formal [legal] rationality" (Balbus, 1973: 18-19). Since conviction on something is virtually sealed at the point of charging, in the court appearances "the question is not guilt or innocence but rather a demonstration of the 'approved way' in which violence can be used legitimately vis-à-vis a given individual" (Blumberg, 1967: 20; see also Bottoms and McClean, 1976; Carlen, 1976; Baldwin and McConville, 1977; Ericson and Baranek, 1981).

The charging practices of detectives are also facilitated by the low visibility conditions of their work within the police organization, and in relation to the court organization. Judges rarely inquire into police practices, especially if the accused enters a guilty plea, and they act *as if* there is no differential selection of offenders and offences (cf. Bottomley, 1973: 221).

Crown attorneys may casually counsel detectives on charging, providing them with the recipe knowledge of how to constitute a "normal crime" (Sudnow, 1965) or "established crime" (Sanders, 1977). However, in our observations detectives rarely consulted with the Crown attorney in the process of laying charges. Detectives were known to have consulted with the Crown attorney regarding the *initial* laying of charges in only three instances. In DC 96, the detectives asked the Crown attorney if any charges were possible in a case involving a couple who had obtained a newly born baby with the consent of the baby's mother, after arranging to have her enter a hospital in another town as the wife of the male member of the couple. In DC 3, the detectives sought the Crown attorney's advice on what status offence charges could be laid against a man with a record for indecent assault (male) whom they defined as "dangerous." In DC 192, the detectives charged the suspect with "buggery," then one week later added "indecent assault (male)" and "contributing to delinquency" charges after consulting with the Crown attorney on what "kicker" charges would ensure a "negotiated" guilty plea settlement.

Similarly, within the detective unit rules of the occupational culture guided detectives in the construction of appropriate charges vis-à-vis attendant evidence. As Sander's (1977: 92) observes, the wide range of possible criminal charges is narrowed when filtered by the occupational culture: "The specific sense of robbery is not provided in 'a bunch of kids grabbing a spray can from another kid,' and any detective who included such charges in his report would be regarded as foolish." In our observations, superordinate officers did not directly supervise detectives, and they were rarely consulted when charges were being laid. Indeed, we observed instances in which detectives explicitly rejected their Detective Sergeant's recommendations regarding charges, whether these recommendations were for more serious charges (DC 36—"wounding" and "attempted rape" instead of "weapon dangerous" and "A.O.B.H."; DC 193—"rape" instead of "attempted rape") or less serious charges (DC 11—lesser charge or private information laid by victim on a threatening telephone call complaint, instead of an indictable charge (*Criminal Code* section 331(1)(a)) laid by the detective).

Within these enabling frameworks, detectives went about their work of charging with conviction. This work consisted of selecting charges that would maximize the detectives' chances for obtaining an outcome they believed was both just and justifiable.

One way to provide maximum leverage is to "charge up" the offence to the most serious category justifiable in the hope of inducing a guilty plea to a less serious offence at the court stage.

> In just about any case the detective can 'show' that a certain set of circumstances has the elements of a crime more serious than he actually

sees the case to be. For instance, the report of the 'attempted murder' was written so that all the necessary elements of an attempted murder were available to the reader; however, the reformulation of the case as a domestic fight was taken to provide 'what really happened.'

Similarly, a detective will often 'show' a suspect what a crime can be 'made' to be if he wants to 'be technical' about it, yet all along the detective does not believe that the case is 'really' an instance of the more serious crime. (Sanders, 1977: 91).

Some research results support the wisdom of charging up to a higher category in relation to the goal of a punitive sentence. For example, a study by the Vera Institute (1977: 13) found that ". . . the more serious the offence charged at arrest in each general category, the stiffer is the sentence likely to be following conviction, whether the conviction was for the felony originally charged, a lesser felony, or a misdemeanor."

DC 43 provides an example of detectives 'charging up' to make their case with regard to the outcome they wanted in court. The detectives arrested a suspect after he was apprehended by an apartment superintendent on behalf of the seven year-old female victim. The victim originally reported that a male youth had lifted her skirt while passing her on an apartment stairwell. The age of the victim posed evidence problems for the detectives; therefore, they proceeded to construct the charge in a way that would ultimately not require a trial with victim testimony but would likely result in a guilty plea.

The detectives' approach was to gain a written statement from the suspect in which he admitted to the incident in a manner that would justify an Indecent Assault (female) charge. However, throughout the interrogation the detectives realized they had very questionable grounds for this charge. Twice during the interrogation the two detectives came out of the interrogation room for a consultation away from the suspect. One detective stated, "I'm getting bored. These are the ones I hate because it's just not clear. We can go with common assault, but I don't know if we have more than that."

The second detective kept on referring to the suspect as "weird" because he was "soft spoken" and slightly "spaced out." This second detective stated, "I think it's all related to a sexual problem . . ." Another factor repeated was that the suspect had no criminal record. The second detective checked through the occurrence file to see if there were any other sex offences committed by a suspect with a similar description. Two occurrences were selected, but they were not utilized. The detectives considered doing a consent search of the suspect's residence to see if there were any other relevant ("pornographic") materials which might help them in their investigation. Finally, one detective stated, "We'll do him for indecent assault (female) and let the Crown decide. If they want to change it to the included offence of common assault then they can."

The detectives proceeded to take a written statement from the

suspect. As indicated in the relevant section of the statement reproduced below, the accused admitted to involvement in the incident
but did not provide an explicit statement about touching the girl's
private parts.

[Accused statement, DC 43]

Accused: [after describing the preliminary events and his reasons for
being in the apartment building]
Then I walked down the stairwell to the second floor
past the door where the second floor is and then those girls
came in. They were walking up the stairs on the outside of
the stairwell and I was walking close to the bannister down
the stairwell. I said, "Hey" to them to catch their attention.
After they got past me the one girl was one step ahead of the
other girl. I was still close to the bannister and that is when
I got turned around and was going to say something to the
kid because I had gotten by them and they hadn't moved.
The one girl noticed me and I didn't think the other girl had
noticed me. I just reached out and flipped her skirt and I
don't know if my hand touched her or not. The girl, once she
noticed that her skirt was flipped, she yelled at me. I looked
at her and then I kept on going down the stairs and went outside out the front door. Then I went home.

Question: Do you wish to add change or take anything out of your
statement?

Accused: I would like to mention I was annoyed at the girls and that is
why I did it.

In the "record of arrest" describing the "facts" of the case, the
detectives constructed an account to justify the Indecent Assault
(female) charge even though it varied from the occurrence report account originally recorded by the patrol officer ("Apparently the
suspect then lifted the victim's short skirt and exposed her under-
garments"), and the statement given by the accused ("I just reached
out and flipped her skirt and I don't know if my hand touched her or
not").

[Record of Arrest, DC 43]

While the accused continued to walk in the stairwell, between the
second and first floors, he was met by the victim and her sister who
were enroute to their apartment located on the second floor.

As the accused passed the victim, he reached out with his hand,
lifted the child's skirt and touched her buttocks.

The victim yelled to the accused, who turned and faced her, and
then the accused continued down to the main floor, where he exited the
building.

Through this process, the detectives provided the prosecution with
the basis for inducing a guilty plea to the lesser included offence of

common assault. At the trial stage, the Assistant Crown attorney, in discussion with detectives, stated that there was insufficient evidence (including unsworn child evidence) for the indecent assault (female) charge. Through discussions among the detectives, the defence counsel and the Assistant Crown attorney, the decision was made to have the accused enter a guilty plea to common assault along with a statement that the accused was willingly undergoing psychiatric treatment.

Another source of leverage in producing convictions is to lay multiple charges. While the law restricts the possibility of gaining multiple convictions on multiple charges arising out of the same fact situation, it does not prohibit the police from laying the multiple charges to maximize their bargaining position at the outset (for a review of this point, see Ericson, 1980: Ch. 6). Moreover, there was no established "offences taken into consideration" practice in the jurisdiction under study, although such practices are legally possible *(Regina v. Robinson* (1969), 49 C.C.C. (2d) 464 (Ont. C.A.)). This is unlike the situation in Britain (e.g., Bottoms and McClean, 1976; Baldwin and McConville, 1977) and in some parts of the United States, e.g., Detroit (LaFave, 1965: esp. 374), and Oakland (Skolnick, 1966). Detectives were not discouraged by legal requirement or administrative device from laying multiple charges.

One exceptional case proved that multiple charging was the norm. In DC 87 the detectives became very angry when Youth Bureau officers apprehended the adult suspect and charged him with only three of six "break and enter" incidents he admitted to. The detectives stated that they would have charged the suspect on all counts, and in addition would have searched the suspect's residence in an attempt to obtain evidence of possible further offences.

From the detectives' viewpoint multiple charging served multiple functions, one or more of which were evident in any particular case. First of all, the practice provided leverage for conviction. It facilitated the opportunity of the Crown attorney to negotiate a guilty plea through the offer of withdrawing some charges. If "kicker" charges were involved—charges "thrown in" to create a worse image of the accused and/or to provide some basis for conviction if the main charge could not be sustained—chances for conviction on something could be increased and the accused could be made to suffer by the charges alone. This relates to a second function of multiple charging, namely creating the maximum possible record against the accused to justify future surveillance and increased leverage in future dealings with him. While adding charges and then withdrawing less important or less substantial charges was not likely to affect the accused person's sentence if he pleaded guilty (because of concurrent sentencing practices), it did provide a more extensive record for the person which could affect future decisions, (e.g., treating the person as a suspect, legitimating charges, denying bail, and increasing sentence on future occasions). Third, charging on each occurrence allowed the detectives to clear each occurrence by charge, thereby swelling both their personal productive appearances and those of the police organization. In sum, detectives charged everyone possible with everything possible as a means of maximizing the chances for convictions; to stamp a more major "criminal" identity on the accused, which served both as an immediate punishment and as a justification for future surveillance; and, to maximize their productive appearances within the police organization.

Multiple charging involved two approaches, with the type of approach varying by whether the case involved "property" occurrences or "interpersonal" occurrences. When property occurrences were involved, suspects were typically charged in relation to each occurrence to set up the framework for a plea settlement whereby the accused would plead guilty to some charge(s) in exchange for the withdrawal of other charge(s) and/or sentence recommendations from the Crown attorney. For example, in DC 98 one accused was charged with 21 counts including "break, enter and theft," "break and enter," "attempted theft," "theft under $200," "possession of stolen property," and "possession of marijuana (NCA 3(1)). These charges included combinations, e.g., theft of items and possession of those items. When the case came to court, the detective, Crown attorney and defence attorney negotiated and settled upon what they regarded as a just and justifiable outcome. They agreed to a 90 day jail term served intermittently, and to 18 months probation, and subsequently had this recommendation accepted by the judge. Two charges (the possession of stolen property and the possession of marijuana) were withdrawn as part of this agreement, and one break and enter charge was withdrawn after the Crown attorney could not find the synopsis while reading out the charges in court, but this was incidental to the overall "package."

In DC 296, the detective started out with the maximal array of charges against each of four accused, and equipped with this framework for negotiation, contacted the accuseds' lawyer to produce a plea settlement. The four accused were each charged on the same offences after a shoplifting "spree." The detective initially charged two counts of theft over $200, three counts of theft under $200, and possession of stolen property over $200 against each accused. After arranging the plea settlement, the "facts" were reconstructed accordingly, along with a strong hint to the Crown attorney that if the settlement was not finalized they were facing a lengthy trial with a parade of witnesses.

[Written Memorandum to the Crown attorney]
To: Crown Attorney
From: [Detective's name]
Ref.: [names four accused] Charged: 2 theft over
3 theft under
1 possession over
I have had occasion to discuss this case with defense counsel [name and telephone number] as well as Crown Attorney [name]. As a

result it has been suggested by [Crown Attorney] that two theft over charges be pled guilty to and that the one possession over charge be amended to read possession under and that the four accused plead guilty to the possession under charge as well. The remaining 3 theft under charges would then be withdrawn.

By having the possession over amended to possession under this covers the balance of stolen property recovered from the 3 stores involved in theft under charges. This would then cover all stores and all charges.

[The Crown Attorney] also advised that all facts would be read into the court and that it be presented as a planned, premeditated scheme executed by four members of one family and that sentence should be accordingly.

[The lawyer] has agreed to these arrangements and will take his chances on sentencing.

I have typed out a further SYNOPSIS which meets the corrected facts and I hope this meets with your approval. In the event this is unsatisfactory all my witnesses will be present in court and have been supoenaed—

Thank you for your consideration.

[Signed by detective]

In "interpersonal" cases, extra charges were added and the facts constructed accordingly in order to develop the image of the accused as a "dangerous" person and thereby maximize the prospects for gaining a conviction on something against a person deemed to be deserving of punishment. Two detailed case examples document this point.

In DC 47 extra charges were sought to construct an image of the suspect as "dangerous" in order to secure a denial of bail, and to parlay everything into a conviction for the main charge of "rape." By their own admission the detectives had questionable evidence for the "rape" charge because the victim had delayed reporting it, and had taken two baths which negated the usefulness of vaginal swab and washing tests. However, there was a shared definition that the suspect deserved punishment. As a supervising detective said while the investigating detective was fishing for charges, "I think something should be done to this guy. You feel like getting some revenge. Even if the charges are withdrawn you can at least embarrass the guy.... Maybe that's not the purpose of the criminal process, but that's what you feel like doing sometimes." This view was reconfirmed much later by the investigating detective as he sat talking with his partner, the court reporter, and a researcher, awaiting the outcome of the trial on the rape charge.

[Tape recorded discussion in the private office of the Crown attorney prosecuting DC 47]

Detective: ... I have been involved in the case for so long that, myself, I feel you lose sort of touch with—you know, you are so prejudiced in the way you feel about it.

> You know and you can watch all the evidence go in but you still think you know there's no doubt in your mind so people that are just . . .
>
> Court reporter: They may have . . .
>
> Detective: That's right, you know, people who have just heard the evidence for a day or two, they don't have the same understanding of the case.
>
> Court reporter: I'm sure there is a point in time that you fellows on the police force must make the conscious decision that this guy has done it and from there on you are doing nothing but proving that that thought is right.
>
> Detective: I think you have to.

In constructing their case, the detectives looked for "kicker" charges. While one detective was taking a statement from the victim, the other detective examined the *Criminal Code* for possible additional charges. The examination centred on finding a charge that would cover the victim's earlier statement that the suspect would not allow her to leave his apartment after the alleged incident. The detective considered the charge of "unlawful confinement" (*Criminal Code* section 247(2)), but eventually decided on "abduction of female" (*Criminal Code* section 248(a)) because, "It carries a heavier penalty." The detective stated that while *Criminal Code* 248(a) was intended for the "white slave" area, it nevertheless seemed applicable in this case. As he was preparing the information, the detective stated to the researcher, "At least it will give us some bargaining power."

The next step in the construction came when the detectives arrested the suspect and executed a warrant to search the suspect's apartment. During the search, the detective took a gun from an ornamental shelf, and later measured it and found that it was a fraction of an inch shorter than the legal length, and thus evidence for a charge of being in possession of a restricted weapon (*Criminal Code* section 91). The suspect was taken to the division station and subsequently charged with rape, abduction of female, and possession of a restricted weapon.

The first major use of these charges was to argue that the accused was "dangerous" enough to be held in custody awaiting trial. This required construction of the information for bail hearing report in a way that would present the worst possible image of the suspect. In relation to the possession of a restricted weapon charge, the detectives noted in the bail information that the "gun" was also being investigated for "armed robbery." Furthermore, the accused's interest in guns was referred to in order to leave the implication that he had intimidated the victim and made her fearful of retaliation.

[Information for Bail Hearing DC 47]
Reasons arresting officer has to believe accused should be held in custody for good of the community or that he may continue his criminal activity.

—The victim fears that the accused will come after her as he knows her address and where she works. The accused had brought out numerous guns and displayed them to the victim just prior to attacking her and raping her.

—one sawed off shot gun .12 gauge which was found in his apt. is being investigated for further offences (armed robbery).

—The accused showed a premeditation when he brought the victim to his apt. when his wife and children weren't there. After he had raped the victim he told her repeatedly that no court would believe her as she had gone to his apt. of her own free will.

The detectives relied upon the facts of the case as they had constructed them in order to make the accused out to be a danger to the community. Facts which would have suggested a competing interpretation were omitted or deflected. For example, the fact that the accused was employed steadily for several years with one firm was mentioned nowhere on the information. The accused's insignificant and unrelated criminal record (one conviction five years previous for taking a vehicle without the owner's consent) was not listed under the "Criminal Record" section of the information for bail hearing form. Instead, this section read, "See CPIC printout which was sent over from H.Q.," suggesting that the accused had a record of some length without indicating how recent it was or its specific content.

The detectives next used the weapons charge, and the account that the accused had displayed his other (legal) weapons to the victim before the alleged rape, at a *voir dire* hearing on the admissibility of the accused's written statement before a Provincial Court judge. During the testimony of the two detectives at this hearing, they were asked to describe the arrest, search, interrogation and release process, and thus had the opportunity to describe the weapons. The judge ruled the statement admissible, and the court then proceeded with a trial on the weapon charge with the *voir dire* evidence admitted for the purposes of the trial. During the trial, one detective was again called to the stand by the Crown attorney. This detective testified as to his expertise with weapons, and stated that he had fired the seized weapon and found it to work. Following testimony from the accused, in which he argued that the gun was an antique and that he had never fired it, the judge found him guilty.

The Crown again called the detective to the stand with respect to sentence. The detective held up a target showing a human form which he said he had fired at with the restricted weapon. The detective said he had fired at a close range and noted that the discharged ammunition spread quickly:

Crown Attorney: Is it deadly?
Detective: Yes, very. This type of weapon is being used more
                often in robberies.
Judge: How old is that gun?
Detective: 10-15 years, it's an old style.

Judge: Antique?

Detective: Not since it has been altered. It's of no value—the
                  R.C.M.P. wouldn't register it.

The judge asked the Crown attorney if he had any further submissions,
and the Crown attorney proceeded to argue for a sentence of imprisonment. However, the judge referred to the subsequent argument by the
defence lawyer that the accused was married and working steadily, in
pronouncing a sentence that included a $350 fine or 35 days in jail,
plus an order prohibiting the convicted person from having any
firearms or ammunition for five years.

The accused went to trial at the Supreme Court level before a
judge and jury. The Crown proceeded to prosecute on the rape charge
after the judge ruled that the abduction of female charge be withdrawn
because it arose out of the same fact situation as the rape. The trial
was preceded by a voir dire hearing concerning the accused's statement to the police. Again the detectives, in describing the arrest and
search process, talked about the seizure of the weapon. When the trial
commenced with the statement admitted, the Crown attempted to introduce into evidence the element that the accused had displayed his
guns to the victim as part of an intimidation strategy prior to the alleged rape and detainment of the victim. However, the judge ruled this
evidence inadmissible.

Throughout these hearings and trials, the strategy of the detectives in collaboration with the Crown attorney was to use the restricted
weapon and display of weapons element to create an image of the accused that might ultimately persuade the judge and jury that he was
the kind of person who might commit rape. It could also be used as
evidence of intimidation by the accused and lack of consent by the victim, an important factor in a case where there was very little physical
evidence. Indeed, there may have been a strategic advantage to having
a separate trial on the weapon charge prior to the trial on the other
charges, because it allowed the Crown to have a violence-related offence registered in the accused's record; this record, in turn, might
have influenced sentence if the accused had subsequently been found
guilty on the rape and/or abduction of female charges.

In DC 3, the suspect was the subject of continuing police
surveillance because of his status as a convicted person for previous
indecent assault (male) offences in relation to juveniles. The suspect's
identity was well known to most detectives, and the suspicion about his
activities was heightened to the point where the Force invested the
resources of its mobile support (under cover intelligence) unit in following him. When the suspect was found in public playgrounds with
younger males, he was charged with vagrancy (*Criminal Code* section 175(e)).

When this matter came to the attention of detectives they decided
to seek other possible charges because they saw the accused as
"dangerous" and in need of being kept "off the streets." The detectives

searched for and discovered a probation order still in force against the accused. The main condition on this probation order prohibited the 27 year-old accused from associating with or communicating with any male person under the age of 21.

One detective telephoned an Assistant Crown attorney and asked for his advice about the most appropriate steps to take against the accused to put further "controls" on him. The detectives mentioned the possibility of laying a "Breach of Probation" charge, and also inquired about the feasibility of proceeding under the "Dangerous Sexual Offender" provisions of the *Criminal Code* section 689. The Assistant Crown attorney not only discouraged these possibilities, but stated that it was not advisable to proceed on the Vagrancy charge because the suspect was not actually found loitering but was engaged in a game of tennis at the time of his apprehension.

The detectives were dissatisfied with this advice and decided to consult the Crown attorney. In the interim, other police officers had again apprehended the suspect and charged him with Vagrancy. The detectives' initial approach to the Crown attorney was in the form of a memo, the essential parts of which read:

> The above named person was just released from [a provincial reformatory] after serving approximately 7 months for Indecent Assault-Male. On [date] he was found by a uniform officer at _____ Tennis Court which is located in a park and he was charged with Vagrancy (e). A few days later I got the information regarding the charge and so I spoke to [an Assistant Crown] about the charge of Vag. (e). Under the circumstances [the Assistant Crown] felt that because [accused's last name] was practicing tennis that he had accounted for himself and was not wandering or loitering. [The Assistant Crown] advised me that he would arrange to have the charge withdrawn on the court date . . .
>
> On [date] our Mobile Support Unit was running [accused's last name] and they followed him to _____ Tennis Court and he was with three juveniles. A uniform officer came over and [accused's last name] was charged with Vag. (e) again.
>
> The writers have been making some checks on [accused's last name] and have found that on [date] [accused's last name] was given a suspended sentence and three years probation with no reporting, however, there were two conditions. One was that he was not to associate or hold any communication with any male persons under the age of 21 years. . . . This probation is still in effect and expires [date].
>
> The writers would like to know which would be the best way to proceed against [accused's last name] to get him back before the courts.
>
> Please see [accused's last name] record which is attached.

The day after this memorandum was written, one detective held a meeting with the Crown attorney about this case. The detective later told his partner that the Crown attorney was "not too excited about it," but suggested that a breach of probation charge should be laid to make their case stronger, and stated that he would not withdraw the second Vagrancy E charge because "it doesn't look good to keep withdrawing them." The detectives did lay the breach of probation charge, and subsequently laid another Vagrancy charge and another breach of probation charge arising out of a separate incident. In this incident, the accused was found associating with the juvenile son of his employer. Charges were laid in spite of the fact that the employer and the son both knew about the accused's record, and did not act as complainants.

The case came to trial, and the accused was planning to enter not guilty pleas on all five counts. However, as he was brought into the prisoner's docket for the trial, he noticed two persons sitting in the courtroom whom he suspected as being surprise Crown witnesses. The accused consulted with his lawyer, who in turn obtained a brief recess to talk with the Crown attorney. The lawyer learned from the Crown attorney that these persons were indeed Crown witnesses, and that they would testify that the accused was associating with their children. This was apparently strong evidence in favour of conviction on the breach of probation charges, and the lawyer worked out a settlement with the Crown attorney whereby the accused would plead guilty to two counts of breach of probation in exchange for withdrawal of the three counts of vagrancy. The accused accepted this arrangement, and a remand was obtained in order to prepare submissions for sentencing. The accused was sentenced to the maximum term of six months imprisonment on each count, to run consecutively for a total of one year, plus a probation order for two years. In passing sentence, the judge stated that one of the warning signals of dangerousness is persistence, and noted that the accused was determined to persist in the face of a court order. The judge told the accused that he had exhausted his credit with the court, and said the maximum sentence was called for in order to protect the young men of the community.

In cases in which the detectives judged their evidence to be questionable, but still thought the suspect deserved to be punished, several options were available. One option was to charge the suspect and pursue prosecution as a stigmatizing process regardless of outcome (e.g., DC 47). A second option was to charge the suspect in order to obtain bail release conditions on him, which would in turn legitimate increased police surveillance and the possibility of getting the person off the streets for violation of bail conditions. A third option was to not charge the suspect, but to use other means to stigmatize him and/or to get controls over him.

Charging suspects with the expressed purpose of "getting controls" through bail conditions was seen as a viable option in interpersonal cases in which there were problems with evidence. For example, in DC 130 an Assistant Crown attorney told a detective that he had been approached by the complainant, who identified a suspect involved in alleged "harassing telephone call" and "watch and beset" occurrences. The Assistant Crown attorney appeared keen to have the suspect charged, although he admitted to the detective that the evidence was "weak." He advised the detective that he wanted the suspect held for a bail hearing so that conditions could be set ordering the suspect to keep away from the complainant. The Assistant Crown attorney added, "I fully expect him to breach these conditions. In fact, I want him to." The suggestion was that a breach would be grounds for further control over the suspect, and also might assist in constructing the image required to produce a conviction.

Similarly, in DC 11 the accused was charged for making a threatening telephone call to his wife, from whom he was separated. The accused was already on charge for a previous incident in which he had threatened his wife with a rifle. The detective decided to charge for the more serious indictable section (*Criminal Code* section 331(1)(a)) rather than to lay a less serious charge or to have the victim lay a private information. In conversation with the Detective Sergeant, the detective said this charge would be more likely to be successful in achieving a denial of bail. Failing this, they could include a condition of release which, given his past behaviour, the accused was likely to break, namely that there be no further communication between the accused and his wife.

In DC 59 the suspect was allegedly involved in two separate incidents of indecently assaulting very young girls (under 7 years of age). As one detective commented, "He knows how to pick his victims," referring to the problem of testimony from victims in this age range. According to the detective involved in a previous investigation on this suspect, he at that time chose a six year-old girl who was partially retarded and who had a speech problem. After a thorough criminal records check revealed that the suspect had no known record, one detective asked the detective partner, "What are we going to do with him?" The detective partner replied, "I know what I would like to do with him [pause]. I think we might have to charge him. We'll charge him and get [bail] conditions. That's the only way to control him—get conditions on him even if the Crown don't take it all the way."[31]

In another case labelled "Indecent Assault (female)," involving young children, the decision was taken to invoke controls over the suspect without laying a charge. The first victim was seven years of age and thus posed problems as a court witness. The suspect was questioned but refused to confess, and the detectives decided to "caution" him. Subsequently the parents of another child in the neighbourhood also expressed concern about the suspect, and another detective team again apprehended and interrogated the suspect. The suspect continued to deny involvement, and he was cautioned again. This second caution was accompanied by a threat that if any more complaints were forthcoming the detective would see to it that the suspect lost his job. In addition, the detective had the suspect submit to being photographed, and this photograph was included in the sex offender photo identification book.

Among the 40 suspects who were not charged, 17 were "cautioned." In relation to 13/17 suspects who were cautioned, the detectives had at least a confession as evidence on which to lay a charge but chose not to charge.

The decision not to charge was related to a number of influences. In some cases the detectives did not charge in exchange for information about accomplices of the suspect, or about other criminal activity (e.g., DC 38, DC 110, DC 121—see Ch. 5).

In other cases detectives felt a charge would go against the expectations of their detective colleagues. For example, in DC 144 the detectives were called to a psychiatric ward of a hospital by a staff member who had discovered marijuana during a search of an inmate's belongings. The detectives questioned this inmate, who provided the name of another inmate as his supplier. The supplier was then questioned and his property searched, revealing more marijuana. However, the detectives simply cautioned the suspects. One detective later stated to his partner that they would be "laughed at" if they had laid charges against psychiatric patients in a hospital setting.

In some cases detectives seemed to accept the explanation of the suspect as grounds for not charging. For example, DC 172 involved the alleged theft of at least 30 tires from the lot of a tire company. When the detectives proceeded to execute a search warrant on the residence of the suspect for this "theft over $200" occurrence, they were greeted by the suspect's mother, who immediately confessed to the offence. The mother explained that she did not know the tires were for sale and that she thought they were scrap. After explaining that the tires were "adjustments" that could be re-sold for $10.00 or more, one detective told the suspect he would only caution her, "Because I don't think you have a guilty mind." This was done against the wishes of the detective's partner, who noted that many of the tires were not used and that "half of them still have the stickers on them."

As we have stressed, the decision to charge took into account the outcomes the detectives wanted to produce. This included the intermediate outcome of the accused's release and the conditions of that release, and the final outcomes of finding and sentence in court. We now turn to an examination of detective involvement in the production of these outcomes, keeping in mind that their charging decisions helped to frame what happened at later stages in the criminal process.

Releasing Accused

While dealing with suspects in custody, detectives must keep in mind the various legal provisions relating to the custody and release of suspects. Similar to other procedural laws relating to detective-suspect transactions, the laws relating to custody and release of suspects are generally enabling for detectives. Detectives are able to *show* conformity with the laws. They are also able to obtain routine acceptance of their release decisions from Justices of the Peace, and to formulate a case for denying bail which at least leads to restrictions on the accused even if the accused is not detained in custody.

In deciding on the form of release from their custody, detectives were directed by the provisions of the *Bail Reform Act*.[32] A general provision of this Act requires detectives to take a suspect before a Justice within 24 hours of arrest. The 24 hours is a maximum period, but the expectation is that the time will be shorter if reasonably possible: "the person shall be taken before a Justice without unreasonable delay and in any event within that [24 hour] period" (*Criminal Code* section 454). Among the 66 arrested suspects in the custody of detectives, we were able to obtain a recording of time in custody for 56 suspects. The mean length of time in custody was 4.55 hours, the median 3.00 hours, and the range .42 to 20.25 hours.

The general requirement of bringing a suspect before a Justice without reasonable delay and within a maximum of 24 hours did not pertain in a number of circumstances. If the detectives decided to release a suspect without charge, they could legally grant an unconditional release of the suspect without the requirement of bringing the person before a Justice, or even a superordinate police officer. It was routine practice for the detectives themselves to release persons who were not charged. All 14 suspects arrested and not charged were released without being brought before a Justice. None of these suspects were detained longer than three hours. Their arrests did not appear in official records of arrest, although some were noted on follow-up investigation reports as having been investigated.

When a suspect is detained and charged with (1) indictable offences under *Criminal Code* section 483, (2) offences in which there is a prosecutorial option of proceeding either by indictment or by summary conviction, or (3) offences punishable on summary conviction only, the detective or officer in charge has the option to release the accused by way of an appearance notice (*Criminal Code* section 452). This notice is given to the accused, and after the release the notice is supposed to be confirmed by a Justice. If it is confirmed by a Justice, the accused must appear in court on the date specified or face the possibility of a further charge for failure to do so. Among the 52 persons in detective custody who were charged, only three were issued an appearance notice, although eight more could have been released on this basis given the legal provisions.

When persons are in custody and charged with offences as outlined in the last paragraph, or with indictable offences carrying a maximum penalty of five years imprisonment or less, the detective has the option of releasing through a promise to appear form issued by the officer in charge (usually a Detective Sergeant or his equivalent in rank in the uniform branch, the Staff Sergeant) without taking the person before a Justice. A total of six accused were released on this basis (*Criminal Code* section 453). All of these persons could have been released through appearance notices.

When a person is arrested and charged with an indictable offence carrying a penalty of more than five years imprisonment, the detective is required to take the accused before a Justice without unreasonable delay. In doing so, the detectives can seek to have the accused released on an undertaking before the Justice that he will appear in court on a specified date; or, the detectives can seek to have the accused continued in custody for a bail hearing at the earliest possible time. The vast majority (43/52) of accused persons in detective custody were brought before a Justice. On detective recommendations, 23 of these accused were released on an undertaking, including one who could have been released on an appearance notice and two who could have been released on a promise to appear. On detective recommendations, 20 of these accused were continued in custody for a bail hearing. In sum, Justices of the Peace followed detective recommendations in every case.

The use of a promise to appear release by an officer in charge rather than an appearance notice occurred in cases where patrol officers had been involved in making the arrest prior to detective contact with the suspect, and /or in cases involving lengthy in custody questioning of the suspect. For example, in DC 89 two youths were arrested by store security personnei, taken into custody by patrol officers, and turned over to detectives who kept them in custody for a further three hours. Using a readily available officer in charge who would routinely issue the promise to appear made this a practical cover for the detective. Indeed, the appearance notice alternative appeared to have been chosen only when the detectives wanted to give the appearance that the accused was never in custody, (e.g., a summary conviction "indecent exposure" case which was handled by the "dial-an arrest" technique (DC 23)).

In three cases the accused were brought before a Justice of the Peace to be released on an undertaking when they could have been released by the police themselves. In DC 295 the accused was charged with three counts of theft under $200 and one count of possession of stolen property under $200. The accused was interrogated and subject to an extensive search of his residence without warrant or consent. The detective may have been trying to *display* legitimacy for his previous actions to the accused by bringing him before the Justice of the Peace.

In DC 43 and DC 93, the accused were charged with "indecent assault (female)" and could have been released on promise to appear forms, because this indictable offence carries a maximum penalty of five years imprisonment. They were both detained for lengthy periods of interrogation; the accused in DC 43 gave a signed statement that was at most a confession to common assault, and the accused in DC 93 gave a statement but refused to sign it. In these circumstances the detectives may have wanted to cover the lengthy period they held the accused in custody by having the Justice of the Peace validate the release to show an apparent review of their actions. Bringing the accused before a Justice of the Peace was also a more "impressive" means of ensuring the appearance of the accused in court.

The main pragmatic concern of detectives was to complete their dealings with the suspect to their own satisfaction while still being able to create the appearance to possible reviewers that the suspect was not being subject to undue restriction. Detectives indicated in different ways that it looked better at the court stage to have processed the accused person at an early stage after his arrest and to have released him from their custody immediately thereafter.

This view was revealed on DS 62. Three detectives and the Detective Sergeant were talking in the general investigation detective office. Eventually one of the detectives raised a question about a suspect held in custody overnight.

Detective: When was he placed in the cells?
Detective Sergeant: 10:45 last night.
Detective: Holy shit . . .
Detective Sergeant: What's wrong with that? You have 24 hours.
Detective: The longer you hold them in the worse it looks in court. They want to know why there is such a delay before you question him.
Detective Sergeant: [jokingly] Tell them that we let him sleep in—it was Sunday morning!

This view was also revealed in the use of a strategy that allowed both the official release of the accused and the continuation of the investigation with the accused. In DC 152 the suspect had been arrested and held in the cells overnight for detective investigation the following morning. The original offence was "theft under $200" involving building materials taken from a construction site, but the uniform branch apparently suspected him of other offences, and turned him over for detective investigation. The suspect was interrogated for approximately one hour, and was then charged and processed. Following this, the accused was officially released on a promise to appear but remained in the detective's custody for a "consent" search of his residence and further questioning. It was 90 minutes after the promise to appear release that the suspect actually was freed from the detective's direct investigative involvement.

As this case illustrates, detectives had, or created, the means to do what they wanted to do in dealing with the suspect before giving up their control over him. If they had reasons for continued custody they were able to hold the suspect for those reasons even if they could not formulate those reasons officially. Other cases illustrate some of the organizational reasons why detectives prolonged custody.

Holding the suspect in for an extended period of time was sometimes seen by detectives as a form of "summary justice" against the person. For example, in DC 170 the suspect was arrested by patrol officers after being caught siphoning gas from another vehicle. A search of the suspect's car revealed large quantities of tobacco, confections, and electronic equipment, and the suspect was arrested and placed in the cells overnight pending detective investigation. The detectives coming in on the morning shift initially took a casual attitude to the investigation, deciding to go to breakfast before the interrogation because, "he's been in the cells overnight, another hour won't hurt him." After breakfast, the detectives spent one hour checking over the property, interrogated the suspect for 90 minutes, checked with the business where the alleged stolen property originated from, then interrogated the suspect once again. Eight hours elapsed from the time the detectives came on duty until the suspect was released before a Justice of the Peace, but the suspect did not confess and was not charged with any offences beyond the original "theft under $200" (siphoning gas). However, the detectives did seize other property believed to be stolen and also gained the "summary justice" of prolonged detention, even though by their own admission they could lay no further charges because of a lack of evidence that would stand up in court.

The mode of custody and time in custody were also influenced by idiosyncratic elements within the police organization. For example, while dealing with the accused in DC 98 on a series of "break, enter and theft" incidents, the detectives planned to release him on an undertaking before a Justice of the Peace. At one point the more senior detective said to his partner, "We'll release him if he can stay with his minister friend. He doesn't have a police record." However, within ten minutes the detective had changed his mind. The detectives had been perusing their files and thought that the accused probably committed other similar offences in the area which they could uncover through further examination of the general occurrence file. This was not in itself grounds for a change of mind, but combined with the detectives' perception that they did not have time to complete this work on the shift because they were required to attend a compulsory meeting with senior officers. The more senior detective stated, "We'll hold him in to Monday [from Friday] to sort out all the charges—see if any more come in." The detectives knew they could get authorization from a Justice of the Peace for either alternative, and opted for continued custody and a bail hearing in face of the meeting with senior officers.

In DC 89 police organizational elements contributed to prolonged custody of the accused, but saved them from a search of their residence. In this case two suspects were apprehended by a store security officer and turned over to a patrol officer in connection with a series of "theft under $200" (shoplifting) occurrences. The detectives completed the interrogation and processing of the suspects within one hour of being assigned the case, and wanted to follow with consent searches of the suspects' residences. However, one detective was Acting Detective Sergeant while the Detective Sergeant was attending a course for a few hours during the shift. The detective held the suspects for two further hours after they were processed, hoping that the Detective Sergeant would return and free him to undertake the searches. However, when the Detective Sergeant still had not returned within this two hour period, the detective had the suspects released on promise to appear notices and did not undertake the searches or other further investigations.

In this relatively minor case the detective decided that further detention was unwarranted. In contrast, in major cases the main concern of detectives was to take whatever time was necessary to complete their investigations in relation to the particular suspect in their custody. In one case of very prolonged custody (DC 193), the suspect was charged with "attempt rape" and then was interrogated repeatedly by a large number of police officers in relation to a series of "indecent assault (female)" incidents that were of some notoriety in the community and the police department. During the intensive investigative effort against this suspect, one detective stated to the researcher that due to the length of the interrogations and the number of detectives involved, confessions from the suspect would be highly questionable for court admissibility purposes. Nevertheless, the detective stated that this was immaterial compared with what he regarded as the most important task for the police organization, namely solving the highly publicized indecent assault (female) occurrences.

In bringing the accused before a Justice of the Peace to obtain a continuation in custody for a bail hearing or a release on an undertaking, detectives could rely upon the same compliance they received in relation to their applications for warrants. We did not observe any instance in which a Justice of the Peace rejected the detectives' recommendation, whether it was for release on an undertaking or for a bail hearing (for similar findings in a British context, see Bottomley, 1970; King, 1971).

This situation meant that the detectives could use the promise of release as a bargaining lever with the accused without the risk of objection from the Justice of the Peace. For example, in DC 222 (cf. 160) three suspects were arrested by patrol officers in relation to a "break, enter and theft" occurrence. The first suspect interrogated refused to confess and was placed back in the cells. The second suspect immediately co-operated in giving a statement that implicated the other two suspects. This co-operative accused was then released on an undertaking while the other two, who refused to confess, were held in for a bail hearing. The detective was explicit about releasing this co-operative accused because of his assistance, even to the point of noting the accused's co-operation immediately prior to noting the form of release on the follow-up report: "On being interviewed by the investigators, accused proved co-operative. He made a written voluntary statement outlining the whole incident and his part in it. Accused released on Promise given before a Justice. . . ."[33]

When detectives arranged to have suspects held in for a bail hearing they confronted the likelihood that the suspect would be released by a Justice of the Peace at that stage. In contrast to several English studies which report that justices follow police recommendations in refusing to grant bail in the vast majority of cases (Gibson, 1960: 31; Bottomley, 1970: 59; King, 1971: 17-19; Bottoms and McClean, 1976: Ch. 8), our data indicate that Justices at bail hearings often did not follow recommendations for custody but did follow recommendations for "conditions" placed upon the person's activities before conviction. Among the 20 accused held in for a bail hearing, eight were denied bail; four were granted bail at their first hearing; five were granted bail at subsequent hearings; and three waived their right to a hearing, including two who pleaded guilty at this point.

Facing the public and contested nature of bail hearings, detectives were forced into doing information work that would accomplish the outcomes they had in mind. If they did not believe their efforts would be successful, and/or could not be bothered doing the extra work involved,[34] they were likely to choose the route of releasing the accused on an undertaking. If they wanted the accused kept off the streets, or restrictive conditions placed on his presence on the streets, they had to make their case.

In preparing for a bail hearing, detectives had to complete an "Information for Bail Hearing" form. This form "begged" information that could be used to justify official decisions, including information about current charges, other charges for which the accused was before the courts, criminal record, reasons why the accused might not appear in court if released, and reasons why the accused should be held in custody "for good of the community or that he may continue his criminal activity." Detectives proceeded to provide the justifications called for. To the extent that detectives were skilled at doing this, one could expect a high correlation between what they wanted and the decisions of the Justices.

In the cases of 15 accused we obtained the detectives' formulated reasons for wanting the accused held in custody as stated in "Information for Bail Hearing" forms. These included criminal record (3); criminal record and serious offence (2); criminal record and instability (occupational and/or domestic) (4); criminal record, serious offence and instability (2); instability (2); and, serious offence and instability (2). Comparable formulations are enumerated in the study by King (1971: 19), which reports "previous convictions" (criminal record) as the most frequently occurring formulation, followed by "no fixed abode" (instability). (See also LaFave, 1965: 186ff).

The information excluded, included, and formulated in particular ways was directed at creating the worst possible image of the accused, which hopefully could be parlayed into getting continued custody or at least some restrictive conditions. We have already considered this process in the case of the accused in DC 47 (pp. 172-74). Another example involved the two accused in DC 88. In this case, the two accused were arrested by a patrol officer after a CPIC check revealed that one accused was a parolee, and a vehicle search revealed nylon stockings, gloves, a knife and pellet gun that were interpreted by the patrol officer to be equipment for a robbery. The detectives interrogated the suspects and charged each of them with "possession of an offensive weapon." The detectives decided to hold both accused in for a bail hearing. For one accused, the formulation in the bail hearing information was largely in terms of his lack of respectability credits.

[Information for Bail Hearing, DC 88].
Reasons arresting officer has to believe accused will not appear on court date and should be held in custody
1—No permanent residence. One listed is a girlfriend's house who is on welfare herself.
2—He has no job.

. . . . .

Reasons arresting officer has to believe accused should be held in custody for good of the community or that he may continue his criminal activity
1—He has no other means of livelihood other than criminal activity
2—The fact that he has no job, has not held a job for some time, and is living with a girl on welfare would indicate that he has no intention of finding a job
3—His good friend, and co-accused has just been released from prison for trafficking in heroin. Did 20 months for a 5 year sentence.

These formulations were the best the detectives could do in the case of this suspect, and can be contrasted with the formulations in the case of the accused in DC 47, where no mention was made of his employment status because he was steadily employed for several years with one company; and, in the "reasons" section, no mention was made of his status as a married man with two children and continued residence in the area.

The other accused in DC 88 was described by the investigating detectives as someone following a criminal career path. In addition, this was the only "information for bail hearing" that included a verbal statement by the accused as part of the justification for why he may not appear in court.

[Information for Bail Hearing, DC 88]
Reasons arresting officer has to believe accused will not appear on court date and should be held in custody
He is on parole and a conviction will likely result in a jail term. The accused stated that if he gets sent to jail once more he'll go "nuts." He stated that it was so hard for him to adjust to society this last time that he knows one more term will finish him psychologically.
Reasons arresting officer has to believe accused should be held in custody for good of the community or that he may continue his criminal activity
His record indicates he has adjusted to a life of crime, especially the more serious crimes. He spent 20 months of a 5 year term for trafficking in heroin.
The fact that a [pellet] gun, a knife, two nylon stockings and two pairs of gloves were found under the seat of his auto while he was driving would indicate that a robbery had been planned, or was about to be planned.

While detectives did not always accomplish the continued custody of the accused, they always got "conditions" on the person's release which were useful to justify surveillance and the possibility of further charges for a breach. As we learned in the previous section of this chapter, "conditions" were sometimes an end in themselves, as was the punitive aspect ("summary justice") of detaining the accused for a bail hearing. In most cases detectives achieved what they wanted out of the process; in any case, they got at least something they wanted. The same finding emerges as we examine detective involvement in transforming accused persons into convicted persons at the court stage.

Convicting Accused

Transforming accused persons into convicted persons was simply the culmination of the work detectives had done up to this point. Detective work at producing information, charges, and forms of release set the stage for securing a conviction in court. This is not to say that detectives ended their work at the point of giving up their custody of the accused. As we document in this section, detectives were centrally involved in plea discussions with defence attorneys and Crown attorneys that led to out of court plea settlements and court registered convictions without a trial. However, these plea discussions, and the outcomes produced from them, were fundamentally shaped by the way the detectives constructed their cases. It was the detectives who provided the "daily menu" (McBarnet, 1979: 33) for transactions in and out of court, and it was typically not in order for lawyers and other agents of the court to order something that was not on this menu.

The forum within which detectives could confirm their convictions was plea transactions with defence lawyers and Crown attorneys. Within this forum there was mutual collaboration based upon implicit trust that the detectives had screened doubtful cases and had brought forward only those cases in which an accused was guilty of something. The task was to engage in behind the scenes agreement as to what the conviction would be on vis-à-vis its implications for sentence, and then to display in court that this outcome was produced within legitimate principles of formal legal rationality and voluntary decisions by the accused (Balbus, 1973: esp. 18-19; see also Carlen, 1976; Ericson and Baranek, 1981). Detectives, and their "agent collaborators" (cf. Blumberg, 1967), were very accomplished at this task. They transacted in terms of their own sense of justice, and then justified the outcome in terms of formal legal-rational principles of justice.

The plea *transactions* were characterized by coercion, manipulation, and/or negotiation (Strauss, 1978) as the parties attempted to achieve the plea *agreements* they had in mind. Typically, they each got something out of the agreements, resulting in a perception of a plea *bargain*. The detectives could ring up their charge credits, and achieve the satisfaction of having their earlier decisions confirmed as the accused was convicted and made "criminal." The Crown attorneys ensured that they obtained a conviction, along with a predictable range of sentence. The lawyers could usually sell their clients on the idea that they achieved leniency in the form of a reasonable sentence and/or the withdrawal of some charges (Heumann, 1978: 32). In sum, they could each secure their own individual interests while giving the collective appearance that the accused had been given a fair deal.

There is a voluminous literature on the topic of plea transactions (e.g., Newman, 1966; Blumberg, 1967; Church, 1976; Baldwin and McConville, 1977; Heumann, 1978; Vera Institute, 1977; Utz, 1978; Cloyd, 1979). Most of the literature concentrates upon the role of lawyers and prosecutors in the plea transaction process, with little or no attention to police involvement. Since most of these studies have been done in United States jurisdictions, the lack of attention to police involvement may reflect the greater involvement of the American prosectuor in the investigation and charging process, compared with his Canadian counterpart. It may also reflect the fact that most of these studies are based in the courthouse setting, and thus miss the work of police-lawyer-prosecutor transactions outside of that setting.

In Canada, one legal commentator (Ferguson, 1972: 5) speculates that there is little direct police involvement in the plea transaction process because the police are under no administrative pressure to dispose of cases. On the other hand, Klein (1974: 219; 1976) interviewed inmates at Prince Albert (Saskatchewan) Penitentiary and found that in their cases extensive "bargaining" with the police was the norm. However, this included "deals" made directly with the police at early stages in the process, as well as deals during the pre-trial stage in court.

Our research documents the extensive involvement of detectives in the plea transaction process.[35] Detectives were known to be involved in transactions with lawyers operating on behalf of 24 accused persons, and with Crown attorneys in the cases of 19 accused persons.[36] Our task is to consider why detectives were involved in these transactions. Our inquiry focusses upon what the detectives gained from participation in these transactions, and what structural features of the law and organization of the court facilitated their involvement.

Detectives were motivated to take part in the plea transaction process to secure convictions which brought them other benefits. As Newman (1966: 232) points out, the conviction decision is *the* pivotal decision in the process, encapsulating what has gone before and what will follow.

A conviction served to confirm the previous decisions of detectives (cf. Laurie, 1970; Reiss, 1971). It announced within the public, legitimate forum of the court that the detectives were correct in proceeding against the accused.

Secondly, a conviction transacted without a public trial prevented close judicial scrutiny or even questioning of how the detectives constructed their case. If the accused pleaded guilty, judges routinely accepted it without an inquiry into how evidence was obtained or what pressures led the accused to his decision. In general, there appears to be little judicial initiative to review prosecutorial discretion on charge reductions, charge withdrawals, and evidence submissions that may be part of a guilty plea transaction. This leaves the police, Crown attorney and defence attorney the latitude to produce a conviction within their own terms according to their own procedures (Grosman, 1969: esp. 28-30; Klein, 1972; Law Reform Commission, 1976: 21).

Third, working out convictions in plea transactions with defence attorneys and Crown attorneys allowed detectives to perpetuate multiple charging practices, which were one basis of police organizational credit. While detectives knew that in most cases they would only get convictions on some charges, the fact that they could justify more charges at the outset allowed them to secure more clearance by charge credits for case occurrences (for examples, see Ericson, 1980: Ch. 6).

Fourth, participating in the plea transaction process to ensure a conviction on something allowed detectives to avoid the extra work involved in going to trial, (e.g., preparing physical evidence; subpoenaing witnesses and taking statements from them; preparing more detailed reports for court; having to appear in court) (cf. Martin and Webster, 1969). While some of these preparations were sometimes engaged in as a means of "levering" the defence into a guilty plea, the effort was never as much as that required in preparing for a full trial.

Transactions between a Crown attorney and the detectives in DC 85 illustrate the detectives' expectation that everything would be resolved by a guilty plea settlement, and his anger when he found out he might be required to prepare the case for trial. In DC 85 the detective charged two accused with multiple counts of break, enter and theft as well as other property offences. He obtained signed statements of confession from each accused, on each of several counts, and recovered some property in relation to some of the occurrences. The potential for work in subpoenaing all the witnesses, bringing the seized property into court, and preparing more detailed briefs for the Crown attorney for trial was enormous. When the Crown attorney indicated that this work might be necessary, the detective baulked, stating that such work was unnecessary in an obvious case for a guilty plea settlement.

> [Tape recorded conversations in Crown attorney's office. Crown attorney on DC 85 talking with another Crown attorney].
>
> "Look at this one, these guys have done about 900 b and e's, and you get 'expected plea of guilty' [written on the file by the investigating detectives], and you know what that means, there are not going to be any witnesses here, so ah . . . the old pressure is on the play Monty Hall.[37]
>
> . . . . .
>
> [Later, the Crown attorney on DC 85 talked with a third Crown attorney].

"I've got 6 b and e's, 3 mischiefs, a theft under, and a possession. There's no brief on the possession and a big scrawl on the front of the dope sheet, "an expected plea of guilty" and you know, "once upon a time there was a break and enter."

. . . . .

[Later, the Crown attorney on DC 85 asked the two detectives to go through each charge against each accused and give more details. The senior detective became upset and started to complain that "the system" was ridiculous because the accused still had not indicated a plea even though there was seized property evidence and signed written statements of confession useable as evidence against them].

Detective: We got voir dires, we got statements, all kinds of stuff, property galore, it's just ridiculous—

Crown Attorney: We'll just go through one at a time, then—

D: It's an injustice as far as dragging people into court and lawyers don't let us know what they're doing, or if they've retained a lawyer or what they're doing.

. . . . .

[After the detective had detailed some charges]

D: The thing is you know, it's ridiculous, how can you take 10 statements from these guys and then they turn around and walk into court without lawyers or anything else and say they're not pleading guilty. Exhibits, just tons, boxes of exhibits, cigarettes and stuff that were stolen, you know, what do we do, bring 20 people into court and sit around on things like this all day, and carry all these exhibits in and get everything lined up, and then not knowing even what these fellows are doing.

. . . . .

[The Crown attorney then attempted to establish the order of charges for the trial, but the detective baulked and again protested that cooperation was needed among all parties to expedite an "obvious" case for guilty pleas. The detective addressed the Crown attorney:]

D: I don't care what you say . . . no way am I going to get all that fucking work and these guys—assholes—walk into court [with] no lawyers, anything, it's just ridiculous.

Subsequently, the detectives, defence attorneys, and Crown attorney arranged a guilty plea settlement that saved the detectives from the extra work.

The law was an enabling feature of detective participation in the plea transaction process. As previously mentioned in the section on "Charging Suspects," and as documented in detail elsewhere (Ericson, 1980: Ch. 6), the law allows the police to lay multiple charges arising out of the same fact situation, even though a conviction cannot be obtained on more than one charge (see *Kienapple v. The Queen* (1974), 15 C.C.C. (2d) 524 (S.C.C.)). The law also allows multiple charges and conviction on each in related offences, e.g., theft of property and being in possession of that property, or possession of a weapon and use of the weapon (see *Côté v. The Queen* (1974), 18 CCC (2d) 321 (S.C.C.)).

The sentencing structure within the *Criminal Code* is also enabling (see generally Newman, 1966; Buckner, 1967: 130-31; Klein, 1974: esp. 13, 19; Alschuler, 1978). High maximum penalties allow detectives to threaten the accused with grave consequences if he does not cooperate. They also introduce the potential for greater unpredictability in the judge's sentencing decisions, again serving as a threat to the accused. The fact that a guilty plea can be a mitigating factor in the judge's sentencing decisions (*R. v. Johnson and Treymayne*, [1970] 4 C.C.C. 64 (Ont. C.A.)) can favour the inducement of a guilty plea. Concurrent sentencing practices on multiple counts can serve to make the defence worry less about the number of registered convictions and more about shopping for a judge and making submissions to him that will ensure a sentence with predictable severity (Grosman, 1969).

The organization of the courts also facilitates plea transactions, and the primacy of police involvement in these transactions. As we have already mentioned, a guilty plea typically ensures that the judge will make no inquiry into how it was produced, thus leaving detectives to construct a case with a concern only for how it can be "sold" in plea transactions with the defence and Crown attorneys. More fundamentally, the Bench in Canada has done little more than assert their disapproval of "plea bargaining" in individual cases (Cousineau and Verdun-Jones, 1979: 294). This has probably contributed to a belief that the practice is sporadic rather than established and widespread. This belief may in turn be one reason why, in contrast to the United States, there has been no systematic inquiry into the phenomenon which might lead to a developed policy.

Among the detective cases followed through to the point of disposition in court, none were known to have involved judges in plea transactions. However, judges making statements in court indicated that they gave tacit approval to plea transactions worked out among detectives, defence attorneys and Crown attorneys. For example, during a court hearing of DC 228 the judge called an early recess for lunch, stating to the Crown attorney, the lawyer for one accused, and the lawyer for the other two accused: "You're all buddies now—we'll take an early lunch and you can discuss this matter over lunch to expedite this matter." The Crown attorney and two lawyers went out to lunch, and were later joined for a brief period by the investigating detective. They negotiated a plea settlement, which included a reduction to attempted theft from attempted robbery for one accused. After lunch they returned to court, where the pleas were duly registered in accordance with this settlement.

In making their case to the Crown attorney, detectives could rely upon several organizational elements which allow them to effect considerable control. One element was that the Crown attorney was dependent upon detectives for the production and construction of evidence. The detectives were obviously more knowledgeable about the details of a case because they had made it, literally. This made Crown attorneys dependent upon detectives, having to trust the detectives' work in order to get on with their own work (cf. Skolnick, 1966: 179).

At the Provincial Court level, Crown attorneys involved in the cases we studied were generally assigned to a courtroom rather than to a case. In consequence, one case could be worked on by a different Crown attorney at each hearing date. This resulted in a Crown attorney being less informed than he would have been if he was assigned a case at the beginning and followed it through to its conclusion. Typically, a Crown attorney would have 20-25 case files on the morning of the court appearance for those cases without having much detailed knowledge of them. Indeed, in many cases the Crown attorney had not even read the case file by the time he was approached by a defence attorney and/or detective about a possible plea transaction (cf. Montagnes, 1978; Ericson, 1980: Ch. 6). In these circumstances, Crown attorneys were very likely to defer to the judgments of detectives in making a deal for guilty pleas.

In the words of a Senior Crown attorney in another Ontario Judicial District, these working conditions do not allow a Crown attorney to deal "with the question of what *should be* in court," and result in a situation where he must rely "almost entirely on the police to have done the right thing at the beginning" (Rickaby, 1975: 29, quoted by Macfarlane, 1979: 56). It is arguable that these organizational elements, rather than the Crown attorney's caseload pressure *per se,* lead him to routinely accept plea arrangements previously worked out between defence attorneys and detectives.[38]

These organizational elements created a situation where detectives and defence attorneys could mutually benefit from working out a plea settlement, then take it to the Crown attorney for his ratification. As one Crown attorney stated in conversation with researchers, very few lawyers called the Crown attorney's office in advance of the court date to discuss Provincial Court cases.

> [Tape recorded conversation in Crown attorney's office]
> "Might be one out of a hundred [lawyers who call], but ah [even] that's not the case, you know they can call me forever, I don't even have the files here even. You can ask me about an impaired driving coming up on some days and I can tell them what it's about. That happens occasionally, very occasionally, someone calls [name] or somebody calls, or somebody up there and "what's this?" I can tell the lawyer what it's all about. Their form of discovery is on set dates in most cases.

The file, the occurrence should be there at that stage and then the other discovery occurs in the morning of the events. My feeling anyway, now some of the better counsel will talk to police officers about it, because they know we don't know anything about it anyway. And just cut right through the nonsense and say, "Can you tell me what this case is about?" The reasonable police officer will go out, if it's somebody they respect, like, happy to talk to them, 'cause the more they know the more good counsel will plead his people guilty.

Thus, detectives contacted defence attorneys, or waited to be contacted by them, in order to discuss the case the detectives had made and the outcomes they would find satisfactory.[39] The research literature has not dealt with these transactions in detail. Moreover, while rules for defence attorneys issued by their Law Society offer guidance on plea agreements with Crown attorneys, they are silent on defence attorney-police transactions; and, while the police Force procedures manual instructs on dealing with Crown attorneys in withdrawing criminal charges, it is silent on police-defence attorney transactions (Macfarlane, 1979: 55-56). Yet, these transactions were a central feature of the pre-trial settlement process. Lawyers sought evidence disclosure, guilty plea agreements, and information relevant to mitigating sentence. In some cases they also sought the detectives' assistance in selling the case, including plea and sentence recommendations, to the Crown attorney (*ibid.*: esp. 102-109; Ericson, 1980: Ch. 6; Ericson and Baranek, 1981: Ch. 4).

Detective work in producing conviction and sentence outcomes in collaboration with other court actors has already been considered in the previous section on "Charging Accused," and in another volume (Ericson, 1980: Ch. 6). At this juncture we shall offer one additional case example to illustrate the nature of detective-lawyer transactions, the elements conducive to detective control over Crown attorneys, and the influence from the Bench.

In DC 129, the accused was charged with robbery after a complaint that someone had forcibly taken money from a parking lot attendant. Furthermore, the accused was later charged for another robbery, along with an accomplice, after a separate incident which allegedly involved repeated punching of the victim and taking money from him. In this second robbery the accomplice was tried separately, and as a result of negotiations between his lawyer, the detective, and the Crown attorney, entered a guilty plea to theft over $200.

Immediately after this, the lawyer for the accused in DC 129 entered into negotiations with the detective regarding the two robbery charges against his client. They held a meeting in an interview room in the courthouse, and included the accused and his parents in the discussion.

The detective indicated to the lawyer that he was willing to accept a guilty plea to robbery [on the second charge] and theft under $200 [on the first charge] and have all his facts read in. The lawyer expressed his concern that the accomplice was allowed to plead to a theft over $200 on the case in which his client was to plead guilty to robbery. The lawyer indicated that the accomplice was more the violent person in that case because he had done the actual beating of the victim while his client had taken the cash. The lawyer suggested that arrangements be made so that his client could appear in front of the same judge at the time the accomplice was sentenced so that he could be dealt with similarly. The lawyer suggested that if this was not done he would stall for time, have a preliminary hearing and elect trial by judge and jury. The lawyer argued that it was unfair that his client should have a robbery charge in his record while the accomplice would only have a theft over record for the same offence. At this point the detective indicated that he was willing to go to trial but would accept no pleas to anything but robbery for the incident involving the accomplice. The lawyer agreed to the detective's terms as long as his client could appear before the judge who had accepted the accomplice's plea to theft over $200 at the time the accomplice was sentenced. The detective suggested that the lawyer arrange this with the Crown attorney.

The detective then went to see a Crown attorney at the County Court building to discuss the case. He explained the agreement he had reached and added that the lawyer would be asking for an intermittent sentence. The Crown attorney stated, "I can't see anything wrong with that. Tell him that we won't make any promises about time though." Later in the afternoon the detective telephoned the accused's lawyer and told him that the Crown attorney was agreeable to the arrangement.

The accused then appeared in court on the robbery charge arising from the offence he had committed alone and entered a guilty plea to theft under $200. At that hearing the lawyer asked for and received a remand with respect to the trial for the second robbery charge, and for the preparation of a pre-sentence report regarding the theft under $200 conviction. Over the following three days, the lawyer again attempted to have the detective and Crown attorney agree to a guilty plea for theft over $200 on the second robbery charge, but his requests were refused. However, the lawyer persisted and finally obtained the detective's agreement for a guilty plea to theft over $200 on the grounds that his client had played a less active role than the accomplice in this offence and yet the accomplice had already been allowed to plead guilty to theft over $200 rather than robbery. A section of the transcript from an interview with the lawyer reveals his perceptions of the negotiation process, including the key role of the detective.

[Interview with the lawyer for the accused in DC 129]
Researcher: Do you think he should have been charged?
Lawyer: Quite . . .
R: With both robberies?
L: Oh, yes, certainly.

R: There was sufficient evidence in other words?

L: Well, there was not only sufficient evidence, he actually made a confession of it, and gave a written statement to the effect.

         . . . . .

R: And did you at any time prior to the day of trial discuss the charges against your client with the detectives investigating the case?

L: Oh yes. Yes ... several times ... [t]he first time that I discussed the matter in person was at the, uh, was the time in court, and this was before any hearing ... [T]he other conversations were by telephone ... And after that they were personal again.

R: What was your purpose in talking with the detectives?

L: Well, my purpose basically is that I try to, uh—I felt that the charges ought to be reduced.

         . . . . .

L: I think what affected the outcome of the case is that although his co-accused was charged with the same offence that he was, and that's [the second one rather than the first one] they were not heard at the same time. And his co-accused came up first, and his counsel, discussing it with the Crown and one of the investigating officers, felt that that particular charge should be reduced to theft over. And the co-accused in fact pleaded guilty on that date to the theft over. And, uh, what I was rather surprised at when I came to court with my client and found that they did not wish to make the same deal with me as they'd made with the co-accused!

R: That's what you discovered?

L: Yes.

R: But that's what you—you did—you ultimately did get that?

L: Yes, I ultimately got that. It appeared to me that the investigating officer says, well, look, we've made a deal with one of the co-accused. We should have somebody charged with robbery here, and since there's two occasions involving your client, it appears that your client should be the one that should plead at least guilty to one of the charges of robbery!

R: So who did you actually get—persuaded? The Crown or the investigating officer?

L: No, the investigating officer. The Crown in this particular case out in [names town] would make no deal of any nature without the consent of the investigating officers. Although I found the practice opposite in some of the other Provincial Courts, in which the Crown really has the biggest say in what is going to happen. It's usually the

investigating officers who say, "Well, it's up to the Crown
to decide on that, and I'll go along with whatever the
Crown says." However, up in [names town] it appears
that the Crown attorneys change so often that they don't
even know who's going to be on what case until the morning of the trial—that they don't have the time to assess it,
and they won't make any decision without the investigating officers.

. . . . .

L: I . . . intimated that . . . I would elect to go before a higher
court, and I would summon the co-accused into court, and
ask him what, uh, he got for his part in the robbery, and I
don't think that a court should deal with two accused in
different ways.

. . . . .

L: Also, I might say that the investigating officer had advised the Crown that he, uh, well, uh, advised the Crown
that it was okay for him to ask for a light sentence in this
case.

It is evident from this interview that the lawyer perceived the
detective as playing a key role in effecting the settlement of guilty pleas
to reduced charges in conjunction with lenient sentencing recommendations. Prior to the opening of court on the day the second case had
been remanded to for trial, the negotiations were completed in the
Crown attorney's office.

[Tape recorded conversation in the Crown attorney's office]
Crown attorney: Let's go right backwards, listen I'll tell you where I'm
going from right now. [The accomplice's] lawyer has
been chasing me around all morning now saying,
"What the hell's happening on the robbery, what's
happening on the robbery?"—number ____ on the
docket.
Detective: Number ____ on the docket?
C.A.:   Ok, now what is number ____?
D: Number ____ will be the [second] robbery . . .
C.A.:   Now what is happening to that robbery, who has pled
to it?
L: Ah, [the accomplice] has already pled to it.
C.A.:   [The accomplice] has pled to the [second]
robbery . . . ?
L: Yes.
D: Pled as a theft over.
L: As a theft over.
D: He was the aggressor in that particular incident.
C.A.:   As a theft over.

D:	Yes. Our suggestion, only our suggestion is ah . . . [the accused] has pled to the theft [under $200] involved in the first robbery.
L:	First robbery which is theft under, that was last time and there is a pre-sentence report on that.
C.A.:	OK.
D:	I would prefer to concede if you are, if, on the [second] robbery . . . if he pled to theft over with all facts read in, and with his statements of admission entered into evidence.
C.A.:	That's fine with me [detective's first name], you have looked very carefully at the file.
D:	I have read his pre-sentence [report] as well, eh.
L:	Yeah, it's an excellent pre-sentence report there.
D:	I would want them [statements] put into the record.
L:	Yeah. His confession as a matter of fact is a good one because it goes into the question of him ah . . . you know drinking 24 beers that day [laugh].
C.A.:	OK. So the robbery is now going to become a theft over.
L:	Yea.
C.A.:	You're going to plead to that, you want me to read in all the facts.
L:	Right.
D:	Read in all the facts, as well as enter those statements . . .
L:	The facts are in that though he has signed that one so . . .
C.A.:	OK.
L:	And his confession [on the second robbery].
C.A.:	Yes.
L:	OK.
C.A.:	Are you prepared for a sentencing this morning as well?
L:	Yes. Yeah because the pre-sentence report is already made, so it's not going to be any different next time.
C.A.:	What are your feelings about sentence, [detective's first name]?
D:	If he pled to the robbery I'd say time. If he pleads to theft I would like to see maybe two weeks, on weekends.
L:	Yes.
D:	He works for _____, eh?
L:	Yeah, he is a good kid.
D:	I think he should get some time, but I think it should be. . .
C.A.:	Intermittent, weekend type of a . . .

D:	Intermittent weekend, but certainly not, not too excessive, easy, maybe 2 weeks. 2 to 4 weeks.
C.A.:	Alright, as opposed to a fine, or . . .
L:	He is going to make restitution, I think one of the terms should be restitution.
D:	An order of restitution as per ah . . . the figures which will be supplied by myself in future . . .
C.A.:	Alright.
D:	I'll get the exact figures.
C.A.:	Alright, OK, well, when that comes up, sit beside me and tell me exactly what the restitution figures are.
D:	I won't have them exactly, but ah . . . both defence counsel are prepared to accept my figure as ah . . . I will receive it from ah . . .
C.A.:	You are prepared to undertake to accept his figure, when it comes forward?
L:	Yes, yes, I think so. Well, I was thinking about two weeks myself on the matter. I think just the idea of being there for a couple of days is enough to, because he's a good kid . . .

In reaching this settlement, the detective was sensitive to the judicial reaction that might ensue if the Crown attorney was required to argue why the accomplice, who took a more active role in the second robbery, was allowed to plead guilty to theft over $200 while the accused in DC 129 was being tried for robbery. At the earlier trial of the accomplice the judge had questioned in open court the reduction of the robbery to theft under $200, saying there appeared to be clear evidence for the robbery charge. However, the judge then stated that he assumed the Crown attorney knew what he was doing. To have again opened up a judicial questioning of the reduction may have led to a negative judicial reaction which the detective wished to avoid.

As documented in Table 6:2, the vast majority of accused in detective cases were convicted on something. Among the 56 accused persons, 45 (or 80 percent) pleaded guilty to at least one charge against them without contesting their case. Another five persons pleaded not guilty to at least one charge, but only two of these persons (both in DC 88) had their case concluded without a conviction. In sum, 48/56 (87 percent) of the accused were convicted on something. Moreover, if we exclude the two persons who failed to appear for court, and the four persons who were subject to a withdrawal of all charge(s) prior to their trial, we find that 48/50 (96 percent) were convicted.[40]

The fact that many accused had some charge(s) withdrawn is not necessarily an indication that they received a "bargain" in the deal. The detectives' practice of charging everyone for everything possible to set the framework for a deal meant that they often expected charge alterations, including many cases in which they knew that some charges could not be sustained if they went to trial. (See the previous

Table 6:2

Plea, Changes In Charge(s), and Finding for Accused
Persons in Detective Cases

Plea, Changes in Charges, and Finding	N	%
Guilty as originally charged	19	33.9
Guilty to some charge(s) after other charge(s) withdrawn	15	26.8
Guilty to reduced charge(s)	4	7.1
Guilty to some charge(s) after some charge(s) reduced and some charge(s) withdrawn	7	12.5
Guilty to one charge; not guilty to one charge and found not guilty	1	1.8
Not guilty to one charge and found guilty	1	1.8
Not guilty to three charges and found guilty to one charge	1	1.8
Not guilty to one charge and found not guilty	2	3.6
No plea—charge(s) withdrawn	4	7.1
No plea—accused failed to appear bench warrant outstanding	2	3.6
Total	56	100.0

section on "Charging Accused"; Ericson, 1980: Ch. 6; Ericson and
Baranek, 1981: Ch. 2, 3, 4). As Heumann (1978: 34) points out, withdrawn charge(s) in cases where there are guilty plea(s) on other
charges must be seen in terms of the total "package" against the accused. Moreover, the prosecutor can easily manipulate the rate of
withdrawn charges, e.g., by redrawing the information and omitting
the charges that he agreed not to prosecute. No matter how it was
done, the main thing for detectives and the Crown attorney was to get a
conviction on something, resulting in what they saw as a just outcome.

Even in cases involving the withdrawal of all charges against the
accused, the detectives achieved particular aims through their charging practices. In these cases detectives saw charging as an end in itself
in terms of "getting conditions" (of bail) on the person even though they
predicted they could not get a conviction on the original charge; in
terms of the stigmatizing influence of the charge on the accused; and/or
as a lever to use against the accused in obtaining something the detectives wanted from the accused. For example, in DC 80 the victim alleged that when she stopped living with her boyfriend, he kept some
property that belonged to her. The detectives executed a search warrant to recover the property, but the culprit refused to turn over two
items allegedly worth several hundred dollars each. In order to "lever"
the suspect into returning these items, he was charged with "theft over

$200." Subsequently the detectives made an arrangement with the accused's lawyer whereby the property was returned to the victim in exchange for a withdrawal of the charge by the Crown attorney, who readily accepted the arrangement.

As we have seen in examining each point of detective decision-making, they were able to accomplish their ends in a routine manner. This accomplishment was based upon predictions about what collaboration they could expect from the other actors in the process, vis-à-vis the work required to make a case to these other actors that would ensure their collaboration. In the final chapter we review the main elements of this work and discuss its implications for what is made of crime in our society.

NOTES

1. We do not have the space for a full legal discussion of arrest, nor is such a discussion necessary in this context. A thorough legal analysis is available in Freedman and Stenning, (1977: 77ff).

2. For example, see *Higgins v. Macdonald* (1928), 50 C.C.C. 353 at 355; *Regina v. Whitfield*, [1970] 1 C.C.C. 129; 10 Halsbury (3rd ed) p 342, para 631.

3. The *Criminal Code*, section 450 states:

450(1) A peace officer may arrest without warrant
(a) a person who has committed an indictable offence or who, on reasonable and probable grounds, he believes has committed or is about to commit an indictable offence,
(b) a person whom he finds committing a criminal offence, or
(c) a person for whose arrest he has reasonable and probable grounds to believe that a warrant is in force within the territorial jurisdiction in which the person is found
(2) A peace officer shall not arrest a person without warrant for
(a) an indictable offence mentioned in section 483,
(b) an offence for which the person may be prosecuted by indictment or for which he is punishable on summary conviction, or
(c) an offence punishable on summary conviction, in any case where
(d) he has reasonable and probable grounds to believe that the public interest, having regard to all the circumstances including the need to
(i) establish the identity of the person
(ii) secure or preserve evidence of or relating to the offence or
(iii) prevent the continuation or repetition of the offence or the commission of another offence,
may be satisfied without so arresting the person, and
(e) he has no reasonable grounds to believe that, if he does not so arrest the person, the person will fail to attend in court in order to be dealt with according to law.

Section 450(2) was passed as part of the *Bail Reform Act* R.S.C. 1970, Ch. 2 (2nd Supp.). This section places the onus on police officers to justify arrests vis-à-vis the criteria in paragraphs (d) and (e), in what are legally seen as less serious offences.

4. See *Kennedy v. Tomlinson et al.* (1959), 126 C.C.C. 175 (Ont. Ct. App.).

5. *R. v. Biron* (1976), 23 C.C.C. (2d) 513, following *Wiltshire v. Barrett*, [1965] 2 All E.R. 271.

6. *R. v. Brezack* (1949), 96 C.C.C. 97 (Ont. C.A.).

7. Another strategy was to justify arrest on one charge for the purpose of interrogating the suspect on other charges. This was a common practice used by both detectives and by patrol officers (Ericson, 1980: Ch. 1, 6). This is not legally problematic if the detective can show that the charge for which he arrested the person is a "real" charge, even if substantially different; and, if he can show that a caution was given to the accused prior to questioning him about the other offences (cf. Kaufman, 1974: 101-106).

8. This suspect was subsequently interrogated for three hours, including a "consent" search of his residence and vehicle before being released without charge.

9. See *Kennedy v. Tomlinson et al.*, note 4.

10. A. T. Lawrence J. in *R. v. Voisin* (1918), 13 Cr. App. R 89. See Kaufman (1974), esp. p. 101:

> The [British Judges'] Rules now clearly provide (in the preamble) that 'nonconformity . . . *may* render answers and statements liable to be excluded from evidence in subsequent criminal proceedings'. This follows a consistent line of jurisprudence, beginning with the dictum in *R. v. Voisin*, and clearly put by Goddard L.C.J. in *R. v. May* when he held that a statement "made in circumstances not in accordance with the Rules, in law . . . is not made inadmissible if it is a voluntary statement." Canadian courts are not, of course, in any way bound by the Rules, but the Rules do "receive respectful consideration as being a useful guide" [quoting Ostler P.M. in *R. v. Vaupotic* (1969), 70 W.W.R. 128 at 131 (B.C.)].

11. Morris reviews the commentary on this point:

> Fisher, in the *Confait* Report draws attention to the ambiguity implicit in the wording of the caution: 'The second half of the caution ('. . . but what you say may be put into writing and given in evidence') assumes that the person *does* talk and may well seem to a simple person to negative the first part, especially when followed by a question or an invitation to speak.' (p. 188). This latter point is made also by Glasbeck and Prentice (1968): '. . . a caution advising him of his right to remain silent loses much of its authority when immediately followed by persistent questioning' (p. 480) . . . Nor does the caution mention that the suspect may, at his own request, terminate the interview, although this right is implicit in the right to silence.

12. The beginning of the statement form reads as follows (example from DC 228):

You are charged with Robbery [suspect initials]

Do you wish to say anything in answer to the charge? You are not obliged to say anything unless you wish to do so, but whatever you do say will be taken down in writing and may be given in evidence.

I [suspect writes name]

[Detective types] If you have spoken to any other Police Officer or to any other person in Authority in connection with this case, I want it clearly understood that I do not want it to influence you in the making of a statement [suspect initials]

Question) Do you understand what you are charged with and the two cautions that I have just read to you?

Answer) Yeah

Question) The [name of Police Force] is investigating an incident earlier this date in which a cab driver was robbed. What if anything can you tell me of this?

13. Wald *et al.*, (1967: 1550) found that even with the *Miranda* legal requirement of informing the suspect of his right of access to a lawyer, detectives did not state this right to 27/108 suspects. Moreover, suspects were rarely offered access to a telephone to make a call to a third party, although they were rarely denied access if they asked for it:

The detectives virtually never forbade a suspect to use the phone, even when they did not want him to call family or friends. We noted only three such cases. Rather, the common technique was simply not to offer to allow the suspect to make a call, or to make such an offer only after some or all of the questioning had occurred.

14. Suspects may also be "wise" to the fact that the presence of lawyers would make little difference in some cases. Ayres (1970: 277) reports that most lawyers he interviewed in connection with an observational study of detective-suspect interrogations,

felt that their presence in the stationhouse would not have altered the outcome of a later trial. The police usually had overwhelming evidence of guilt when an arrest was made, the lawyers said, and thus the suspects generally had little choice but to plead guilty.

15. See Beck, J. in *Gottschalk v. Hutton* (1921), 36 C.C.C. 298. See generally Freedman and Stenning (1977: 119ff). *Criminal Code* section 103(1) allows a police officer to search the person of a suspect whenever he "believes on reasonable grounds that an offence is being committed or has been committed against any of the provisions of this Act relating to prohibited weapons or restricted weapons." The *Narcotic Control Act* R.S.C. 1970, Chap. N-1 section 10(1) allows a police officer to:

(a) without a warrant enter and search any place other than a dwelling-house, and under the authority of a writ of assistance or a warrant issued under this section, enter and search any dwelling-house in which he reasonably believes there is a narcotic by means of or in respect of which an offence under this Act has been committed;
(b) search any person found in such place; and
(c) seize and take away any narcotic found in such place . . .

As we discussed in relation to arrest, the definitions of "reasonable grounds" and "reasonable belief" are open to wide interpretive latitude, and they can easily be constructed retrospectively if evidence is found. See note 16.

16. See Skolnick (1966: esp. 224) for an analysis of factors within the police occupational culture, including the pragmatic orientation of detectives, which deflect the potential for control of the American exclusionary rule.

17. The construction of the case against the accused in DC 47 is described and analyzed in more detail in the following section entitled, "Charging Suspects."

18. A similar "success" rate, with similar explanations exists in the area of police applications for judicial authorization for "electronic surveillance." According to the *Toronto Globe and Mail,* 9 January, 1980, "Police in Ontario were granted 265 authorizations for electronic bugging in 1978 for possible offences under the Criminal Code, a 19 percent increase from the previous year. An annual report by Attorney-General Roy McMurtry says none of the 237 applications for authorizations of wiretaps or 28 applications for renewed electronic eavesdropping was refused by the Ontario judges who heard them in secret." (See also the editorial comment, "The Perfect Ones," *Toronto Globe and Mail,* 12 January 1980; Mann and Lee (1979: 170-71).

19. See *R. v. Moore* (1922), 63 D.L.R. 472 (Alta. C.A.) at 473:

Clearly what the statute requires is not merely that the constable is to have information which justifies him in making an oath that he has reasonable ground for belief, but that the magistrate himself should be satisfied by information on the oath of an officer that there is (in fact and in truth) reasonable ground for belief upon which the magistrate, in his discretion, may grant a warrant . . . Discretion in the Act must mean judicial discretion and I am at a loss to see upon what ground (the justice of the peace) can exercise proper discretion without some specific facts to guide him. Otherwise it seems to me he is nothing more than an automaton in the hands of the constable, which was surely not intended that he should be.

20. In the "old days" before the new police, the system of private justice was particularly advantageous to the Justices:

'The greatest criminals in the town,' Horace Walpole had written in 1742, 'are the officers of justice. There is no tyranny they do not exercise, no villainy in which they do not partake' ... The degradation which the office of constable underwent in London and other towns in the eighteenth century, was made all the worse by the corruption of the urban justices. The honest exercise of a justice's functions was such a disagreeable business in large towns, and so full of risk for those who were not expert in the law, that very few persons of standing would undertake it ... [T]he general body of their Worships was composed of ignorant and often rapacious individuals. Many tolerated and encouraged disorder as a source of income, and sold warrants and summonses like articles of commerce, their houses or offices being known as 'justice shops.' Moylan (1929: 11).

21. See McRuer, C.J. in *R. v. Washer* (1947), 92 C.C.C. 218 (Ont.):

The question is always one of discretion resting on the trial Judge, and that is a discretion to be exercised with great caution." And, earlier, "The question of whether a statement made by an accused person when in custody charged with a crime is admissible or not is always to be determined in the particular circumstances of the case."

22. See Freedman and Stenning (1977: 146-47):

It used to be thought that in Canada the courts had a discretion to exclude even statements which were technically admissible as voluntary, if they had been obtained in some manner which the courts felt was somehow "unfair" to the accused. In *R. v. Wray*, [1970] 4 C.C.C. 1, however, the Supreme Court of Canada made it clear that judicial discretion can virtually never be used in this way to exclude admissible confessions. The court said that judicial discretion could only be used to exclude evidence 'the admissibility of which is tenuous and whose probative force in relation to the main issue before the Court is trifling,' and when the admission of such evidence would be 'gravely prejudicial to the accused'. This is the only test of 'unfairness' which the Courts may apply in exercising their judicial exclusionary discretion [[1970], 4 C.C.C. 1, at 17 (per Martland, J.]. Clearly, confessional statements by an accused will rarely, if ever, meet this test, since they will almost always be of more than 'trifling probative force' in relation to the issue of the accused's guilt or innonence.

23. *R. v. Lawrence* (1949), 7 C.R. 464 (Ont.) McRuer, C.J.:

Where the discovery of the fact confirms the confession—that is, where the confession must be taken to be true by reason of the discovery of the fact—then that part of the confession that is confirmed by the discovery of the fact is admissible, but further than that no part of the confession is admissible.

24. Detectives are instructed to isolate a suspect from settings (e.g., his home) where he may feel more aware of his rights and have others to offer moral support. "In his office, the investigator possesses all the advantages. The atmosphere suggests the invincibility of the forces of law." (O'Hara, 1956, cited in the *Miranda* decision and noted by Wald *et al.*, 1967: 1534n).

25. As discussed in Chapter 2, we were excluded from systematic access to interrogations. The researchers were present for the *entire* interrogation of only nine suspects although they were able to witness parts of other interrogations, and to overhear some or all of still others.

26. In performing this trick, detectives were following the "bible" of the interrogation art, Inbau and Reid (1967: 66):

> Where the case is one of a theft of money or property by means of larceny, embezzlement or burglary, the interrogator should refer to the reported loss in terms of just about double or triple the actual amount involved ... The interrogator should then suggest that the actual amount of the loss may be much less than reported, that perhaps nothing but money was taken, or that the person or company reporting the loss may be trying to cheat the insurance company covering the risk by adding to the loss actually sustained.

27. As Inbau and Reid (1967: 107-08) suggest, it may be just as useful to make up a test that will deceive the suspect. They suggest the threat of a "truth serum" test. If the suspect refuses, this can be taken as an indication of guilt. If the suspect agrees, another round of deception must be entered into: "If a subject does ultimately agree to take a truth-serum test, the interrogator can then resort to an impressive pretense of trying but failing to arrange for a test at that time."

28. The *Criminal Code* states that the charge of "possession" requires knowledge that the item was stolen (section 312), and carries a maximum penalty of two years imprisonment "where the value of what comes into his possession does not exceed two hundred dollars" (section 313b).

29. Even police administrators do not hide the fact that the presumption of guilt has displaced the presumption of innocence in Anglo-American legal jurisdictions. For example, Sir Robert Mark, former Commissioner of the Metropolitan London police, is quoted as stating:

> The procedural safeguards for the suspect or accused in our system of criminal justice are such that committal for trial, involving the participation of lawyers and bench, is itself an indication of strong probability of guilt.

[Quoted by Alderson and Stead, 1973: 16; McBarnet, 1976: 175].

30. For example, a Connecticut prosecutor related his orientation to Heumann (1978: 104):

> Say an old lady is grabbed by a kid and knocked to the ground and her pocketbook taken as she is waiting for the bus. We'd be as tough as anybody on that one, whether you call it a breach of the peace or a rob-

bery. We'd be very tough. And in this case there would be a good likelihood of the first offender going to jail, whatever the charge we give him. The name of the charge isn't important. We'd have the facts regardless.

31. This stated strategy was not carried out. Immediately after the shift on which this statement was made, this detective was transferred out of the general investigation unit. The other detective made no attempt to contact the suspect, and eventually "filed" the occurrence. This disposition was justified by reference to the evidence problems.

32. Essential parts of this Act are included in the *Criminal Code*, Part XIV. For references on this Act, see Scollin (1972), Ontario Crown Attorney's Association (1976).

33. The nature and extent of "bail bargaining" from the accused's viewpoint is documented by Bottoms and McClean (1976: 200ff) and Ericson and Baranek (1981: Ch. 2).

34. In the study by King (1971: 41), it was found that "Almost twice as much information was given when the police raised objections to bail compared to those cases where they did not oppose bail or expressed no view either way." This suggests the extra "information work" involved in making a case for custody.

35. Documentation on this involvement is provided in a number of studies connected with the research programme at the Centre of Criminology, University of Toronto, including Ericson (1980), Ericson and Baranek (1981), Macfarlane (1979), Macfarlane and Giffen (1981), and Wilkins (1981).

36. "Known" transactions were ascertained from any available data within the research programme at the Centre of Criminology, University of Toronto, especially lawyer interviews and tape recorded conversations in the Crown attorney's office. These figures likely underreport the total number of instances in which detectives were involved in plea transactions. In the research programme sample as a whole, which included cases generated by patrol officers (Ericson, 1980), as well as cases generated by detectives in the present study, lawyers reported plea transactions with Crown attorneys in the cases of 53/80 accused, and with the police (mainly detectives) in the cases of 31/80 accused. All but four cases of plea transaction involving the police also involved a Crown attorney. Lawyers said they had *some discussion* with the police in two-thirds of the cases (Macfarlane, 1979: 85).

37. Monty Hall is the name of the host on a former television "quiz" programme called "Let's Make a Deal."

38. In this connection, Heumann (1978: esp. 28-30) makes a compelling argument that case load pressure is not a cogent explanation for the high volume of cases disposed of by guilty pleas. Heumann provides historical documentation from the State of Connecticut to show that most cases have always been disposed of by guilty pleas, even in periods when case volume pressures were not apparent.

39. Sanders (1977: 127) reports that the California detectives he observed would initiate these discussions at a very early stage: "In cases where the suspect did not cop out, the detectives would often work with the defence lawyer to get a confession."

Skolnick's (1966: 133) observations in Oakland, California revealed that detectives constructed their written case accounts with a sensitivity to the likelihood that defence attorneys would scrutinize them and use them in their transactions:

> The State's rules of criminal discovery are interpreted in Westville [Oakland] as obliging the prosecutor to permit the defence to examine police arrest reports. Consequently, the police do not report as the significant events leading to arrest what an unbiased observer viewing the situation would report. Instead they compose a description that satisfies legal requirements without interfering with their organizational requirements.

40. Most studies report high rates of conviction. McBarnet (1976: 172) reports a Scottish conviction rate of 91% for all cases (1974); an English rate of 82% in Crown Courts and 94% in Magistrates courts; and a Sheffield rate of 98.5% in Magistrates courts based on the study by Bottoms and McClean (1976). In the United States, Heumann (1978: 28) reports that in the Connecticut Superior Courts from 1880-1954, "The mean percentage of trial to total disposition ratio . . . is 8.7 percent." His contemporary observational study in three Connecticut court jurisdictions confirms these historical data. In a study in New York City, the Vera Institute (1977: 133) documents "a system dominated by plea bargaining, in which only 2.6% of the cases ended in trial." In Canada, Friedland (1965: 89) reports that 69% of the accused persons in his sample drawn from the Toronto Magistrates Courts pleaded guilty.

Chapter 7

Conclusions and Implications: Crime as Detective Property

In this chapter we summarize what has gone before in order to make conclusions with implications for what might come next. This exercise entails relating the data to our theoretical interests, and using both data and theory to inform questions of policy.

Crime as Detective Property

We have examined detective work in terms of the working ideology and attendant actions of its practitioners. Detectives work within organizational structures which allow them to get the job done in ways that can be routinely justified and made legitimate to the various audiences they deal with. Detectives have relative autonomy within the police organization; an array of enabling laws at their disposal to formulate their actions; and, a positional advantage in the court organization which allows them to have influence on outcomes through informational control vis-à-vis a set of rules within which they can formulate their case. Together, these elements assist detectives in making their working environment predictable, and their work of making crime and criminals routine. Detectives are able to make cases of citizen conflict the property of the crime control organization, and especially of the police organization, serving their interests as well as, and sometimes instead of, the interests of the citizen (Christie, 1977; see also Law Reform Commission, 1974: esp. 20-21).

Of course, we have not argued that detectives can do whatever they please. Detectives work within limits, using a restricted range of organizational rules to ensure that what they do can be made justifiable. Within these limitations detectives proceed to make what they can of their cases.

The many questions concerning how detectives do their work all relate to central questions concerning control of the process. Who controls the process? How is this control accomplished? What is achieved from this control? This is essentially a matter of discretion or power, defined in terms of the relative autonomy of detectives vis-à-vis the organizational influences they must take into account, and which they must make part of their accounts. Theoretically, this matter is central to sociological concern with how social control is related to the reproduction of social order. Politically, this matter is important in considering the extent to which citizens can make their daily lives predictable, experiencing both the feeling of security and actual security within the framework of a police and criminal law process that does not interfere in unpredictable, uncontrollable, unjust ways. As Holdaway (1979: 11) states in his introduction to a collection of contemporary articles on policing, "The central historic policy issues remain: who controls the police, how can the police be rendered effectively accountable?"

Our theoretical interest in control, and our epistemology based in social action theory, have relevance to these policy questions. We do not conceive detectives as automatons who simply respond to the stimulus of organizational influences. We view detectives as having an interpretive capacity, able to take into account organizational influences in the formulation of action that reflects these influences. This introduces a volitional element. This element serves as an analytical device, but also suggests a value preference. In allowing for the human capacity to make choices within a limiting framework of "causes," volitional sociology has a political character because it suggests that one's subjects could have acted otherwise.

> If sociology allows for a choice on the part of human actors, then it can blame, by the way it assigns causes, any of the people involved, since they could have chosen not to do what they did. This has consequences for the political character of sociological analysis. Volitional sociologies perform this service for the heros they identify.
> (Becker and Horowitz, 1972: 58).

Of course, the criminal law process itself "operates *as if* human beings have free choice" (Packer, 1968: 132; see also 74-75). In doing so, it is aimed at bolstering ideals that are "far more significant than even the prevention of socially undesirable behavior" *(ibid.).* The inclusion of choice allows imputation of responsibility, and this imputation is central in deciding what control (punishment) should be meted out (Ericson, 1975: Ch. 5). Just as criminal offenders are treated as if they operate with freedom of choice within the limiting conditions of their social circumstances, so detectives and other criminal control agents can be treated as if they operate with freedom of choice within the limiting conditions of their organizational circumstances. They are responsible for their actions and must be judged accordingly.

Our research has described and analyzed the process by which detectives make events into crimes and people into criminals. Detectives, and the organization on whose behalf they operate, should be held responsible for what they make. As Manning (1977: 7-8) points out, most members of the public see the police as makers of crime and hold them responsible for it.

Although people are aware of an enormous range of private definitions of "crime," "order," the "law" and "immorality," they grant to the police legitimacy in providing operational definitions of these phenomena, and they defer in large part to police definitions of crime and the law. Official information about crime and deviance, as a result, is now considered equivalent to the available information on crime and deviance in the society (J. Douglas, 1971: 68ff). Consequently, the public seeks to hold the police, and not the society at large, responsible for what they define as a rise in crime and lawlessness. Perhaps more accurately it could be said that the public alternates between a scapegoat theory of crime (often accepting police projections about the causes of crime, such as 'the economic situation' or 'drugs' or 'permissiveness') and blaming the police for failing to control it.

The research we have undertaken helps us to understand the choices that detectives make, and therefore can enlighten us on where and to whom we should allocate blame and impute responsibility. By examining detective work with reference to the organizational frameworks within which this work is carried out, we can appreciate that much of what detectives do is framed by conditions (e.g., low visibility) and structures (e.g., police organizational, court organizational, and legal rules) which are not of their own making. At this juncture it is worthwhile to review these elements so that we can have them in mind whilst addressing their implications for the control of detective work.

The rules detectives used were bound in with their accounts of their actions for official purposes. The rules which applied or could be applied were taken into the account, literally, as the detectives formulated a case outcome. They had considerable autonomy in doing this, within the range of legitimate justifications organizationally available, because of the low visibility conditions of their work.

Detectives were subject to police organizational rules, but these were translated and integrated into their everyday working practices. The governing rules among their fellow detectives sustained practices that "got the job done" while defining the limits of tolerable "easing" behaviour in relation to the administration. The demands of supervisory officers had to be taken into account, especially at the stage of mobilizing a case and at the stage of providing a written justification for the disposition of a case. At the point of mobilization this was not problematic because detectives shared with their supervisors the need for immediate and sustained attention to cases with suspects in custody, identifiable suspects and/or serious allegations. The only minor disagreements at this point concerned cases in which supervisors ordered special attention for "PR" purposes. At the point of case disposition, there were also few problems because detectives had mastered the range of accounts that would make their decisions acceptable to their supervisors. In general Detective Sergeants were treated as colleagues whose opinion might be sought in certain matters, and ignored if it did not accord with the way in which the detectives wished to make their case.

Similarly, while the rules of the court and its agents were taken into account by detectives, there was little direct court supervision over what detectives did in making their cases. Crown attorneys were rarely consulted in the initial laying of charges. The organization of Crown attorney work, which often led to the same case being worked on by different Crown attorneys at different court hearings, meant that Crown attorneys regularly deferred to detective judgements about "the facts" and what charges could and should be sustained from them. With most accused pleading guilty, there was little attention from the Bench as to how and why that outcome was produced. While detectives were undoubtedly controlled by feeling that they had to work within the expectations of the Crown attorney and the Bench, typically they knew how to show conformity with these expectations while still making what they wanted out of their cases.

As stressed in our introductory comments in Chapter 1, detective work has always been information processing work. Moreover, in the vast majority of cases this did not involve lengthy and painstaking effort at gathering physical clues, interviewing witnesses, and generating informants. Rather, it involved relying upon established sources and techniques to obtain information, and the use of resourcefulness and recipe knowledge to make the information into a justifiable basis for a particular case disposition. As enumerated in Chapter 3, detectives spent most of their time generating information and producing written accounts from it. Their actions were oriented primarily to producing accounts of their actions to the various audiences they were called upon to deal with. These accounts were prospectively planned for by making predictions about what would be a justifiable case outcome, and retrospectively constructed from the raw material of information received to dispose of the case.

In dealing with victim-complainants, detectives had to work matters so that the case became police "property" (cf. Christie, 1977) and yet appeared to be worked on behalf of the victim-complainant's interests. The rules for accomplishing this work were derived from the occupational culture of fellow detectives.

When nothing could be done within the framework of detective operations, detectives would "file" the case. If detectives had no significant investigative priorities, or the victim-complainant was ascribed a special status, or the victim-complainant made inquiries, the detectives would "PR" a case of this type, providing a gloss that "real detective work" was being done in order to cool out the victim-complainant.

When detectives were uncertain if anything could be done, they sometimes sought further information from victim-complainants. This information could be used to pursue further investigation. Alternatively, if detectives perceived that they were being used (i.e., that they were becoming "property" to be used on behalf of the victim-complainant's personal troubles), they sometimes "unfounded" the case and thereby defined it out of their "crime work" sphere of operation.

In still other cases the detectives had a definite disposition in mind and sought victim-complainant cooperation to justify this disposition. Sometimes the disposition was decided in advance because detectives used the victim-complainant's case as property to trade off for other commodities of value to the police organization. In other cases the detectives decided upon a non-charge disposition to save the time and· effort involved in prosecuting a case that was in their mind justifiable but questionable. In these cases detectives sometimes gave different accounts to different interested parties. Victim-complainants were manipulated into accepting the detective's disposition for the case (e.g., "caution" rather than "charge" of the suspect), and then referred to by the detective in his written police organizational justification for the disposition (e.g., "cautioned" on the basis of the "victim's wishes").

In sum, detectives and victim-complainants sometimes shared the case as property, each obtaining mutual advantage by what the detectives did with it. However, when detectives defined the case as *entirely* the victim-complainant's property it was "unfounded," deemed not to be a "crime" and therefore not a matter for detectives. On the other hand, when the case was taken over and used *entirely* as detective property to deal with other matters, it remained within the detectives' sphere of "crime" work.

Detective dealings with suspects and accused persons had similar elements to their dealings with victim-complainants. The only major difference was the more direct relevance of legal rules in dealing with suspects and accused persons. Legal rules relating to the control of suspects (arrest, access to a third party), the use of suspects in the production of information (right to silence, search, interrogation), charging suspects, conditions for the release of suspects, and producing convictions in court, enabled detectives to maintain considerable autonomy in transforming suspects into accused, and accused into convicted "criminals." This work was also facilitated by rules within the occupational culture (e.g., pertaining to interrogation techniques). It was also enabled by the rules of the court organization whereby Justices of the Peace routinely dispensed what detectives asked for, and Crown attorneys routinely deferred to detective judgements about plea settlements worked out with defence attorneys.

In dealing with suspects and accused, detectives maintained a tight control on the case as police property. Suspects and accused could only benefit from this property by giving the detectives other property which they valued (e.g., information about other suspects and suspected activity) in exchange for concessions from detectives; or, by allowing the detectives to gain what they wanted from the property they had (e.g., agreeing to plead guilty in exchange for charge reductions, charge withdrawals, sentence recommendations, etc.). While suspects, accused, and their lawyers occasionally perceived a bargain in this process (see Ericson and Baranek, 1981: Ch. 4), detectives knew that in making these deals they were not decreasing the profitability of their enterprise.

In summary, a central message of our research is that cases became the property of detectives on behalf of the police organization and the supporting agencies of crime control. As detectives exercise their property rights over a case, the case becomes transformed with reference to the organizational structures which pertain (the occupational culture of detectives, as it filters community organization, police organization, court organization, and legal criteria). This process was designed to meet the needs of the citizenry, and it often does. This process did meet the needs of detectives, facilitating their working designs.

Again, we emphasize the transactional nature of the process. We do not argue that detectives typically acted unilaterally and coerced whatever outcomes they had in mind. They were interdependent with the patrol branch, influenced by the way patrol officers formulated their accounts of incidents and by the capability of patrol officers to apprehend or at least identify suspects. They were interdependent with informants who, whether acting on behalf of organizations or as individuals, were defined solely in terms of what informational commodities they had to offer detectives in exchange for being able to use some aspect of the police as property. They were interdependent with victim-complainants who also controlled vital information and could use it in exchange for the use of the police as property. They were interdependent with suspects and accused, whose compliance eased the task of making a case that would yield convictions without the public contest of a trial.

All of these transactions had the potential for being characterized by coercion, manipulation, and/or negotiation *from all sides.* However, the conclusion from our work is that detectives had the upper hand in most transactions. This conclusion may in part be a reflection of the fact that we have concentrated upon the process from the viewpoint of detectives, and we have therefore emphasized their strategic powers because we know most about them. If we scrutinized cases from the viewpoint of informants, suspects, accused persons, lawyers and Crown attorneys, we might well have discovered some ways in which they manipulated and coerced detectives. In response to this, we can state that we did observe persons in these roles as they dealt directly with detectives, and their responses form part of our observations. Moreover, related research on some of the detectives' cases also suggests that the detectives often had the upper hand (Ericson and Baranek, 1981 on the accused; Macfarlane, 1979; Macfarlane and Giffen, 1981 on lawyers). Furthermore, our analysis of the structure of the law, court organization, and police organization, and of citizen deference to the authoritative aura of the detectives' office, suggests that criminal process structures are explicitly designed to give detectives the upper hand. Detectives, as rational and pragmatic actors, simply make innovative use of the resources that have been given to them to control the process.

Within the organization of the criminal process, discretion varies inversely with formal status. Detectives have effective control over the process because of their positional advantage in relation to other agents and agencies. Their control over information production, selection and use allows detectives to substantially influence what becomes a "crime" and who becomes a "criminal." This is of major importance in understanding the way the criminal process differs from the way it is conceived by some socio-legal theorists.

The principle of legality is supposed to function to provide effective limits on the power of State agents to judge and punish. However, as we have seen, many laws are written and used in a manner which enable detectives to do what they want to obtain what they want. Detective practices are facilitated further by the low visibility conditions of their work, which allow them to be *the* definers of reality about a case, and to construct "facts" about the case which are treated as legitimate because they take into account the rules which are supposed to govern the process. In sum, detectives are typically able to work *within* the legal provisions of their office to accomplish their mandate. These legal provisions, and the other organizational elements we have analyzed, help to ensure that in conjunction with their patrol officer colleagues (cf. Ericson, 1980), detectives have great power to judge and punish.

There is no statutory duty in Canada for full enforcement of the law (Cameron, 1974). However, it seems to be part of popular belief, fuelled by the way police organizations "sell" their work to obtain more resources (Ericson, 1980: Ch. 7), that law enforcement is "full" according to the criteria outlined by Goldstein (1960):

> Minimally, then, full enforcement, so far as the police are concerned, means (1) the investigation of every disturbing event which is reported to or observed by them and which they have reason to suspect may be a violation of the criminal law; (2) following a determination that some crime has been committed, an effort to discover its perpetrators; and (3) the presentation of all information collected by them to the prosecutor for his determination of the appropriateness of further invoking the criminal process.

Our data clearly indicate that many reported events were not investigated; many events made into "crime" involved no effort to discover the perpetrators; and, information was very rarely presented to the Crown attorney before detectives had charged an accused and planned a prosecution. In brief, detectives did not even attempt full enforcement. They enforced selectively, in the context of organizational criteria.

The concept of full enforcement, and its corollary "underenforcement," are only meaningful within a legalistic perspective. When we understand detective work organizationally, as we have done in this book, we realize that these concepts are not helpful because their realization is impossible (and probably undesirable). As Manning (1977: 248-49) argues:

> Since rules are always embedded in ambiguity and surrounded by the opinions of conflicting publics, officials are constantly adjusting to the enforcement problem in expedient terms—by applying the rules at their disposal to the advantage of their organizations and to themselves (Merelman, 1969) . . . [M]ost rule enforcement persists as a practical option because it is useful for enforcement agencies . . . The term "underenforcement" is misleading because it assumes a legalistic perspective in which all laws are to be enforced all the time against all violators. This is a dramaturgical fiction meant to serve as a deterrent and is not the practice in law enforcement nor the expectation of the courts. Underenforcement tends to occur in the case of low-visibility violations (few people are aware of their occurrence) and where there is little chance that non-enforcement will "come back"—that someone will complain, demand an arrest, or make public the delict (LaFave, 1965). In other words underenforcement can be seen as a matter of dramatic necessity—the events provide too few of the materials required for a potent performance that will be available to significant audiences.

The concepts of full enforcement and underenforcement also lack meaning when we consider the meaning of "crime" as it was constituted in the work of the detectives we studied. The majority of cases (59 percent) were "filed" by detectives, usually after little or no investigative effort. While these cases officially stood as "crimes," it was usually only because a patrol officer and/or detectives accepted the account of the victim-complainant that what he said occurred did occur. There was no extensive investigative effort which might have led detectives to "unfound" the case, or to transform it into quite a different matter. A further 20 percent of cases were cleared by "caution" of a suspect and/or made "unfounded" by detectives. Many of the cases involving "cautioned" suspects apparently lacked evidence for a charge, and could have been classified as "no crimes" along with the "unfounded" cases. The other 21 percent of the cases resulted in clearance by charging a suspect. Only in this small minority of cases was evidence made public (i.e., reported to other actors in the process) to justify a "crime" designation. However, even in some of these cases, detectives charged predicting that they did not have the evidence to secure a conviction; their charges were directed at securing other ends, such as bail release conditions. In the vast majority of cases, what was made of the case remained within the exclusive preserve of the detectives and their organizational accounting system.

These findings allow us to appreciate that what detectives make of cases can only be meaningfully understood with reference to the organization of their work, and especially the organization they work for. Among other things, this appreciation allows us to understand what goes into the making of information which senior police administrators and other politicians use for other purposes. Ironically detectives, and the organization on whose behalf they operate, help to make the very thing they are supposed to combat. The most fundamental way in which they control the process is to make, literally, what can be subject to control by others.

Prospects for Change

Within the present organization of the criminal process there is a certain inevitability to police control of it. This can lead to a tendency to accept the inevitable, rather than asking what alternatives can be imagined, and perhaps made feasible. It is not our intention to explore all possible alternatives in every detail, a task that would require at least another volume. However, we wish to address some of the well known arguments for alternatives and the issues they entail.

As one should be able to appreciate in reading this book, we are dealing with matters of importance to all citizens. The police have an extremely influential role in defining the relation of the State to society (Hall, *et al.*, 1978; Taylor, 1980). They are supported in this role by powers that are granted to them alone, powers which can be used to disrupt freedom and stigmatize. What the police do in using these extreme powers over citizens is a barometer of dealings with citizens by other State agents in lesser exercises of authority. Indeed, in this role the police, supported by the other agents of the criminal process, are responsible for reproducing the State's reputation as a moral agent. In turn, this is a means by which those at the upper end of society's scheme of things maintain their legitimacy and hegemony (cf. Ignatieff, 1978: 167).

We are unlikely to experience a fundamental change in the police without a fundamental change in the inequality structure that supports them. Even if this came about, we would end up with a new police supporting a new status quo; and, the new status quo would in turn support their police by creating enabling conditions for police work (cf. Thompson, 1979: 325). Moreover, we know that the transitional period in changing the status quo can result in particularly brutal and arbitrary acts (as witnessed by contemporary events in Iran); and, we also know that "new sensibilities" about egalitarian forms of State control have resulted in repressive policies when put into practice by a new status quo (as witnessed in the Soviet Union) (cf. Cohen, 1979; Downes, 1979).

If we accept the existing status quo, we are faced with the dilemma that "order breeds not peace of mind but greater anxiety and recurring demands for more order" (Ignatieff, 1978: 218; see also Taylor, 1980). The perpetual demand for more "policing" of every type has been a feature of our society over the past two decades, and it has been met with an enormous expansion of the "crime control industry" along with other forms of State control over the population (Foucault,

1977; Friedenberg, 1980). This escalation of the "war on crime" in Canada has yet to realize its limits (Ericson, 1980). It is fuelled by reference to vague criteria such as "order" and "security," concepts which are well suited to escalation because they are elastic, they carry a virtuous ring, and they contain a built-in self-justification: who can object to a people's efforts at maintaining order and preserving security? (cf. Black, 1977: 11), quoted in Chomsky and Herman, 1979: 5).

An alternative to this conservative reaction is the liberal call for a toleration of diversity. Thus, liberal legal scholars state that, "One purpose of the criminal law ought to be to protect as much deviant behavior as society can tolerate" (J. Goldstein, cited approvingly by Griffiths, 1970: 367n; see also Packer, 1968). This has been echoed by liberal social scientists, especially those within the labelling or social reactions school (e.g., Schur, 1973; Ericson, 1975: Ch. 5), but also by those who are apparently further to the left (Taylor, et al., 1973, 1975). The problem with this approach is that what first appears as greater enlightenment leading to a more tolerant approach can end up being more punitive (Cohen, 1979). For example, deinstitutionalization of inmates can cause greater problems for both society and ex-inmates, unanticipated by liberal rhetoric (Scull, 1977); and, calls for an "enlightened" view of particular substantive offences can lead to proposals for legal change which indicate a more punitive reaction against the target population (e.g., the "rape" issue, cf. Clark and Lewis, 1978).

Obviously, there are problems with any move that is made. In light of this, any move must be made with caution, taking into account what we know about similar moves that have been made in other jurisdictions, and in other spheres of organizational life.

In terms of the control of police discretion or power, we must recognize that no matter what changes are attempted, police officers will still have some latitude for choice. The task is to have police officers operate within an acceptable range of choices, putting limits on what they can do in the context of those interests we wish them to serve (cf. Cameron, 1974: 46-47; Thomas, 1974: 139). Of course, there have been recurring attempts to do this employing various approaches, including revision of legal rules, changing the organization of the court, and altering the administration of police forces to incorporate a "professional" orientation with well trained officers.

The procedural and substantive criminal law have always been seen as a bulwark of police power, and there have been repeated calls to maintain and enhance the enabling elements. Beattie (1977: 49, citing *British Colonist*, 6 February 1846: 3) quotes a letter to a newspaper editor in Upper Canada in 1846 regarding the need for greater powers of search:

> Now were the law here in this respect as it is in Scotland, that a *general* search warrant could be issued, society would be purged of these pests ["thieves"] ... The objections that could be made to a general search warrant are frivolous in comparison with the good that

would result from it. No honest man whose name is above suspicion would care for the banditt's entering his house, and saying he had a general search warrant to look for stolen goods; neither would a search take place there—although, for effect, (the same as in Scotland) they might at first visit a few houses known to be entirely above suspicion. I trust the press will agitate this point, and that the legislature will amend the law in this particular, as the state of the country loudly calls for such amendment.

Canadian procedural and substantive criminal law has not been subject to substantial changes since Confederation, and the codification in 1892 (Mewett, 1967). Where the legal legitimations have proved inadequate for police purposes, the call has been to legally legitimate practices which were formerly illegal (cf. Mann and Lee, 1979, concerning the contemporary investigation of "wrongdoings" by the RCMP). Canadian criminal law and procedure has been internationally known as very punitive in support of the forces of "lawnorder." For example, an American Bar Association report in 1922 ("For a Better Enforcement of the Law," 589-591, cited by Douthet, 1975: 322-23), in condemning "molly coddling and sympathy by misinformed and ill-advised meddlers" as the "cause" of a high crime rate in large American cities, referred approvingly to the situation in Canada of more severe criminal penalties "causing" lower crime rates: "the theory there seems to involve protection to the public, with only a secondary concern for the criminal."

It is arguable that this theory is still the one which Canadians would like their system of "lawnorder" to be based upon, as evidenced by their attitudes to certain issues (e.g., capital punishment, see Chandler, 1978), and their apparent support for the rapid growth of the crime industry (Friedenberg, 1980; Ericson, 1980: Ch. 7). Citizens seem to accept the media portrayal of police work, that a certain amount of deviant excess by detectives and other police officers is necessary to keep the lid on the excessive deviance that is said to permeate our society (cf. Hurd, 1979: 127).

In this supportive climate, there is little chance that a new law designed to limit police practices will have its intended effect if it is seen by line officers as interfering with the interests of police work. As Greenawalt (1974: 248) concludes, police officers will always innovate in response to changes in rules. In doing this, police officers are no different than workers in other bureaucratic organizations. Prison guards translate new due process rules for disciplining inmates into the framework of rules by which they have always maintained the upper hand over inmates (Harvard Center for Criminal Justice, 1972). Similarly, industrial workers maintain their own structure of control while incorporating management efforts to alter this structure (e.g., Ditton, 1977). In any bureaucratic work organization, "What a new set of rules is not likely to do is make any fundamental changes in an already organized set of practices" (Imersheim, 1977: 40). In the police organization, "Any modification of the rules governing police activity will be unsuccessful so long as the rule-changes are seen as illegitimate by many policemen. They are likely to be seen as illegitimate if they conflict with the demands made upon them and with the view of the world emanating from the policeman's role" (Chambliss and Seidman, 1971: 392).

The filtering of legal rules through the organization of detective work means that we must analyze this organization in order to understand detective use of criminal law and procedure among other rule systems. Our analysis reveals that the law does not rule; rather, detectives use law and other rules to control the process. The existence of organizational "recipe" rules creates predictability for detectives in their work, but unpredictability for those who are not intimately familiar with these rules and the organization they support.

One meaning of the rule of law is that "government in all its actions is bound by rules fixed and announced beforehand—rules which make it possible to foresee with fair certainty how the authority will use its coercive powers in given circumstances . . . Within the known rules of the game the individual is free to pursue his personal ends and desires, certain that the powers of government will not be used deliberately to frustrate his efforts" (Hayek, 1944: 72-73). Since the legal rules as codified are not the operable rules of the game, but are translated along with other organizational rules as detectives account for their actions, and since the use of these rules organizationally is not fixed, and not generally known outside of the organization of detective work, citizens cannot adequately predict and guide their actions in dealing with detectives, who thereby gain the upper hand.

In this research we have documented the many ways in which detectives make their work predictable. Detective control over their rules of operation means that they can make things less predictable for those with whom they deal, and this is a primary means by which they control the process. In the context of these findings, it is not possible to sustain the argument that the introduction of legal rules alone will fundamentally influence the process and detective control of it. If detectives, and other agents of the system on whose behalf they operate, want to disadvantage someone or some group, procedural rules are not likely to stand in the way (cf. Griffiths, 1970: 381n).

Procedural laws can have the effect of giving strength to detective conduct they were supposed to restrain (Skolnick, 1966: 12). As we have seen, in almost all cases detectives are able to use them to their advantage, or get around them legally, without problems. As McBarnet (1976, 1979) concludes in her analysis of Scottish and English law, procedural rules are explicitly *for* crime control, not an impediment to it.

Another possibility for change is to alter the organization of the criminal process. An altered organizational structure might bring about ways to increase the visibility and accountability of detective work. Instead of the occasional disciplinary control wave against detective conduct, based upon a "rotten apple" theory of individual misconduct, the police administration and the courts should take action in relation to the structural conditions that produce misconduct: ". . . external control should be designed in a manner that reinforces the internal systems of discipline upon which primary dependence continues to be placed. They should not be oriented toward the control of individual misconduct, but rather should be directed at a review of the conditions that make such misconduct possible" (Goldstein, 1967: 171).

As we have repeatedly emphasized, the primary condition enabling detective autonomy is the low visibility of their work to other criminal control agents. As they are making a case to other agents, detectives can control information, and rely upon trusting relationships, to secure confirmation of their decisions. Detectives can manage routine approval of the case reports and decisions from the Detective Sergeant. They can secure their case against an accused before a lawyer has an opportunity to review it; the lawyer is thereby limited in giving adequate advice because he has no independent basis for discovering what happened in interrogation or how the detectives made their case. Detectives receive almost invariable compliance from Justices of the Peace in the granting of warrants, release on an undertaking, and bail conditions. They can use the organization of Crown attorney work to create a dependency whereby the detective takes an instrumental role in working out a guilty plea settlement with the defence. Detectives can also rely upon judges to ratify convictions without inquiry into how they were produced, thereby enhancing police authority.

The obvious recommendation is to increase the potential for review at each of these points, and to break down the cooptation of these other agents by detectives. This would enable a greater potential for adversariness at each stage of the process. However, there are many problems with putting into effect such a recommendation. Administrative rules are subject to the same translation process within the organization of detective work as legal rules. Moreover, as Utz (1978: 5) argues, more abuse may come from failures of co-operation than from collaboration in producing a mutually agreed upon just and justifiable disposition. For example, one of the few ways in which a lawyer might gain advantage for his clients is to become involved in ongoing relationships with detectives and Crown attorneys, gaining some insight and access to the recipe knowledge, rules, and other organizational elements by which they do their work.

Detective supervisors, lawyers, Justices of the Peace, Crown attorneys, and judges would have to be there themselves to independently assess detective construction of a case. They could not do this on a systematic basis. Moreover, given the structure of laws which enable detectives to make their cases within wide limits of justification, it might rarely make a difference if other parties were present. For example, the availability of a lawyer to participate in the interrogation process on his client's behalf appears to make little difference to case outcomes, although it may slightly enhance plea settlement possibilities (Ayres, 1970). Even when lawyers have been available at the police custody stage, they have been rarely used by the accused (Medalie *et al.*, 1968), and detectives have found ways to get around their disruptive potential (*ibid;* Wald *et al.*, 1967). Of course, increasing contacts among detectives, lawyers and other criminal control agents would likely enhance rather than break down the potential for cooptation.

In the jurisdiction we studied, the production of court outcomes took place backstage in discussions among detectives, lawyers and Crown attorneys. This process appears to be very similar to the process by which civil dispute settlements are worked out (cf. Ross, 1970; Heydebrand, 1977; Heumann, 1978: 149; Foucault, 1979). In this process, the judge serves more as an agent of ratification than adjudication. In the vast majority of cases the accused pleads guilty, and since the common law system accepts a guilty plea without proof, there is no inquiry in court concerning the construction of the case. Yet, the reported legal decisions concerning procedures used in case construction are based upon the small minority of cases that do result in trial, and contribute to a popular belief that trials do characterize the disposition of cases (Heumann, 1978: 13). Perhaps organizational and legal changes would be more fruitfully and realistically directed if they were concerned with the protection of persons who plead guilty rather than the present almost exclusive emphasis upon the protection of those who claim innocence.

Detective control over information also limits the potential for effective administrative review of their decisions by judges. As Williams (1974: 164) observes, "The absence of sufficient information is one reason why it would be unrealistic to expect the courts to investigate and control the discretionary powers of the police in their law enforcement, especially those concerned with prosecutions, through the familiar process of judicial review of administrative action."

In face of the limited potential for control of the police through changes in legal rules, or through changes in the organization of the criminal process as it relates to review of detective decisions, some would argue for greater emphasis on internal regulation within the police force. One element of this is to put faith in police administrative rule-making, shifting the onus for formulating rules away from the legislative bodies conferring police power to the police themselves (e.g., Davis, 1969). This would entail an effort to formalize, and thereby make more widely known, the organizational rules within which detective actions are framed. Another element of this professionalization of the police service is the argument for more formal training of the police as part of a wider programme based upon the belief that proper socialization is the best means of control. This approach of leaving it up to the authorities to regulate themselves, and to deal with problems of authority through the assertion of more authority, is a favourite response in Canadian government (Friedenberg, 1980; Hagan and Leon, 1980).

The professionalization alternative has been with us a long time. As mentioned in Chapter 1, there were nineteenth century experiments in London's new police to appoint "gentlemen of good education and social standing" as detectives in the hope that they would be less susceptible to corruption and improve the standards of the work. Early social scientists also advocated professionalism as a means of correcting unacceptable behaviour by workers (e.g., Durkheim, 1933, first published in 1893).

Contemporary social scientists continue to examine the professionalization alternative, and its implications for social control. Analyses of various occupations and professions point to the way in which professionalization enhances autonomy and control by the occupational group over what they do. Calls for professionalization serve as ideological preparation for the expansion (in size and control) of the industry or business in question. As it becomes established, the professional aura provides an ideal basis to justify the exercise of power, legitimating it as authority. It also allows members of the professional group to enhance the lucrative aspects of their employment, often to the relative disadvantage of those they are supposed to be serving, to the point where the professional is more in need of the client than the client is in need of the professional's ministrations (Friedenberg, 1975; McKnight, 1977). In many areas of occupational life—social work, doctoring, lawyering, and industrial management—professions have been shown to be "disabling" for citizens and enabling only for professional members (Illich et al., 1977). In the correctional sphere of the criminal process, there has been extensive documentation of the negative ramifications of professionalization (e.g., Kittrie, 1971; Mitford, 1973; Ericson, 1974, 1978; Ellis, 1979).

In the case of the police, the professionalization alternative has also been scrutinized and criticized. Some (e.g., Lambert, 1970; Cain, 1972) have argued that professionalization might have the effect of curtailing excesses of police power. Others (e.g., Skolnick, 1966; Norris, 1973; Manning, 1977) have pointed out that professionalization is usually accompanied by technological trappings and public relations efforts which give only the appearance of change, with no substantial alteration in the training and operating procedures of line officers.

Blumberg and Niederhoffer (1970: 10-12) depict police professionalization as the "Holy Grail" of the American police reform movement, and go on to state that "professionalism intensifies the demand for self-policing and autonomy." Some (e.g., Cain, 1972) argue that professionalization is associated with government control. Robinson (1975) claims that a professionalized police force may serve politicians even better than a force over which they have more direct control because they can displace responsibility when there are problems, and take credit when the police can display competence. Others (e.g., James,

1979: 70) contend that "the mystification of professionalization" may be associated with "a freedom from government control and a clouding of the actual practices of policing as it is performed by lower ranks."

One thing is certain, professionalization does not increase visibility of police actions. Line detectives are still able to filter administrative rules, incorporating them into their rules of practice, which remain known only to members of the detectives' occupational culture. The administration is still able to filter knowledge from inside their bureaucracy to inquisitive citizens on the outside. As Thomas (1974: 148) states in arguing against Davis' (1969) proposal for administrative rule-making, "there is a tendency both on the part of law enforcement agencies and paroling agencies whose decision-making is not open to continuous public assessment, to conceal the criteria on which they operate, partly out of a natural defensiveness and partly because some case can be made out for preserving the confidentiality of such criteria."

Of course, this is not just a matter of defensive concealment. The protection of professionalism, and the need to further enhance the professional imagery, can lead to selective construction of information about crime and other police business. "Since professionalism can only be achieved or maintained as long as the police have high prestige in the public eye, there is a powerful tendency to cover up, to falsify reports and statistics of crime to maintain that prestige. Every bureaucracy is ultimately a self-serving instrument supportive of its own world views and the decisions it has already made or is about to make; the police are no exception" (Blumberg and Niederhoffer, 1970: 12).

In light of this, perhaps all we can hope for is to socialize police officers according to criteria that seem appropriate at the time. We can start with the "empty vessel" of the new recruit, and pour in all the right ingredients until he is full of goodness. However, we know that socialization through formal training is unlikely to accomplish the task. For example, lawyers claim that their extensive legal training does not prepare them for the reality of their work, and they must learn the recipe knowledge within their occupational environment before they can "really go to work" and do a competent job as judged by their peers (Packer and Ehrlich, 1972: 14; Heumann, 1978: 48; Macfarlane, 1979). This is part of the experience common to any occupational group that has formal training: as the worker becomes socialized into the working realities of his job, he learns that the reality taught in formal training is inadequate, and often irrelevant.

In summary, giving more authority to the police authorities through professionalization in the hope that internal control will function as a panacea is unlikely to do anything but enhance police autonomy. When this solution is examined closely, it cannot even be seriously entertained as a possibility for control of the police. Rather, it serves the interests of control by the police.

Obviously there is little potential for a *major* reduction in police power via any of the approaches we have considered: legal change, organizational changes within the criminal process, and organizational changes in the police Force (professionalization). Indeed our empirical study, along with other socio-legal research, points to the fact that the entire system—the law, the organization of the courts, and the police organization—is ideally designed to ensure that detectives control the making of crime and criminals. Tinkering with one or two elements within the system cannot have an impact on how the entire system operates. As we have argued, individual changes in rules are routinely incorporated into the existing system of rules to accomplish things in much the same way as they have always been accomplished. Without radical change of the system, we cannot avoid the fact that the police will continue to control the process through their positional advantage vis-à-vis other organizations for crime control, and through the legal and organizational structural resources bestowed upon them.

We are not advocating suspension of efforts at tinkering with the present system, if for no other reason than the fact that such efforts are obviously better than giving in completely to the forces of "lawnorder." However, we must be constantly wary of how tinkering efforts often only give the appearance of change. They can end up giving more legitimacy to the existing system and thus greater power to the police.

We are not saying that there are no present controls over detectives that limit what they can do in their work. Some obvious controls remain. For example, we discovered that judges did not become involved in plea discussions regarding sentence with detectives, the Crown attorney, or defence attorney. Judges only heard sentence *recommendations* from the Crown attorney and/or defence attorney, and did not have to take these recommendations into account. In consequence, they maintained the upper hand by making things somewhat unpredictable for the detectives, Crown attorney and defence attorney, who all sought a sentence outcome that fit their sense of justice vis-à-vis the circumstances of the case. The detectives, Crown attorney and defence attorney could individually or collectively manipulate aspects of the case, and "judge shop," in order to increase the predictability of the outcome they wanted, but the judge still held the final power in his sentencing discretion.

Furthermore, some controls are "invisible"in the sense that they are never actualized behaviorally because the detective predicts, based upon the rules of the game, what the outcome will be. The detective is unlikely to make application to a Justice of the Peace if he predicts it will be turned down; to charge if he thinks the Crown attorney will not accept it; to suggest a sentence recommendation if he predicts it is likely to be viewed as unreasonable by the other parties. The rules, the expectations of others, must be taken into account, and used in accounts, even if they are used to reject a particular course of action. As Bittner (1970: 24) states,

[T]he norms observable in open court reach down and govern even the process of its evasion. In the criminal process, like in chess, the game is rarely played to the end, but it is a rare chess player who concedes defeat merely to save time. Instead, he concedes because he knows or can reasonably guess what would happen if he persisted to play to the end. And thus the rules of the end-game are valid determinants of chess-playing even though they are relatively rarely seen in action.

Obviously, we need much more research before we can state confidently that what we want does not already exist. Sometimes changes are introduced without the requisite knowledge of what already exists, and therefore of what is being changed. An example of this is the implementation of "diversion" schemes in various Canadian jurisdictions without adequate knowledge of the nature and extent of existing police practices in "diverting" cases through their decisions not to record an occurrence, investigate, and/or charge a suspect (cf. Law Reform Commission, 1974, 1974a, 1975; Ericson, 1977; Solicitor General of Canada, 1979a). Sometimes policies are developed for economic or political reasons, but formulated as if they are for the betterment of a just system of criminal control (Scull, 1977). If we have ongoing research monitoring our present system, we can evaluate the extent to which "criminal justice" policy talk is an excuse for political actors whose interests are located elsewhere (cf. Ericson, 1980: Ch. 7).

Our research specifies how detectives exist on de facto legitimacy as well as on legitimacy conferred by the organizational forums within which they operate. This is a very good reason for ongoing research that monitors what they do and how they go about doing it. If we are ever to approach equality of opportunity for the various parties who have stakes in the criminal process, then we must strive to ensure that each party can take informed decisions with predictable outcomes. This can only come about if each party knows the rules by which the other parties operate. Research helps to articulate the organizational rules of detective operations, which should help others in undertaking and assessing their dealings with detectives.

In addition to this pragmatic function, ongoing research can serve a more general educational function. The beginning of a police state requires not only a well equipped and zealous police, but also an indifferent public. The lack of major public reaction to recent revelations about police activities in Canada, including systematic crimes by the R.C.M.P. (Mann and Lee, 1979) and systematic brutality by the Waterloo Regional Police Force, is not a good sign. Within my value system, it is a sign of greater health when people question authority than when they accept it because it apparently serves their immediate self-interests. Research can contribute to this healthy question as an ongoing enterprise.

In stating this, we are referring to the demystification function of research. All socio-legal research has demystifying elements because it involves a different way of looking at the facts and a different discourse from that used by research subjects or other "publics." "A myth is, of course, not a fairy story. It is the presentation of facts belonging in one category in the idioms belonging to another. To explode a myth is accordingly not to deny the facts but to re-allocate them" (Ryle, 1949, quoted by Scull, 1977: 3). Demystification shows that things are not as integrated as they appear to be; that special interests control the environment rather than everyone serving for the interests of everyone else; that there is conflict when there appears to be consensus; and, that the authority the myth supports is not firm and fixed but tacit and tenuous, built up in mundane, everyday transactions in a myriad of social settings. Demystification serves questioning, and leads to an awareness that given the somewhat relative and mutable nature of what was previously taken for granted as fixed, there may be possibilities for change.

Of course, social scientists are not immune from mystifying through the accounts they give in their research. It is interesting to note that some of the major themes Hurd (1979: 131-34) identifies in television detective shows are also themes in academic writing and research on the police: police vs. crime, law vs. rule, professional vs. organization, authority vs. bureaucracy, intuition vs. technology, comradeship vs. rank. Social scientists are not free from the societal images of the phenomena they study, and without conscious and concientious effort they may end up reproducing the myths which restrict knowledge and inhibit the search for alternatives.

Moreover, demystification itself can serve the forces of alienation rather than change, resulting in inaction, withdrawal, selfish individualism, privitization.

> An apparently radical plot can hide a conservative trap.
>
> This is to contradict those liberal sociologists who write about the social construction of everyday life. They tend to see de-mystification of social interaction and social processes as a necessary preliminary to radical structural change. In many circumstances, however, it is demystification itself which, by allowing the individual to distance himself from the social arrangements to which he is a party, gives him a sense of satisfaction with his own lot which is incompatible with a desire for change ... Recognition of the arbitrary nature of our domestic arrangements, of our work tasks, of our leisure pursuits does not so much provide premises upon which political action may be constructed, in which the concept of work and family might be attacked, instead they give the individual a slightly decreased sense of social commitment, a further warrant for that cynicism about social life which carries with it such a satisfying sense of the importance of oneself as an individual. (Cohen and Taylor, 1976: 35-36).

In order to avoid that familiar journey of 360 degrees distance, only to end up at the point of origin encircled by conservatism, it is essential to increase one's knowledge of the possible courses to take. In charting the desired course for detective work, we need to know more about how it compares with work in other types of organizational settings, how it compares with similar police work done in other jurisdictions, and how it has operated historically vis-à-vis other organizations and institutions of social control.

The history of social control does inform us that each new sensibility about how to order the population becomes transformed into a measure of repression at least as great as that which preceded it. This is so because in society as a whole there has not been fundamental change in the structure of power, but only in the tools by which this power is exercised. As modern day power tools, detectives are well equipped to get the job done efficiently and effectively. They do not labour manually. They are but one of the many vectors of power which contribute to the machinery of State control. In the last analysis, their enabling power resources within the law, the organization of the criminal process, the organization of the police force, and the community they police, must be seen in this light. While detectives make crime into police property, it serves interests of power much greater than their own.

A Response

to *Making Crime: A Study of Detective Work* from The Board of Commissioners of Police in the Jurisdiction under study, pursuant to the agreement between the Board and the Centre of Criminology of The University of Toronto*

The agreement between the Centre of Criminology of the University of Toronto, and the Board of Commissioners of Police in the jurisdiction under study, permits the Board to answer, and have included in any report, any criticisms of police procedures and/or conduct of individual police officers.

The Board and the Chief of Police, then and now, are convinced that research into the criminal justice system is necessary to a growing knowledge and understanding of it, the true ingredients of its improvement. Indeed, we accept the support of such research as an obligation. There are other obligations. The law and the policies and processes of criminal justice, while obviously complex and often not well understood, rest on a fragile and changing consensus that continually tends to restore the balances of our various needs for security and of rights and freedom. These dynamics are much a part of law enforcement and all in society must be unremittingly sensitive to them. The obligation, then, that is implicit in research is a particularly heavy one. Much of this obligation is one of reporting with a solicitude for completeness and accuracy of facts, for adequacy of analysis, and, for caution in drawing conclusions. We emphasize that this research obligation must be particularly compelling in the law enforcement field. The immediate, potential impact of the report of such research extends well beyond scholarly debate, and onto those vital concerns of the community.

The Board believes that the report dictates that it exercise its option to respond.

---

* The publisher and the author have agreed to include this response to *Making Crime* at the request of the Board of Commissioners of Police in the jurisdiction under study. Their response has been printed verbatim.

The Board of Commissioners of Police in the jurisdiction under study were asked to identify the jurisdiction and to have the names of Board members listed on this page. This request was made on the principle that authors who stand by their work symbolize their responsibility for it by putting their names on it. The Board of Commissioners of Police decided not to be identified with their response.

We take exception to many of the report's statements, but will respond to a lesser number. We assume that at this point, the reader will have read the report. Our response is organized according to: first, the system or method used in the work to analyze and report data; second, the incompleteness of data; and, third, important problems of fact. Any particular theory of deviancy that may have been reflected in the report is not germane to this response.

Related to the first are the opening paragraphs of chapter two which sketch in the reliance on the "epistemology of symbolic interactionism" (p. 23), a way of thinking and the conforming research method. As a brief recall, the former is indicated by the quote from Rock, "valid knowledge is held to reside neither in the subject nor in the object but in the transactions that unfold between them . . ." (p. 23). The latter, the method, is observation of detectives at work as the source of information. We cannot claim especial familiarity with this highly particularistic discipline of symbolic interactionism, although we are informed of it. The reporting of information obtained is, apparently, the recounting of the phenomena observed and as the report notes in chapter two, interpretation hinges on the products of the transaction within the phenomenon, e.g., an arrest. The adequacy of such descriptive study is largely dependent upon the observer's understanding of and insight into the phenomenon being studied. Whether the research process conformed to the strictures of such symbolic interactionism is left to others—it is a scientific judgment though not divorced from the issue of validity. The aspect of concern here is the reportorial freedom the method permits. Indeed, Rock in his book cited in the report, states that words are usable for their connotative meaning as much as for their precision in denoting meaning. Connotation requires that associations or ideas be added by the reader. The reporting of the research information in this case, clearly, rests in large part on the latter, the connotative, and it seems to us therefore, to require much care. The report, we believe, exploits this permissiveness in the use of words. Inferences from a recounting are invited of a reader and often, compelled. From this aspect arises the negative cast of much of the report; we are concerned with such negativisms for their validity is difficult to assess in this mode of reporting, and their impact on the reader problematic.

There are numerous examples which illustrate this point; but only a few will be mentioned in emphasis. The recounting of one detective's excessive drinking habits (p. 64) compels the inference that he was dismissed from the Force as a result of being "pushed outside the protective ring of his colleagues" due to a "shared belief" that the 'drinking detective's' problems were creating high visibility and therefore inviting administrative scrutiny of the entire office which would ultimately affect everyone's interests. Neither stated nor implied is that senior administrative personnel were aware of the problem, were genuinely concerned for the detective's welfare, were involved in counselling with the detective, and in fact had arranged for and provided leave for therapeutic treatment. It was not until he could no longer undertake his responsibilities as a peace officer that he was dismissed from the Force, a dismissal originating from administration, not in concert with his colleagues and not predicated upon any ostracism by them. The difficulty, of course, in reporting unfolding transactions, in this case between the 'drinking detective' and his colleagues, is that the product of the transaction, the dismissal of the detective, is presumed to result in valid knowledge. Unfortunately, it does not; the recounting results in a misinterpretation, it being ignorant of the relevant processes which impinge upon the reality produced.

A similar problem arises in relation to a perceived antagonism between the general assignment and special services detectives (pp. 61-62). In recounting the frustration of one detective, an informal conversation is cited about a murder case being investigated by special service detectives but about which the 'frustrated detective' had information. The compelling inference is that because of perceived obstacles, the 'frustrated detective' did not provide the murder investigators with essential information. While the words may reveal the frustration of the detective, the transaction cannot assume a reality based on whether or not crucial information was communicated to the special investigators. The connotation is that it wasn't; yet, there is neither evidence of that nor concern in the reporting of information for related transactions from which a conclusion about the situation could be drawn. The method of reporting demands considerable interpretive latitude. The account has not recognized the rules of co-operation in the Force and the impact is suggestive of officer negligence.

A third example which we will relate here, but which is by no means a final example, concerns the recounting of an 'indecent exposure' case (p. 101) wherein investigative activity is interpreted as being a "public relations pitch," aimed at completing the "necessary 'face work' with the victim and her parents." The case, apparently, was "subsequently 'filed' with no further investigative activity." The inescapable inference, of course, is that the detectives' primary motivation was not to apprehend a sex offender but to convince the victim's parents that they were "doing what detectives are supposed to do" (p. 100), and to "provide a gloss" (p. 102), so that, presumably, the victim's parents would not later complain of inaction. It is difficult for the reader to infer anything else from the recounting since there is not enough detail about the case to make an informed judgment about detective action. Nevertheless, that the case was 'filed' with no further investigative activity is a conclusion which only serves to enhance the compelling inference. What is not stated is that the case was 'filed' in an active modus operandi file for later comparison with similar offences, thus providing a potential for additional evidence of suspect identity. Clearly what was left unsaid would have precluded the conclusion that there was no further investigative activity and would therefore have altered the meaning.

We believe, as laymen, that the report carries beyond this reportorial latitude in its repeated use of idiom. Shorthand terms are acceptable—we all use them—if meaning is shared. With idiom, if no meaning is commonly shared, interpretation on the part of the reader is demanded, for precise meaning is not deducible from the words themselves. Two of the major examples are "low visibility" and "cover." Neither receive direct, primary definition in the report. "Cover" *by inference*, is a creative act of solely self-serving value. The use of the term is extensive; careful reading is required to avoid pitfalls of interpretation. The meaning appears to be that it is a powerful motivator to act in a certain way because of a negative, extrinsic threat. This use is so extensive as to remove from much of the report indications that detectives act through a positive, intrinsic process related to organizational and social values. Thus, readers are frequently reminded that detectives are driven to continuously maintain "low visibility" to counter threats against their self interest. The threat seems to arise from a failure to meet "organizational demands" or to avoid them. "Organizational demands" in turn, are undefined idiom.

Deficient in reporting as this is, and productive of the negative colouration of detective motivations as it is, this aspect is more serious for it relates to the core of the research.

The problems of supervision have been well known in police forces from their inception. They derive from the discretion of patrol and detective officers exercised beyond the direct observation of supervisors. Only some forms of supervision can be practiced. Given these supervisory limitations, then, this perspective further suggests that there must be appropriate mechanisms in place that ensure accountability through administrative practices. Thus, a judicial capacity to review, for example, the nature of obtaining a confession or of making an arrest is an accountability process. These are expanded upon through police force practices that in the report are labelled "organizational demands," but which are neither defined nor even the subject of enquiry.

The important process of supervising through accountability is largely, then, in the report, converted to idiom, and consigned to a borderline position beyond analysis. Yet, and we emphasize this, the dynamics of accountability bear directly on discretion, the stated focus of the study. We deal with such administrative practices in another context below; they are of relevance to any police administration as much as to scholarly study.

This portion of our response can be closed with a reflection on

the process or the technicalities of symbolic interactionism. The report properly discusses the interactions related to implementing the research within the Police Force, and related problems. Such problems are common and commonly reported. The subculture of detectives, as the report notes, was problematic, and detectives in turn found the presence of the researchers presenting pragmatic, ethical and legal problems. The researchers were observers, recorders of transactions and in some ways fell prey to that subculture. The incident involving an "unprocessed warrant" was a practical joke (p. 152). Other practical jokes, *which were documented* by Detective Sergeants, were played on the researchers by the detectives, including exaggerating what they would do, or had done, for informants, deliberately writing up false follow up reports and other documents and leaving them in conspicuous places for the researchers; and, signing arrest and search warrants in the name of justices of the peace, convincing researchers that they would be used but later throwing them out.

There is a so-called detective subculture; the work requires a leavening of humour and shared idioms in the face of the demands of that work and the demands of administrative directions. Notwithstanding the warnings given the researchers in this regard, the report suggests that the subculture did not enter into the understanding of the observers; they lacked the insight so necessary to the mode of research they undertook.

A proposal to use symbolic interactionism within an organization, we are advised, may well not yield the informed consent required of any such proposed research. It seems that the nature of the reporting as described above, poses an ethical problem in seeking such consent. The experience we now have testifies to that, and, for example, this problem is set out in the Rock (1979) text, cited in the report.

This response now turns to questions of completeness of data. Simplistically, the observation method used may not bring into the immediate attention of the observer much that guides and directs the work of detectives, the policies, regulations and day-to-day directions of the Police Force. Rules, legal, administrative, or informal, however, are central to this report and ". . . it is the researchers' task *to ferret out* these rules as they are conceived and used in the everyday actions of detectives" (p. 11; emphasis added). Administrative rules do have a reality as they are ". . . conceived and used . . ." but are not fully understandable unless the actual rule is identified and its ends known. In other words, the conception of a rule and how it is used can not be analyzed without knowing what the rule is. The reader is left to make a series of inferences about the nature of rules, what they intend, and what they subsequently permit in relation to an end. This is aggravated by the report's failure to acknowledge, to inform the reader, that rules were not sought out and that the accounting lacks this explanatory resource. Equally, in this accounting, generally, there are no consistent indications of a post-incident interview of a detective, a confirmatory probe, of how rules were "conceived and used," a most acceptable and sensible method. The introductory pages of the report, chapter one, discuss such rules in general and point to some relation with the exercise of discretion. Elsewhere, much is devoted, and properly so, to the legal rules of arrest, administering cautions, and others. Such descriptions, though cursory, assist in an understanding of detective actions. Administrative rules were not so identified and described.

As we have already indicated, the rules are not described nor ferretted out but repetitively alluded to as "organizational demands" in relation to "cover" and "visibility." This is a grave deficiency and the cost is an equal deficiency in our understanding of the products of discretion. Rules, as the report notes, do enable, but they also direct and control actions to known ends. The products of this direction, their success or lack thereof, are surely an issue. Within policing, there is a substantial body of governing regulation and law, and of administrative policy, practice and procedure. The report is silent on this directing and accounting; these dynamics are submerged by the imputation of the motive of "cover," and one therefore has to ask the fundamental question—'Do these interpretations result in valid knowledge?"

The report discusses with clarity and brevity, that the detective is at the intersection of demands from several sources; he mediates these according to the criteria of these sources or groupings, and he is given powerful tools but is to be, and to remain, accountable. Whether he is made effectively accountable, and whether he mediates demand according to organizational, legal and social ends are questions which move one into the difficult areas of scientific objectivity, and to the borders of political/social beliefs and ideology. At least at the operating (the micro) level, these questions demand an elaboration of disclosure and analysis, as was done with some legal rules. To repeat, any formal group acts towards certain ends and will have rules that direct action toward those ends but limit means. The rules will obviously have enabling features with all groups acting to exploit their limits. At this operating level, the compatability of detectives' goals and those of the Police Force is relevant. The careful reader will note what the report might and perhaps should have—that the more enabling dynamic is the weight of evidence of guilt; but, given this, there is a countervailing and escalating compulsion on the detective to ensure the alleged suspect, in turn, is accountable regardless of status. On this point, and in context with the report, it can be said that, "obviously, we need much more research before we can state confidently that what we want does not already exist" (p. 225).

The source of information was the observation of detectives. The field workers were to have adjusted their work schedules according to those of the detectives with whom they were attached, including overtime. They were with them for "most activity" with the exception of "when detectives were required to attend court on their days off; if this included a non-sample case, the field workers usually did not attend" (p. 25). There is an implicit assumption that matters addressed by the detectives with their colleagues and others while attending court on days off were directly connected with the charge before the court on that day. Such is not the case; thus, potentially valuable interactions were not observed, both in relation to sample cases and others. This is particularly potent in consideration of the statement that "detectives were known to have consulted with the Crown Attorney regarding the initial laying of charges in only 3 instances" (p. 167). Detectives in the offices under study, during the research period, committed in excess of 2600 hours to court attendance while off duty. While averaging is subject to criticism on the face of it, it is nevertheless worth noting that on average, each detective had 58 hours and each team over 110 hours. It is, in our opinion, a serious oversight to have disregarded this potentially useful source of data.

Overlooked are the rules of evidence generally; their influence pervades reported case accounts, but go unnoticed except to the scrupulous reader. Noted elsewhere, assessing weight of evidence in minor offences is within a detective's discretion. As such, the rules of evidence are both critical to decision-making, and, enabling. Readers will recall the incident in which a tavern customer was considerably bruised (pp. 113-114). The recounting implies that detective discretion permitted the decision to charge the customer rather than the "bouncer" with assault. In actuality, the customer attacked the "bouncer" with a knife; the evidence of that, together with its seriousness, simply could not sustain an original charge of assault against the latter. The "bouncer," acting on behalf of the owner, was countering force with force to effect an arrest. Whether more force was used than was necessary in the circumstances was an issue independent of but collateral to the original assault. Hence, there were two distinct issues—the original assault, and the excessive use of force to counter the assault. The reach of the rules of evidence is apparent in the transaction and its outcome; the failure to separate the issues, or even address the second, creates confusion and ignores the more substantive issue that rules of evidence are a compelling influence on officer discretion.

We can speculate that these deficiencies in the report have led to the failure to explore some hypotheses. As the report states, patrol officers are required to turn over most cases immediately to detective Bureaux. One effect may be that detectives function in part to restore order somewhat in the manner of patrol officers. An analysis of detective discretion may well have resulted in this conclusion—some data are available. As one moves into the area of criminal offences, that discretion diminishes. The detective's work comes under increasing scrutiny from immediate supervisors; for major crime investigations, little or no discretion survives. Perhaps it is paradoxical that the more experienced the detective, the less discretion he has. The deficiencies in the report are ones of a presumption about the detective function and generalizing from the work of general assignment detectives, who investigate the more minor offences, to all detectives, especially to those in offices concentrating exclusively on serious crime. In numbers, specialized detectives out number the general assignment detectives. Exclusive of the specialized Youth Bureau, and as the report notes, in 1980, 8.6% of the total Police Force was engaged in general assignment work, and 10.6% on the more specialized work. The study of specialized detectives was open to the researchers; but, they chose to limit their sample though not the generality of conclusions.

In summary, on this part of our response addressing incompleteness of data, there is a serious deficiency in the report in its failure to account for the specifics of legal or administrative control, and its purposes, on discretion. This is surprising in view of the attention paid to control of the police in the final chapter. Such has led to the general, and we believe adversely critical, imputation to detectives of a negative motivation of "cover," consistently vague in its meaning. This has resulted in a report that avoided the central issue of accountability and directing on discretion, and perhaps failed in achieving new knowledge in the area. These parts of the report, and there are many, have a triteness of account as a result, and tend to take the reader through a series of imperfect accounts of detective behaviour.

We now turn to important problems of fact, problems which cannot be divorced from either of our first two concerns, the method of reporting and inadequacy of data, since the very deficiencies therein contribute to these problems. It is distressing that problems of fact exist at all. The report states that "detectives did not work as sleuths (which) meant that their work was not dependent on technology . . ., nor on physical evidence clues" (p. 90) and in support cites in an end note that of the 295 cases studied, "85.8% involved no physical clues whatsoever." The criminal identification (forensic) services of the Force assisted the general assignment detectives of the study, during the study period, with collecting physical evidence in 61 robbery investigations, 21 rapes and attempted rapes, 25 other sexual offences, 162 thefts from automobiles, 51 arsons, 849 shopbreaks, 478 housebreaks, in addition to 42 composite drawings and thousands of photographs, fingerprint charts and scale drawings.

There are other generalized conclusions; only a few will be

mentioned. There is insufficient support for the conclusion that it was detective practice to charge "everyone possible for everything possible" (p. 165ff.). The report notes that a number of suspects were not charged at all (pp. 82, 178-179), further that "a total of 101 charges were laid in relation to the 51 persons charged" (p. 43); averaging the latter to "two charges for every person charged" (p. 43) does not enhance understanding. More definitive would have been a documentation of the proportion of the 51 who were charged with more than one offence, the numbers of charges laid against them, and the number of charges that were not, but could have been laid. Moreover, while the report presents some information as to the number of cases that were the subject of a plea transaction process (pp. 187-188, 206), it is unable to sustain the very generalized conclusion in relation to multiple charging that everyone possible was charged with everything possible, when it is simply not the case.

It is a complication of the research strategy that by a distancing from what the detectives take for granted, such as institutional arrangements, the observer can, at best, be tentative in his conclusions. The conclusion on page 98 that "detectives had to produce 'necessary paper' . . . within the police organization, according to criteria that made it appear that investigative efforts were expended" is not well supported by the examples of detectives doing a rather cursory, if any, investigation of theft cases and formulating reports consistent with a more thorough investigation. What perhaps is confounding is an assumption that there was a "force requirement of providing a written justification for dispositions" as though administrative talk is in the form of 'justification' rather than action. The meaning one draws from a series of transactions is highly dependent upon one's understanding of the processes involved and unless one can transcend the immediate phenomenon, through thorough investigation of the rules, as mentioned above, one cannot hope to disentangle the features, map out their connections and understand their effects (Rock, 1974). The inevitable result is to create a warped sense of fact. Such is the case when the report hastily concludes that "in short, this section (of the criminal code) justifies deadly force against escaping suspects" (p. 138). As the report earlier noted, the section only justifies as much force as is necessary to prevent escape, *unless the escape can reasonably be prevented in a less violent manner* (emphasis added). Further dictates of effecting use of force provisions include a consideration of the nature and seriousness of the offence. The question of accountability and review, as addressed above, is most pertinent; what the report calls an "arsenal of means available to police officers" (p. 138) must be assessed both on that basis as well as on a thorough understanding and adequate summary of the law. Quite properly, the limits of the report preclude intensive examination of the law as it is applied or translated by police officers; this is evident in the report's discussion of the laws of arrest, search and seizure. Necessarily, then, extreme caution must be exercised in drawing hasty conclusions, or in overly simplifying or generalizing from only perfunctory analyses. In this context, then, it is difficult to understand the basis on which the report is able to conclude that, even though cautioning a suspect only becomes an issue if the suspect is charged, "it is very easy for the police officer to manipulate the caution so that it does not inhibit his construction of the case" (p. 144). Retrospective justifications and giving the appearance of procedural regularity, are, like "low-visibility" and "cover", ill-defined but imputed motives of the detective. The imputations are serious—lack of systematic access to interrogations was, admittedly, a problem. Conclusions about administering right to silence cautions and practices in the taking of statements and confessions, then, must unavoidably be modified in light of this problem and the incompleteness of data it generated. Interrogation techniques cited in the Calgary City Police training manual (pp. 158-159) can neither be generalized across Police Forces nor used to fill the void left by lack of direct access and observation in the Force studied—it is simply not sufficient support for the statement that ". . . rules of police practice direct the detective to use suspects to whatever degree they can be exploited" (p. 159). Artifacts of this nature are common; not having 'ferreted out' the rules, or the policies, as is the researcher's task, has contributed to these artifacts.

The lack of access to interrogations must be the subject of elaboration since, as the report carefully notes, the problem was critical to the research. The report did not directly address the fact that the Crown Attorney gave explicit direction, when the problem became known, that researchers were not to be permitted access since it would seriously jeopardize the admissibility of statements and ultimately case outcome. The report glosses over this, and instead renders an interpretation that the underlying motivation was a concern by detectives that "researchers would not collaborate in the versions of the truth the detectives wished to construct" (p. 33). This is a cogent example of the research tendency to construct negativistic interpretations without clearly understanding the methods of investigation and interrogation. Moreover, we are annoyed that the report complains about non-access when it was never agreed to, although initially some access was thought possible. We recognize that a gap occurs in the research and resulting deficiencies merit observation in the report; but, an agreement freely entered into surely merits a responsible recognition of an obligation that subsequent, plaintive comments are out of place.

In summary, then, to this third major area of concern, related to problems of fact, it is vital that facts be reported accurately.

Facts, in themselves, however, are meaningless; it is their interpretation and use which is crucial to the research enterprise. The assumption that "everything is subject to interpretation and then formulation as it is given the status of information and is presented as 'factual'" (p. 23) is typical of the report; but, it is heavily reliant on the researcher's interpretations and shared understandings of the phenomenon under study. We are of the opinion that a major part of this report has suffered from a lack of circumspection in drawing meaning.

There is another issue which we feel obligated to address. The Board, in agreeing to support the research projects within the patrol (as yet unpublished) and the detective divisions, accepted the likelihood that extensive research information collection would reveal deviations from administrative rules. The Board, the Chief of Police, and his senior officers, however, are not complacent. Some aspects must be placed in historical context—amalgamating smaller municipal forces into a Regional Force is not without its problems. Diverse training practices and policies under which officers operated prior to amalgamation continued to be manifested after the inception of the Regional Force. Intensive efforts by senior administrators during those early years, which included the research period, were directed towards clarifying policy, changing and raising policing standards and in effecting mechanisms for the control of institutional deviance. Other deviations, such as engaging in non-police activity while on duty, are attributable to the practice of permitting reasonable flexibility with regard to time use in return for not claiming every quarter hour overtime worked, as is the detectives' prerogative. To have recorded data pertinent to such non-police activity (pp. 45-46), and yet not to have similarly recorded unclaimed overtime, or claimed overtime (amounting to over 7000 hours in the subject period and averaging 154 hours per detective, in addition to the 2600 hours of court time already noted) reduces the efficacy of the data pertaining to how police officer time was spent. Some personal business must be conducted during normal business hours, hence the controlled flexibility permitted. Police officers must cope with the stress of irregular and often lengthy hours. Instead of counting the number of hours spent at breakfast and lunch, perhaps focus should have been placed on the manifestation of the detective's job regimen on his behaviour.

We do not, however, accept illegal activity and are gravely concerned about the allegations of such misconduct on pages 38 and 153-154. There is a legal and moral requirement on us to act on the face of the allegation, regardless of source, notwithstanding the difficulties posed for the investigation of an incident occurring several years earlier. We do not condone officers 'lefthanding' search warrants (signing a justice of the peace's name). Such activity would result in criminal charges and dismissal from the

Force. We have already investigated the incident, and have evidence on which to seriously question the basis of the allegation. We are dismayed that principal researchers have not, by virtue of the ethnics of research on human subjects, co-operated in providing factual data to us to support this most serious allegation. Surely, there are bounds to the ethics of engaging in research of this nature —criminal wrongdoing by officers is not a fait accompli; it is intolerable. In a sense, we are stymied, and if there is a lesson to be learned, it is that the limits of academic freedom must be examined and questioned; the university is not outside the canons of the law, notwithstanding the difficulty that such limitation may pose for the research enterprise. Researchers and universities must be held accountable, and it is a dilemma which they must face and with which they must wrestle.

The Board well realizes that no research report, especially one as extensive as this, and however carefully prepared, can be immune to criticism. We have responded, critically, to some portions of it, but have been cognizant of the scholarly effort that is inherent in it. Research into the work of detectives is, indeed, rare; no ground-breaking study such as this can be comprehensive and free of problems. The reader will note that as a result, and with wisdom, conclusions in the text are tentative. While in many aspects the report is disappointing in terms of its probative value, there are some merits to the report; there is a revelation of a few of the enormous complexities of the nature of detective policing; and there is an insightful attempt to further identify the tangle of issues involved in policing. The Board's position is that the processes of criminal justice are complex and must be subject to study if they are to preserve the delicate balances society requires. The researcher has obligations, as stated at the outset, if the results of his research are to contribute to a growing knowledge of the dynamics of the criminal justice system. While it may be a matter of debate amongst scholars, it is the Board's position that the report has not met these obligations and has not adhered to the scientific rigours of reporting.

A Reply

to the Response of The Board of Commissioners of Police
from Richard V. Ericson

The response of the Board of Commissioners of Police is welcomed as a historical moment in the annals of social research: it surely marks the first time that a group of officials and politicians has attempted to engage the discourse of "this highly particularistic discipline of symbolic interactionism." While I find the early part of the response heavy going and difficult, I fully understand the thrust of the response.

Organizations facing a difficult or impossible mandate must establish ways of manipulating appearances in order to perpetuate the image that they are doing what it is that people think they do. In the policing business, much is made of crime and the presumed capability of dealing with it through specialized techniques of criminal investigation and law enforcement. The fact is that the causes of, and correctives to, harmful human conduct, whether designated criminal or otherwise, lie well beyond the control capabilities of the police and other forces of governmental social control.

The response to my book from the Board of Commissioners of Police highlights very particular aspects that are of concern to them, and offers very particular explanations and justifications for these aspects. It appears to me that they are concerned with those very aspects which question the conventional wisdom about detective work and which portray detectives as ordinary human beings. The fact is that most crimes cannot be solved, and the only reasonable thing left for detectives to do is to finesse the case with the complainant. The fact is that when faced with review procedures on their decisions that are mere form, detectives will routinely take the approach that it is only a matter of form and that they can therefore proceed to accomplish what they want. The fact is that when a decision is taken by a detective, things will be constructed so as to maximize the chances for a just and justifiable outcome from the detective's perspective. As the book documents, in the face of structural facilitators and impediments to their work, detectives act in a very reasonable and skillful manner.

I could dispute many points raised in the response, but this is not necessary since the intelligent reader can appreciate the nature of the response in light of my model for understanding detective work and my findings. I therefore shall make only a few illustrative points.

Some of the points raised in the response nicely confirm my own position. For example, at this juncture (March 1981), four years after the completion of the fieldwork and just prior to publication, I am given yet another "new" explanation for why we did not have systematic access to interrogations: "The Crown attorney gave explicit direction, when the problem became known, that researchers were not to be permitted access since it would seriously jeopardize the admissibility of statements and ultimately case outcome." Surely this reason supports my interpretation that the central (and fully understandable) concern was that another version of events might jeopardize the case the detectives wished to construct, and that they could not reasonably predict or ensure collaboration from researchers in their construction.

While we did not usually attend court with detectives on their days off, substantial data were collected about detectives in the court context through other components of the research programme at the Toronto Centre of Criminology, especially the Crown attorney study and the lawyer study.

As explained in Chapter Two, we focused upon general investigation detectives because of the wide range of matters coming to their attention. In comparison Special Services detective units specialized in very particular and restricted areas of investigation. Notwithstanding this, we wished to spend time with proactively oriented detectives who would provide contrast with the reactively oriented general investigation detectives. We therefore requested observational attachment with morality unit officers, but our request was denied.

In their response the Board of Commissioners of Police contend that the occupational subculture is characterized by "practical jokes," rather than practical rules and techniques for getting the job done as emphasized in the book. This allows them to make the further contention that the researchers "fell prey" to various "practical jokes": "The incident involving an 'unprocessed warrant' was a practical joke. Other practical jokes, *which were documented* by Detective Sergeants, were played on the researchers by detectives, including exaggerating what they would do, or had done, for informants, deliberately writing up false follow up reports and other documents and leaving them in conspicuous places for the researchers; and, signing arrest and search warrants in the name of justices of the peace, convincing researchers that they would be used but later throwing them out."

From the viewpoint of the Board of Commissioners of Police this interpretation may well be both practical and amusing. However, I do not find it funny because it suggests serious problems with some of our data. The reader is referred to Chapter Two for a very detailed outline of our observational methodology.

Is the Board of Commissioners of Police seriously contending that even though we spent more than 1,400 hours over eleven months within general investigation units, we were unable to sort out what detectives were doing as a practical joke and what they were doing as practical elements in the construction of cases? Could we be subject to such massive deception over this extensive period of fieldwork? We know that detectives are highly skilled at constructing cases, but are they skilled enough to accomplish such massive deception? This certainly contradicts the fieldwork record of social researchers who have continually documented in varied settings that subjects quickly adjust to the presence of fieldworkers and return to their usual practices. Indeed, subjects must do so to continue a competent performance within their usual social roles. It also contradicts what one would expect of workers committed to their organization, who would surely attempt deception in a manner intended to create a positive image rather than a negative one.

More fundamentally, it must be stressed that all official documents at our disposal pertaining to case investigations came from one of two sources. All case documents were photocopied with permission through police headquarters several months after the completion of fieldwork. When accused were charged, persons working on the Crown attorney study, the accused study, and/or the lawyer study, photocopied with permission of the Court Administrator the "package" of documents prepared by the detectives for the Crown attorney, as well as other court documents. Is the Board of Commissioners of Police claiming that "false follow-up reports and other documents" manufactured for the purpose of deceiving researchers were part of the permanent case records in police headquarters, part of the package of documents given to the Crown attorney to be used in prosecution, and part of the permanent court records?

The response is but another example of how the police make a case. I do not accept the case made by the Board of Commissioners of Police. While many of our findings may properly be viewed as making a novel contribution to social inquiry, they are not fiction.

Of course, the final analysis and judgment will be made by the reader.

Bibliography

Alderson, J. C. and Stead, P. J. (1973) *The Police We Deserve,* Wolfe: London.

Alschuler, A. (1968) "The Prosecutor's Role in Plea Bargaining." *University of Chicago Law Review* 36: 50-112.

Alschuler, A. (1978) "Sentencing Reform and Prosecutorial Power: A Critique of Recent Proposals for 'Fixed' and 'Presumptive' Sentencing." *University of Pennsylvania Law Review* 126: 550-577.

Angell, J. (1971) "Toward an Alternative to the Classic Police Organizational Arrangements: A Democratic Model." *Criminology* 9: 185-206.

Ayres, R. (1970) "Confessions and the Court" in A. Niederhoffer and A. Blumberg (eds.) *The Ambivalent Force.* Waltham, Mass.: Ginn.

Balbus, I. (1973) *The Dialectics of Legal Repression.* New York: Sage.

Baldwin, J. and McConville, M. (1977) *Negotiated Justice: Pressures to Plead Guilty.* London: Martin Robertson.

Banton, M. (1964) *The Policeman in the Community.* London: Tavistock.

Barnard, C. (1938) *The Functions of Executives.* Cambridge: Harvard University Press.

Bayley, D. (1977) "The Limits of Police Reform" in D. Bayley (ed.) *Police and Society.* Beverly Hills: Sage.

Beattie, J. (1977) *Documents Illustrating Attitudes Towards Crime and Punishment in Upper Canada, 1830-1850.* Toronto: Centre of Criminology, University of Toronto.

Becker, C. (1974) "Discretionary Clearances: Observations on Police Screening Strategies" in Law Reform Commission (Canada) *Studies on Diversion.* Ottawa: Information Canada.

Becker, H. and Horowitz, I. (1972) "Radical Politics and Sociological Research." *American Journal of Sociology* 78: 48-65.

Benson, J. (1977) "Innovation and Crisis in Organizational Analysis." *The Sociological Quarterly* 18: 3-16.

Berger, P. and Luckmann, T. (1966) *The Social Construction of Reality: A Treatise in the Sociology of Knowledge.* Middlesex: Penguin.

Bittner, E. (1967a) "Police Discretion in Emergency Apprehension of Mentally Ill Persons." *Social Problems* 14: 278-292.

Bittner, E. (1967b) "The Police on Skid Row: A Study of Peace Keeping." *American Sociological Review* 32: 699-715.

Bittner, E. (1970) *The Functions of the Police in Modern Society.* Rockville, Maryland: NIMH.

Bittner, E. (1974) "A Theory of the Police" in H. Jacob (ed.) *The Potential for Reform of Criminal Justice*. London: Sage.

Black, D. (1968) *Police Encounters and Social Organization: An Observation Study*. Ph.D. dissertation, University of Michigan.

Black, D. (1972) "The Boundaries of Legal Sociology." *Yale Law Journal* 81(6): 1086-1110.

Black, D. (1976) *The Behavior of Law*. New York: Academic Press.

Black, J. (1977) *United States Penetration of Brazil*. Philadelphia: University of Pennsylvania Press.

Block, P. and Weidman, D. (1975) *Managing Criminal Investigations*. Washington: L.E.A.A., U.S. Government Printing Office.

Blumberg, A. (1967) *Criminal Justice*. Chicago: Quadrangle.

Blumberg, A. (1970) "The Practice of Law as a Confidence Game: Organizational Cooptation of a Profession" in A. Niederhoffer and A. Blumberg (eds.) *The Ambivalent Force*. Waltham, Mass.: Ginn.

Blumberg, A. and Niederhoffer, A. (1970) "The Police in Social and Historical Perspective" in A. Niederhoffer and A. Blumberg (eds.) *The Ambivalent Force*. Waltham, Mass.: Ginn.

Bottomley, A. (1970) *Prison Before Trial*. London: Bell.

Bottomley, A. (1973) *Decisions in the Penal Process*. London: Martin Robertson.

Bottomley, A. and Coleman, C. (1979) "Police Effectiveness and the Public: The Limitations of Official Crime Rates." Paper presented to the Cambridge Conference on Police Effectiveness, Cambridge, England, July 11-13.

Bottoms, A. and McClean, J. (1976) *Defendants in the Criminal Process*. London: Routledge and Kegan Paul.

Brown, L. and Brown, C. (1973) *An Unauthorized History of the RCMP*. Toronto: James Lorimer.

Buckner, H. T. (1967) *The Police: The Culture of a Social Control Agency*. Ph.D. thesis, University of California at Berkeley.

Buckner, H. T. (1970) "Transformations of Reality in the Legal Process." *Social Research* 37: 88-101.

Cain, M. (1971) "On the Beat" in S. Cohen (ed.) *Images of Deviance*. London: Tavistock.

Cain, M. (1972) "Police Professionalism: Its Meaning and Consequences." *Anglo-American Law Review* 1: 217-231.

Cain, M. (1973) *Society and the Policeman's Role*. London: Routledge and Kegan Paul.

Cameron, N. (1974) "The Control of Police Discretion." draft manuscript, Toronto: Centre of Criminology, University of Toronto. 91 pp.

Camus, A. (1963) *The Fall*. London: Penguin.

Carlen, P. (1976) *Magistrates' Justice*. London: Martin Robertson.

Center, L. and Smith, T. (1973) "Crime Statistics—Can They Be Trusted." *American Criminal Law Review* 11: 1045-1086.

Chaiken, J. (1975) *The Criminal Investigation Process: Vol. II Survey of Municipal and County Police Departments*. Santa Monica, Rand Corporation.

Chambliss, W. (1969) *Crime and the Legal Process*. New York: McGraw-Hill.

Chambliss, W. and Seidman, R. (1971) *Law, Order and Power*. Reading, Mass.: Addison-Wesley.

Chan, J. (1980) *Cheap Punishment or Costly Control: An Analysis of Penal Reforms in the Welfare State*. M.A. dissertation, Centre of Criminology, University of Toronto.

Chan, J. and Doob, A. (1977) *The Exercise of Discretion with Juveniles*. Centre of Criminology, University of Toronto.

Chandler, D. (1976) *Capital Punishment in Canada*. Toronto: McClelland and Stewart.

Chatterton, M. (1976) "Police in Social Control" in *Control Without Custody*. Cropwood Papers, Institute of Criminology, University of Cambridge.

Chatterton, M. (1979) "The Supervision of Patrol Work under the Fixed Points System" in S. Holdaway (ed.) *The British Police*. London: Edward Arnold.

Chibnall, S. (1979) "The Metropolitan Police and the News Media" in S. Holdaway (ed.) *The British Police*. London: Edward Arnold.

Chomsky, N. and Herman, E. (1979) *The Washington Connection and Third World Facism*. Montreal: Black Rose Books.

Christie, N. (1977) "Conflicts as Property." *British Journal of Criminology* 17: 1-15.

Church, T. (1976) "Plea Bargains, Concessions and the Courts: An Analysis of a Quasi-experiment." *Law and Society Review* 10: 384-388.

Clark, J. and Sykes, R. (1974) "Some Determinants of Police Organization and Practice in Modern Industrial Democracy" in D. Glaser, *Handbook of Criminology*. Chicago: Rand-McNally.

Clark, L. and Lewis, D. (1978) *Rape: The Price of Coercive Sexuality*. Toronto: Women's Educational Press.

Cloyd, J. (1979) "Prosecution's Power, Procedural Rights, and Pleading Guilty: The Problem of Coercion in Plea Bargaining Drug Cases." *Social Problems* 26: 452-466.

Cobb, B. (1957) *The First Detectives*. London: Faber and Faber.

Cohen, S. (1979) "Guilt, Justice and Tolerance: Some Old Concepts for a New Criminology" in D. Downes and P. Rock (eds.) *Deviant Interpretations*. Oxford: Martin Robertson.

Cohen, S. and Taylor, L. (1976) *Escape Attempts: The Theory and Practice of Resistance to Everyday Life*. London: Allen Lane.

Coleman, J. (1973) "Loss of Power." *American Sociological Review* 38: 1-17.

Cook, K. (1977) "Exchange and Power in Networks of Interorganizational Relations." *The Sociological Quarterly* 18: 62-82.

Courtis, M. (1970) *Attitudes to Crime and the Police in Toronto*. Toronto: Centre of Criminology, University of Toronto.

Cousineau, D. and Verdun-Jones, S. (1979) "Evaluating Research into Plea Bargaining in Canada and the United States: Pitfalls Facing the Policy Makers." *Canadian Journal of Criminology* 21: 293-309.

Cox, S. et al. (1977) *The Fall of Scotland Yard*. London: Penguin.

Dalton, M. (1959) *Men Who Manage*. New York: Wiley.

Davis, K. (1969) *Discretionary Justice*. Baton Rouge: Louisiana State University Press.

Day, R. and Day, J. (1977) "A Review of the Current State of Negotiated Order Theory: An Appreciation and a Critique." *The Sociological Quarterly* 18: 126-142.

Dell, S. (1971) *Silence in Court*. London: Bell.

Ditton, J. (1977) *Part-Time Crime*. London: Macmillan.

Ditton, J. (1979) *Controlology: Beyond the New Criminology*. London: Macmillan.

Donzelot, J. (1979) *The Policing of Families*. New York: Pantheon.

Doob, A. and Kirschenbaum, H. (1972) "Some Empirical Evidence on the Effect of s. 12 of the Canada Evidence Act Upon an Accused." *Criminal Law Quarterly* 15: 88-96.

Douglas, J. (1971) *American Social Order*. New York: Free Press.

Douthet, N. (1975) "Police Professionalism and the War Against Crime in the United States, 1920-30s" in G. Mosse (ed.) *Police Forces in History*. Beverly Hills: Sage.

Downes, D. (1979) "Praxis Makes Perfect: A Critique of Critical Criminology" in D. Downes and P. Rock (eds.) *Deviant Interpretations*. Oxford: Martin Robertson.

Durkheim, E. (1933) *The Division of Labour in Society*. New York: Free Press.

Ellis, D. (1979) "The Prison Guard as Carceral Luddite: A Critical Review of the MacGuigan Report on the Penitentiary System in Canada." *Canadian Journal of Sociology* 4: 43-64.

Ennis, P. M. (1967) *Criminal Victimization in the United States: A Report of a National Survey*. Washington: U.S. Government Printing Office.

Ericson, R. (1974) "Psychiatrists in Prison: On Admitting Professional Tinkers into a Tinkers' Paradise." *Chitty's Law Journal* 22(1): 29-33.

Ericson, R. (1975) *Criminal Reactions: The Labelling Perspective*. Farnborough: Saxon House.

Ericson, R. (1977) "From Social Theory to Penal Practice: The Liberal Demise of Criminological Causes." *Canadian Journal of Criminology and Corrections* 19: 170-191.

Ericson, R. (1978) "Penal Psychiatry in Canada" in W. Greenaway and S. Brickey (eds.) *Law and Social Control in Canada*. Scarborough: Prentice-Hall.

Ericson, R. (1980) *Reproducing Order: A Study of Police Patrol Work* (forthcoming). Toronto: University of Toronto Press.

Ericson, R. and Baranek, P. (1981) *The Ordering of Justice: A Study of Accused Persons as Dependents in the Criminal Process*. (forthcoming).

Etzioni, A. (1961) *A Comparative Analysis of Complex Organizations*. New York: Free Press.

Feeley, M. (1973) "Two Models of the Criminal Justice System: An Organizational Perspective." *Law and Society Review* 7: 407-425.

Ferguson, G. (1972) "The Role of the Judge in Plea Bargaining." *Criminal Law Quarterly* 15: 26-51.

Fontana, J. (1974) *The Law of Search Warrants in Canada.* Toronto: Butterworths.

Foucault, M. (1977) *Discipline and Punish.* London: Allen Lane.

Foucault, M. (1979) "On the Concept of the 'Dangerous' Individual in Nineteenth Century Legal Psychiatry" in D. Weistub (ed.) *Law and Psychiatry: A Symposium.* Toronto: Pergamon.

Freedman, D. and Stenning, P. (1977) *Private Security, Police and the Law in Canada.* Toronto: Centre of Criminology, University of Toronto.

Friedenberg, E. (1975) *The Disposal of Liberty and Other Industrial Wastes.* New York: Doubleday.

Friedenberg, E. (1980) "The Punishment Industry in Canada." *Canadian Journal of Sociology* 5: 273–283.

Friedland, M. (1965) *Detention Without Trial.* Toronto: University of Toronto Press.

Friedland, M. (1978) *Access to the Law.* Toronto: Methuen.

Gibson, E. (1960) *Time Spent Awaiting Trial.* London: H.M.S.O.

Giddens, A. (1976) *New Rules of Sociological Method.* London: Hutchinson.

Glasbeck, H. and Prentice, D. (1968) "The Criminal Suspect's Illusory Right of Silence in the British Commonwealth." *Cornell Law Quarterly* 53: 473.

Glaser, B. and Strauss, A. (1967) *The Discovery of Grounded Theory: Strategies for Qualitative Research.* Chicago: Aldine.

Goldstein, H. (1967) "Administrative Problems in Controlling the Exercise of Police Authority." *Journal of Criminal Law, Criminology and Police Science* 58: 160-172.

Goldstein, H. (1970) "Police Discretion: The Ideal versus the Real" in A. Niederhoffer and A. Blumberg (eds.) *The Ambivalent Force.* Waltham, Mass.: Ginn.

Goldstein, J. (1960) "Police Discretion not to Invoke the Criminal Process: Low Visibility Decisions in the Administration of Justice." *Yale Law Journal* 69: 543.

Gooderson, R. (1970) "The Interrogation of Suspects" *Canadian Bar Review* 48: 270-307.

Gouldner, A. et al. (1977) "The Production of Cynical Knowledge in Organizations." *American Sociological Review* 42: 539-551.

Greenawalt, K. (1974) "Perspectives on the Right to Silence" in R. Hood (ed.) *Crime, Criminology and Public Policy.* London: Heinemann.

Greenwood, P. et al. (1975) *The Criminal Investigation Process: Volume III Observations and Analysis.* Santa Monica: Rand Corporation.

Griffiths, J. (1970) "Ideology in Criminal Procedure, or a Third 'Model' of the Criminal Process." *Yale Law Journal* 79: 359-417.

Griffiths, J. and Ayres, R. (1967) "A Postscript to the *Miranda* Project:

Interrogation of Draft Protesters" *Yale Law Journal* 77: 305-306.
Grosman, B. (1969) *The Prosecutor.* Toronto: University of Toronto Press.
Grosman, B. (1975) *Police Command: Decisions and Discretion.* Toronto: MacMillan.
Hagan, J. (1981) *Righting Wrongs: A Study of Victim Involvement in the Criminal Justice System* (forthcoming).
Hagan, J. and Leon, J. (1980) "The Rehabilitation of Law: A Social-Historical Comparison of Probation in Canada and the United States." *Canadian Journal of Sociology* 5: 235-251.
Hall, S. et al. (1978) *Policing the Crisis.* London: Macmillan.
Harney, M. and Cross, J. (1960) *The Informer in Law Enforcement.* Springfield: Charles Thomas.
Harvard Center for Criminal Justice (1972) "Judicial Intervention in Prison Discipline." *Journal of Criminal Law and Criminology* 63: 200-228.
Hatherill, G. (1964) "The Means of Interrogation." *Medico-Legal Journal* 32: 164-175.
Hawkins, G. (1976) *The Prison: Policy and Practice.* Chicago: University of Chicago Press.
Hayduk, L. (1976) "Formulations in Police Work: Some Observations and Related Theoretical Concerns." *Canadian Journal of Sociology* 1: 463-479.
Hayek, F. (1944) *The Road to Serfdom.* Chicago: University of Chicago Press.
Helder, H. (1978) "Power Relationships and Proactive Police Searches." unpublished paper, Toronto: Centre of Criminology, University of Toronto.
Heumann, M. (1978) *Plea Bargaining: The Experiences of Prosecutors, Judges and Defense Attorneys.* Chicago: University of Chicago Press.
Heydebrand, W. (1977) "Organizational Contradictions in Public Bureaucracies: Toward a Marxian Theory of Organizations." *The Sociological Quarterly* 18: 83-107.
Hogarth, J. (1971) *Sentencing as a Human Process.* Toronto: University of Toronto Press.
Holdaway, S. (1979) *The British Police.* London: Edward Arnold.
Holzner, B. (1972) *Reality Construction in Society.* (2nd ed.) Cambridge, Mass.: Schenkman.
Hosticka, C. (1979) "We Don't Care What Happened, We only Care About What Is Going to Happen: Lawyer-client Negotiations of Reality." *Social Problems* 26: 599-610.
Hurd, G. (1979) "The Television Presentation of the Police" in S. Holdaway (ed.) *The British Police.* London: Edward Arnold.
Ignatieff, M. (1978) *A Just Measure of Pain.* London: Macmillan.
Ignatieff, M. (1979) "Police and People: The Birth of Mr. Peel's 'blue locusts'." *New Society* (30 August): 443-445.

Illich, I. et al. (1977) *Disabling Professions*. Don Mills: Burns and MacEachern.

Imersheim, A. (1977) "Organizational Change as a Paradigm Shift." *Sociological Quarterly* 18: 33-43.

Inbau, F. and Reid, J. (1967) *Criminal Interrogation and Confessions*. Baltimore: Williams and Wilkins.

James, D. (1979) "Police-Black Relations: The Professional Solution" in S. Holdaway (ed.) *The British Police*. London: Edward Arnold.

Kadish, M. and Kadish, S. (1973) *Discretion to Disobey: A Study of Lawful Departures from Legal Rules*. Stanford: Stanford University Press.

Katz, M. (1974) "Violence and Civility in a Suburban Milieu." *Journal of Police Science and Administration* 2: 239-249.

Kaufman, F. (1974) *The Admissibility of Confessions*. Toronto: Carswell.

Kelling, G. et al. (1979) "Policing: A Research Agenda for Rational Policy Making." Paper presented to the Cambridge Conference on Police Effectiveness, Cambridge, England, July 11-13.

King, M. (1971) *Bail or Custody*. London: Cobden Trust.

Kirkham, G. (1974) "From Professor to Patrolman." *Journal of Police Science and Administration* 2: 127-137.

Kittrie, N. (1971) *The Right to be Different*. Baltimore: Johns Hopkins Press.

Klein, A. (1972) "Plea Bargaining." *Criminal Law Quarterly* 14: 289-305.

Klein, J. (1974) *Official Morality and Offender Perceptions of the Bargaining Process*. Ph.D. Dissertation, Department of Sociology, University of Alberta.

Klein, J. (1976) *Lets Make a Deal*. Lexington, Mass.: Lexington Books.

Koenig, D. (1975) *R.C.M.P. Views of Themselves, Their Jobs and the Public*. Victoria: Research Report, University of Victoria.

Kokis, R. (1977) "Domestic Violence: A Study of Police Non-Enforcement." M.A. Dissertation, Centre of Criminology, University of Toronto.

LaFave, W. (1965) *Arrest: The Decision to Take a Suspect into Custody*. Boston: Little Brown.

Lambert, J. (1970) *Crime, Police and Race Relations*. London: Oxford University Press.

Laurie, P. (1970) *Scotland Yard*. London: Bodley Head.

Law Reform Commission of Canada (1973) *Evidence: Compellability of the Accused and the Admissibility of his Statements*. Study Paper. 44 pp.

Law Reform Commission (Canada) (1974) *The Principles of Sentencing and Dispositions*. Ottawa: Information Canada.

Law Reform Commission (Canada) (1974a) *Studies on Diversion*. Ottawa: Information Canada.

Law Reform Commission (Canada) (1975) *Diversion*. Ottawa: Information Canada.

Law Reform Commission (Canada) (1976) *Criminal Procedure: Control of the Process.* Ottawa: Information Canada.

Leigh, L. (1975) *Police Powers in England and Wales.* London: Butterworths.

McBarnet, D. (1976) "Pre-trial Procedures and the Construction of Conviction" in P. Carlen (ed.) *The Sociology of Law.* Keele: Department of Sociology, University of Keele.

McBarnet, D. (1979) "Arrest: The Legal Context of Policing" in S. Holdaway (ed.) *The British Police.* London: Edward Arnold.

McCabe, S. and Sutcliffe, F. (1978) *Defining Crime: A Study of Police Decisions.* Oxford: Basil Blackwell.

McDonald, L. (1976) *The Sociology of Law and Order.* London: Faber.

McKnight, J. (1977) "Professionalized Service and Disabling Help" in Ivan Illich et al. *The Disabling Professions.* Don Mills: Burns and MacEachern.

McMullan, J. (1980) "Maudits Voleurs: Racketeering and the Collection of Private Debts in Montreal." *Canadian Journal of Sociology* 5: 121-143.

Macfarlane, D. (1979) *Lawyering in the Lower Courts: Making the Best of Bad Cases.* Unpublished Research Report, Toronto: Centre of Criminology, University of Toronto.

Macfarlane, D. and Giffen, J. (1981) *Lawyering in the Lower Criminal Courts: Making the Best of 'Bad' Cases.* (forthcoming)

Mann, E. and Lee, J. (1979) *R.C.M.P. vs. the People.* Don Mills: General Publishing.

Manning, P. (1971) "The Police: Mandate, Strategy and Appearances" in J. Douglas, *Crime and Justice in American Society.* Indianapolis: Bobbs-Merrill.

Manning, P. (1972) "Observing the Police: Deviants, Respectables and the Law" in J. Douglas (ed.) *Research on Deviance.* New York: Random House.

Manning, P. (1977) *Police Work.* Cambridge, Mass.: MIT Press.

Manning, P. (1977a) "Rules in Organizational Context: Narcotics Law Enforcement in Two Settings." *The Sociological Quarterly* 18: 44-61.

Manning, P. (1979) "Organization and Environment: Influences on Police Work." Paper presented to the Cambridge Conference on Police Effectiveness, Cambridge, England, July 11-13.

Manning, P. (1979a) "The Social Control of Police Work" in S. Holdaway (ed.) *The British Police.* London: Edward Arnold.

Manning, P. (1980) *The Narcs' Game.* Cambridge, Mass.: M.I.T. Press.

Martin, J. P. and Webster, D. (1969) *The Police: A Study in Manpower.* London: Heinemann Educational Books Ltd.

Medalie, R. et al. (1968) "Custodial Police Interrogation in our Nation's Capital: The Attempt to Implement Miranda." *Michigan Law Review* 66: 1347-1422.

Menzies, R. (1978) "Canadian Police Practices in Entry, Search and Seizure: Reasonable and Probable Grounds for Abuse." M.A. dissertation, Toronto: Centre of Criminology, University of Toronto.

Merelaman, R. (1969) "The Dramaturgy of Politics." *Sociological Quarterly* 10: 216-241.

Mewett, A. (1967) "The Criminal Law, 1867-1967." *Canadian Bar Review* 45: 726-740.

Miller, W. (1977) *Cops and Bobbies*. Chicago: University of Chicago Press.

Miller, W. (1979) "London's Police Tradition in a Changing Society" in S. Holdaway (ed.) *The British Police*. London: Edward Arnold.

Mitford, J. (1973) *Kind and Usual Punishment: The Prison Business*. New York: Vintage Books.

Montagnes, C. (1978) *Coming Apart: An Examination of the Daily Management of Prosecution Caseloads in Provincial Court*. M.A. dissertation, Toronto: Centre of Criminology, University of Toronto.

Morris, P. (1978) "Police Interrogation in England and Wales." A Critical Review of the Literature prepared for the U.K. Royal Commission on Criminal Procedure.

Morrison, W. (1975) "The Northwest Mounted Police and the Klondike Gold Rush" in G. Mosse (ed.) *Police Forces in History*. London: Sage.

Moylan, J. (1929) *Scotland Yard*. London: Putnam.

Muir, W. (1977) *Police: Street Corner Politicians*. Chicago: University of Chicago Press.

Newman, D. (1966) *Conviction: The Determination of Guilt or Innocence Without Trial*. Boston: Little Brown.

Norris, D. (1973) *Police Community Relations*. Lexington, Mass.: Lexington Books.

Ontario Crown Attorney's Association (1976) *Bail Reform—1976: A Manual for Law Enforcement Officers*. Toronto: Ontario Crown Attorney's Association.

Packer, H. (1968) *The Limits of the Criminal Sanction*. London: Oxford University Press.

Packer, H. and Ehrlich, I. (1972) *New Directions in Legal Education: A Report Prepared for the Carnegie Commission on Higher Education*. New York: McGraw-Hill.

Pepinsky, H. (1975) "Police Decision-Making" in D. Gottfredson (ed.) *Decision-Making in the Criminal Justice System: Reviews and Essays*. Rockville, Md.: NIMH.

Pepinsky, H. (1976) "Police Patrolmen's Offense-Reporting Behavior." *Journal of Research in Crime and Delinquency* 13(1): 33-47.

Ramsay, J. (1972) "My Case Against the R.C.M.P." *MacLean's* (July): 19.

Reiss, A. (1968) "Police brutality—Answers to Key Questions." *Transaction* (July-August): 10-19.

Reiss, A. (1971) *The Police and the Public*. New Haven: Yale University Press.

Reiss, A. (1974) "Discretionary Justice" in D. Glaser (ed.) *Handbook of Criminology*. Chicago: Rand McNally.

Reiss, A. and Black, D. (1967) "Interrogation and the Criminal Process." *Annals* 374: 47-57.

Reiss, A. and Bordua, D. (1967) "Environment and Organization: A Perspective on the Police" in D. Bordua (ed.) *The Police: Six Sociological Essays.* New York: Wiley.

Reith, C. (1943) *The Police and the Democratic Ideal.* London: Oxford University Press.

Renton, R. and Brown, H. (1972) *Criminal Procedure According to the Law of Scotland.* London: Green.

Rickaby, D. (1975) "Crisis in the Criminal Courts—Justice or Chaos?" *Crown's Newsletter* (April): 14-34.

Robinson, C. (1975) "The Mayor and the Police" in G. Mosse (ed.) *Police Forces in History.* London: Sage.

Rock, P. (1976) *Making People Pay.* London: Routledge.

Rock, P. (1979) *The Making of Symbolic Interactionism.* London: Macmillan.

Rock, P. (1979a) "The Sociology of Crime, Symbolic Interactionism and some Problematic Qualities of Radical Criminology" in D. Downes and P. Rock (eds.) *Deviant Interpretations.* Oxford: Martin Robertson.

Ross, H. (1970) *Settled Out of Court.* Chicago: Aldine.

Rubinstein, J. (1973) *City Police.* New York: Farrar, Strauss and Giroux.

Ryle, G. (1949) *The Concept of the Mind.* London: Hutchinson.

Salhany, J. (1972) *Canadian Criminal Procedure.* Toronto: Canada Law Book Company.

Sanders, W. (1977) *Detective Work.* New York: Free Press.

Sanders, W. (1974) *Sociologist as Detective.* New York: Praeger.

Schur, E. (1973) *Radical Non-Intervention.* Englewood Cliffs, N.J.: Prentice-Hall.

Scollin, J. (1972) *The Bail Reform Act: An Analysis of Amendments to the Criminal Code Related to Bail and Arrest.* Toronto: Carswell.

Scull, A. (1977) *Decarceration.* Englewood Cliffs: Prentice-Hall.

Seeburger, R. and Wettick, R. (1967) "Miranda in Pittsburgh—A Statistical Study." *University of Pittsburgh Law Review* 29: 1-26.

Seidman, D. and Couzens, M. (1974) "Getting the Crime Rate Down: Political Pressure and Crime Reporting." *Law and Society Review* 8: 457-493.

Shearing, C. (1977) *Real Men, Wise Men, Good Men and Cautious Men: A Study of Culture, Role Models and Interaction Within a Police Communications Centre.* Ph.D. Thesis, Toronto: Department of Sociology, University of Toronto.

Shearing, C., Farnell, M., and Stenning, P. (1980) *Policing for Profit.* Toronto: University of Toronto Press.

Sherman, L. (ed.) (1974) *Police Corruption.* New York: Anchor Books.

Silver, A. (1967) "The Demand for Order in Civil Society: A Review of Some Themes in the History of Urban Crime, Police, and Riot" in D. Bordua (ed.) *The Police: Six Sociological Essays.* New York: Wiley.

Silverman, D. (1970) *The Theory of Organizations.* London: Heinemann.

Skogan, W. (1975) "Public Policy and Public Evaluations of Criminal Justice System Performance" in J. Gardiner and M. Mulkey (eds.) *Crime and Criminal Justice: Issues in Public Policy Analysis.* Lexington, Mass.: Lexington Books.

Skogan, W. (1976) "Crime and Crime Rates" in W. Skogan (ed.) *Sample Surveys of Victims of Crimes.* Cambridge, Mass.: Ballinger Press.

Skolnick, J. (1966) *Justice Without Trial.* New York: Wiley.

Skolnick, J. and Woodworth, J. (1967) "Bureaucracy, Information and Social Control: A Study of a Morals Detail" in D. Bordua (ed.) *The Police: Six Sociological Essays.* New York: Wiley.

Solicitor General of Canada (1979) *Selected Trends in Canadian Criminal Justice.* Ottawa: Communication Division, Ministry of the Solicitor General of Canada.

Solicitor General of Canada (1979a) *National Inventory of Diversion Projects: An Update.* Ottawa: Communication Division, Ministry of the Solicitor General of Canada.

Sparks, R. et al. (1977) *Surveying Victims: A Study of the Measurement of Criminal Victimization, Perception of Crime, and Attitudes to Criminal Justice.* London: Wiley.

Steer, D. (1970) *Police Cautions—A Study in the Exercise of Police Discretion.* Oxford: Basil Blackwell.

Strauss, A. (1978) *Negotiations.* San Francisco: Jossey-Bass.

Sudnow, D. (1965) "Normal Crimes: Sociological Features of the Penal Code in a Public Defenders Office." *Social Problems* 12: 255-272.

Sykes, R. and Clark, J. (1975) "A Theory of Deference Exchange in Police Civilian Encounters." *American Journal of Sociology* 81(3): 584-600.

Taylor, I. (1980) "The Law and Order Issue in the British and Canadian General Elections of 1979: Crime, Populism and the State." *Canadian Journal of Sociology* 5: 285–311.

Taylor, I. et al. (1973) *The New Criminology.* London: Routledge and Kegan Paul.

Taylor, I. et al. (eds.) (1975) *Critical Criminology.* London: Routledge and Kegan Paul.

Thomas, D. (1974) "The Control of Discretion in the Administration of Criminal Justice" in R. Hood (ed.) *Crime, Criminology and Public Policy.* London: Heinemann.

Thompson, E. P. (1979) "On the New Issue of Postal Stamps." *New Society* 50: 324-326.

Turk, A. (1969) *Criminality and Legal Order.* Chicago: Rand McNally.

Turk, A. (1973) "Review of *The New Criminology*" Mimeo., Toronto: Centre of Criminology, University of Toronto.

Turk, A. (1977) "Class, Conflict and Criminalization." *Sociological Focus.* 10: 209-220.

United States National Crime Commission (1967) *Task Force Report: The Police.* Washington: U.S. Government Printing Office.

Utz, P. (1978) *Settling the Facts: Discretion and Negotiation in the Criminal Courts.* Lexington, Mass.: Lexington Books.

Vera Institute (1977) *Felony Arrests: Their Prosecution and Disposition in New York City's Courts.* New York: Vera Institute.

Wald, M. et al. (1967) "Interrogations in New Haven: The Impact of Miranda." *Yale Law Journal* 76: 1521-1648.

Watson, N. and Sterling, J. (1969) *Police and Their Opinions.* Washington: I.A.C.P.

Weick, K. (1969) *The Social Psychology of Organizing.* Reading, Mass.: Addison-Wesley.

Westley, W. (1951) "The Police: A Sociological Study of Law, Custom, and Morality." Ph.D. Dissertation, University of Chicago.

Wilkins, J. (1981) *The Prosecution and the Courts.* (forthcoming).

Williams, C. (1961) "The Criminal Law and Public Opinion: Some Police Reactions." *Criminal Law Review*, pp. 359-367.

Williams, G. (1960) "Questioning by the Police: Some Practical Considerations." *Criminal Law Review*, 325-346.

Wilson, J. (1968) *Varieties of Police Behavior.* Cambridge, Mass.: Harvard University Press.

Wilson, J. (1978) *The Investigators.* New York: Basic Books.

Wilson, J. and Boland, B. (1979) "The Effect of Police on Crime." *Law and Society Review* 12: 367-390.

Wilson, O. (1962) *Police Administration.* New York: McGraw-Hill.

Witt, J. (1973) "Non-coercive Interrogation and the Administration of Criminal Justice: The Impact of Miranda on Police Effectuality." *Journal of Criminal Law, Criminology, and Police Science* 64: 320-332.

Younger, (1966) "Interrogations of Criminal Defendants—Some Views on Miranda v. Arizona" *Fordham Law Review* 35: 165.

Zander, M. (1978) "The Right of Silence in the Police Station and the Caution" in P. Glazebrook (ed.) *Reshaping the Criminal Law.* London: Stevens.

Index